T0381132

A COMPENDIUM
to the
BIBLE

A THEOLOGICAL STUDY

MICHAEL J. BYRNE

WESTBOW
PRESS®
A DIVISION OF THOMAS NELSON
& ZONDERVAN

WestBow Press books may be ordered through booksellers or by contacting:

WestBow Press
A Division of Thomas Nelson & Zondervan
1663 Liberty Drive
Bloomington, IN 47403
www.westbowpress.com
844-714-3454

ISBN: 979-8-3850-0538-3 (sc)
ISBN: 979-8-3850-0539-0 (hc)
ISBN: 979-8-3850-0540-6 (e)

Library of Congress Control Number: 2023915778

Print information available on the last page.

WestBow Press rev. date: 11/13/2023

And He said, "Go, and tell this people:
Keep on hearing, but do not understand;
Keep on seeing, but do not perceive.
Make the heart of this people dull,
And their ears heavy,
And shut their eyes;
Lest they see with their eyes,
And hear with their ears,
And understand with their heart,
And return and be healed."
—Isaiah 6:9–10

Contents

Prologue

All scriptures given in this book are taken from the New King James Version of the Bible.

> I looked when He opened the sixth seal, and behold, there was a great earthquake; and the sun became black as sackcloth of hair. And the moon became like blood. And the stars of heaven fell to the earth, as a fig tree drops its late figs when it is shaken by a mighty wind. Then the sky receded as a scroll when it is rolled up, and every mountain and island was moved out of its place. And the kings of the earth, the great men, the commanders, the mighty men, every slave and every free man, hid themselves in the caves and in the rocks of the mountains, and said to the mountains and rocks, "Fall on us and hide us from the face of Him who sits on the throne and from the wrath of the lamb! "For the great day of His wrath has come, and who is able to stand?" (Revelation 6:12–17)

> After these things I saw four angels standing at the four corners of the earth, holding the four winds of the earth, that the wind should not blow on the earth, on the sea, or on any tree. Then I saw another angel ascending from the east, having the

seal of the living God. And he cried with a loud voice to the four angels to whom it was granted to harm the earth and the sea, saying, "Do not harm the earth, the sea, or the trees till we have sealed the servants of our God on their foreheads." (Revelation 7:1–3)

And this gospel of the kingdom will be preached in all the world as a witness to all the nations, and then the end will come. (Matthew 24:14)

But when the grain ripens, immediately he puts in the sickle, because the harvest has come. (Mark 4:29)

In the writing of this book, certain assertions have been made:

1. The Bible, as translated from the original texts and handed down to us in the form of the New King James Version, is the revealed knowledge of God.
2. The Old Testament is written as an historical record of the world and of a specific nation.
3. God used individuals of that nation and the nation itself to reveal Himself to humanity.
4. The Old Testament reveals God's nature and the nature of humanity.
5. The Old Testament points to promises made by God—to characters and writers of that book—in regard to that nation and humanity.
6. As was instructed to Moses on Mount Sinai, the tabernacle that he was directed to construct was a copy of the True Tabernacle.
7. The Old Testament—with all of its stories, commands, and regulations—is a physical representation of the spiritual

promises that God has made to humanity, it is in its entirety a copy of the True.

8. The terms Christ and Messiah are used interchangeably.

This work will be viewed as controversial and challenging to the existing beliefs of each and every reader. What follows will require more than just the human spirit to understand. It brings to mind the parable of the sower:

> Then He spoke many things to them in parables, saying: "Behold, a sower went out to sow. And as he sowed, some seed fell by the wayside; and the birds came and devoured them." (Matthew 13:3–4)

> When anyone hears the word of the kingdom, and does not understand it, then the wicked one comes and snatches away what was sown in his heart. This is he who received seed by the wayside. (Matthew 13:19)

And as was done by those who received the seed by the wayside, the birds will come and pick apart every morsel of truth and be satiated with their lies and contentions.

The majority of this work is supporting texts from the Bible. Although it is not exhaustive, it is hoped that enough texts have been included to validate the claims that are being made. The narrative has been limited as much as possible to avoid misrepresenting the scriptures. The subjects have been arranged so that each subject builds on the preceding subjects. There is much overlap between subjects.

Certain claims may be difficult to grasp because of current and historical beliefs. A certain familiarity with scripture will aid in the understanding of this work, but it is not necessary. A complete reading of the work should be made before making any final judgments.

The Bible, of course, should be referenced in its entirety. It is not intended that anyone should blindly believe anything; severe criticism is both expected and accepted.

Be assured that the following is not some idle tale.

Chapter 1

ALL SCRIPTURE HAS BEEN GIVEN FOR INSTRUCTION

Whom will he teach knowledge? And whom will He make to understand the message? Those just weaned from milk? Those just drawn from the breasts? For precept must be upon precept, precept upon precept, Line upon line, line upon line, Here a little, there a little. For with stammering lips and another tongue He will speak to this people, To whom He said, "This is the rest with which You may cause the weary to rest," And, "This is the refreshing"; Yet they would not hear. But the word of the LORD was to them, "Precept upon precept, precept upon precept, Line upon line, line upon line, Here a little, there a little," That they might go and fall backward, and be broken And snared and caught. (Isaiah 28:9–13)

Therefore thus says the LORD God: "Behold, I lay in Zion a stone for a foundation, A tried stone, a precious cornerstone, a sure foundation: Whoever believes will not act hastily." (Isaiah 28:16)

1

All Scripture is given by inspiration of God, and is profitable for doctrine, for reproof, for correction, for instruction in righteousness that the man of God may be complete, thoroughly equipped for every good work. (2 Timothy 3:16–17; emphasis added)

And so we have the prophetic word confirmed, which you do well to heed as a light that shines in a dark place, until the day dawns and the morning star rises in your heart; *knowing this first, that no prophecy of Scripture is of any private interpretation,* for prophecy never came by the will of man, "but holy men of God spoke as they were moved by the Holy Spirit. (2 Peter 1:19–21; emphasis added)

But there were also false prophets among the people, even as there will be false teachers among you, who will secretly bring in destructive heresies, even denying the Lord who bought them, and bring on themselves swift destruction. And many will follow their destructive ways, because of whom the way of truth will be blasphemed. (2 Peter 2:1–2)

For the word of God is living and powerful, and sharper than any two-edged sword, piercing even to the division of soul and spirit, and of joints and marrow, and is a discerner of the thoughts and intents of the heart. And there is no creature hidden from His sight, but all things are naked and open to the eyes of Him to whom we must give account. (Hebrews 4:12–13)

Chapter 2

THE HIDDEN MYSTERY
OF THE GOSPEL

"Behold, the days are coming," says the Lord God, "That I will send a famine on the land, Not a famine of bread, Nor a thirst for water, But of hearing the words of the Lord. They shall wander from sea to sea, And from north to east; They shall run to and fro, seeking the word of the Lord, But shall not find it." (Amos 8:11–12)

Now to Him who is able to establish you according to my gospel and the preaching of Jesus Christ, *according to the revelation of the mystery kept secret since the world began* but now made manifest, and by the prophetic Scriptures made known to all nations, according to the commandment of the everlasting God, *for obedience to the faith.* (Romans 16:25–26; emphasis added)

However, we speak wisdom among those who are mature, yet not the wisdom of this age, nor of the rulers of this age, who are coming to nothing. *But we speak the wisdom of God in a mystery, the hidden wisdom which God ordained before the ages for our glory,* which none of the rulers of this age knew; for had they known, they would not have crucified the Lord of glory, But as it is written: *"Eye has not seen, nor ear heard, Nor have entered into the heart of man The things which God has prepared for those who love Him." But God has revealed them to us through His Spirit.* For the Spirit searches all things, yes, the deep things of God. For what man knows the things of a man except the spirit of the man which is in him? *Even so no one knows the things of God except the Spirit of God.* Now we have received, not the spirit of the world, but the Spirit who is from God, that we might know the things that have been freely given to us by God. (1 Corinthians 2:6–12; emphasis added)

But the natural man does not receive the things of the Spirit of God, for they are foolishness to him; nor can he know them, *because they are spiritually discerned.* (1 Corinthians 2:14; emphasis added)

But even if our gospel is veiled, it is veiled to those who are perishing, whose minds the god of this age has blinded, who do not believe, lest the light of the gospel of the glory of Christ, who is the image of God, should shine on them. For we do not preach ourselves, but Christ Jesus the Lord. (2 Corinthians 4:3–5; emphasis added)

And consider that the long-suffering of our Lord is salvation—as also our beloved brother Paul, according to the wisdom given to him, has written

4

> to you, as also in all his epistles, speaking in them
> of these very things, in which are some things hard
> to understand, *which untaught and unstable people*
> *twist to their own destruction, as they do also the rest*
> *of the Scriptures.* (2 Peter 3:15–16; emphasis added)

The Gospel has been hidden from time immemorial. It was first revealed to us some two thousand years ago by a young Jewish man named John, who went about baptizing people, and it was later expounded upon by Jesus of Nazareth. In the first century AD, after the death of Jesus, the Gospel was preached throughout the civilized world. The Gospel received much opposition, as is revealed to in the book of the Acts of the Apostles.

Most people are aware of the early church martyrs, executions in the Colosseum, and Christians being fed to the lions. We have works of art showing Christians being impaled and burned to death. The founding fathers of Christianity were jailed and executed for their beliefs. Christians were hunted down and murdered. All of the writers of the letters to the Christian communities warned of the false doctrines that were permeating throughout the world and to be on their guard against them.

When Christianity first came on the scene, it created such an upheaval of current beliefs that there was widespread retaliation against it. The facts state that by AD 70, the leaders and vocal members of the Christian community had all but been executed, incarcerated, or forced into hiding.

Christianity was more than a thorn in the side of the Roman Empire. As political entities go, Rome was no different than the times we live in today. After doing everything they could to destroy and eradicate Christianity, they ended up creating their own homogenous Christian faith. They transposed everything pagan onto Christianity and eliminated everything that was Christian from it. It may have been one of the greatest fetes of diplomacy in political history. They smoothed the conflict between the existing religions and created a new state religion.

The major point of contention between Jews and Christians was that the Christians professed that Jesus was the only begotten Son of God, the Firstborn of creation. Jews, as do Muslims today, believe that there is only One God, and He did not beget a Son.

Believing that Jesus is God's only begotten Son is the key to the faith that empowers us to overcome temptation and sin. Not believing that Jesus is the only begotten Son of the Father will leave a person in the same situation that the seven sons of Sceva, a Jewish chief priest, found themselves in when they tried to exorcise a demon. Acts 19:14–16 describes how the seven sons called on the name of Jesus, trying to imitate Christians doing the same thing. Having no faith in who Jesus was, the demon-possessed man arose and beat the seven sons senseless.

The efforts of politicians and religious leaders to bring about peace between the current religions involved efforts of reconciliation. That reconciliation has given us today what has become known as Christianity, a pale ghost of the Way that was preached in the beginning. It pacified everyone; Christianity became ritual and celebratory. If you try to be a nice person, go to church on Sunday, attend Easter and Christmas services, say your prayers, give to the local charity, and acknowledge you're a sinner, God will forgive you. These are all pagan beliefs. Worshipping national and community deities was encouraged—just as various Christian sects today are encouraged to worship the likes of the queen of heaven and her entourage.

Included in Jesus's preaching was His recollections of how all of the prophets who had been sent to Israel before Him were rejected and many of them were tortured and executed.

> Others were tortured, not accepting deliverance,
> that they might obtain a better resurrection. Still
> others had trial of mockings and scourings, yes, and

of chains and imprisonment. They were stoned, they
were sawn in two, were tempted, were slain with
the sword. They wandered about in sheepskins and
goatskins, being destitute, afflicted, tormented—of
whom the world was not worthy. They wandered
in deserts and mountains, in dens and caves of the
earth. (Hebrews 11:35–38)

Since the beginning of time, humanity has attempted to eradicate
any knowledge of God and His plans for humanity. People have
continued in the pursuits that Eve began in the Garden of Eden.
Since Eve, mankind has chosen to build their own temples and
churches, and to follow the dictates of their own hearts.

Because of humanity's obstinacy, God surreptitiously inspired
a select number of men to document various histories and writings
of the Israelites in the Old and New Testaments. Throughout these
histories and writings, God intervened in such a way that when
they were recorded, they would actually paint a mosaic of God's
intentions and purposes towards humanity.

Even theologians have theorized that two of the Gospels in
the New Testament alluded to a preceding document, which is
commonly referred to as the Q Source. They assume that this
document was either destroyed or shared orally. Theories of written
and oral traditions and beliefs of the Bible abound.

The Bible, in its entirety, is the source of an encrypted message
from God to humanity. As has been documented in the Bible, the
writers of the books of the Old Testament did not fully understand
what they were writing. Various writers revealed various aspects of
God's final plan for humanity.

The encrypted message that is contained in the Bible could
better be identified as the Gospel. Paul, as did the other Apostles
and writers of the New Testament, used the Old Testament to preach
the Gospel.

> Then Paul, as his custom was, went in to them, and
> for three Sabbaths reasoned with them from the
> Scriptures, explaining and demonstrating that the
> Christ had to suffer and rise again from the dead,
> and saying, "This Jesus whom I preach to you is the
> Christ." (Acts 17:2–3)

Paul did not use cleverly devised cliches to convince his audience. He used painstaking arguments that could not be refuted. Arguments that took days and weeks to fully develop in order to convince the few. These were tough crowds, but with the aid of God's Holy Spirit the Gospel was preached orally. The letters written by Paul and the other writers of the New Testament, were letters of exhortation, building on doctrine that had already been preached and believed. Trying to understand the Gospel from the hodgepodge of minuscule fragments of God's design found throughout the New Testament can be an extremely difficult enterprise and one that has never yet been fully realized.

The current understanding of the Gospel is left to the recitation of a few Bible verses, but a full understanding and explanation of that Gospel is a challenge that has yet to be met.

What has been hidden for almost two thousand years is now revealed.

Chapter 3

THE LOAVES AND THE FISHES

A Prophecy of End-Time Events

And when Jesus went out He saw a great multitude; and He was moved with compassion for them, and healed their sick.

When it was evening, His disciples came to Him, saying, "This is a deserted place, and the hour is already late. Send the multitudes away, that they may go into the villages and buy themselves food."

But Jesus said to them, "They do not need to go away. You give them something to eat."

And they said to Him, "We have only five loaves and two fishes."

He said, "Bring them here to Me."

Then He commanded the multitudes to sit down on the grass. And He took the five loaves and the two fish, and looking up to heaven, He blessed and broke and gave the loaves to the disciples; and the disciples gave to the multitudes.

So they all ate and were filled, *and they took up twelve baskets of the fragments that remained.*

> *Now those who had eaten were about five thousand*
> *men*, besides women and children.
>
> Immediately Jesus made His disciples get into
> the boat and go before Him to the other side, while
> He sent the multitudes away.
>
> And when He had sent the multitudes away,
> He went up on the mountain to pray. Now when
> evening came, He was alone there. (Matthew
> 14:14–23; emphasis added)

> However, many of those who heard the word
> believed; and the number of the men came to be
> *about five thousand*. (Acts 4:4; emphasis added)

The feeding of the five thousand was prophetic. Jesus blessed the
loaves and the fishes and had the disciples distribute them. After
everyone had eaten, twelve baskets of leftovers were collected by the
disciples.

This prophecy was fulfilled in Acts 4:4. The five thousand men
who ate of the loaves and fishes represented the five thousand men
who were first converted. The twelve baskets of leftovers represented
the twelve apostles whose mission was to first proselytize the world.
They, together with the first-century church, represent the firstfruits
of the body of Christ. That Jesus immediately had the disciples get
into the boat once the feeding of the multitude was finished portends
to the duration in which the Gospel was first made available to the
early church.

The Second Feeding of the Multitude

> Then great multitudes came to Him, having with
> them the lame, blind, mute, maimed, and many
> others; and they laid them down at Jesus's feet, and
> He healed them. So the multitude marvelled when

they saw the mute speaking, the maimed made whole, the lame walking, and the blind seeing; and they glorified the God of Israel. Now Jesus called His disciples to Himself and said, "I have compassion on the multitude, because they have now continued with Me three days and have nothing to eat. And I do not want to send them away hungry, lest they faint on the way." Then His disciples said to Him, "Where could we get enough bread in the wilderness to fill such a great multitude?" Jesus said to them, "How many loaves do you have?" And they said, "Seven, and a few little fish." So He commanded the multitude to sit down on the ground. And He took the seven loaves and the fish and gave thanks, broke them and gave them to His disciples; and the disciples gave to the multitude. So they all ate and were filled, and they took up seven large baskets full of the fragments that were left. Now those who ate were four thousand men, besides women and children. (Matthew 15:30–38)

Assuredly, I say to you this generation will by no means pass away till all these things take place. (Matthew 24:34)

The second feeding of the multitude is prophetic of the Gospel, which is to be preached, and the resulting conversion that will take place at the end of this age. The original time frame for the Gospel that was preached after Christ's resurrection lasted one generation. John the Baptist began his preaching in approximately AD 29, and Jesus began His ministry in approximately AD 36. The destruction of the second temple was in AD 70.

At the time of the destruction of the second temple or shortly thereafter, Christianity as preached by the apostles had all but ceased to exist. We are now entering into the end of the ages. This period of time will only last one generation. Remembering Moses—a physical representation of the True and how his ministry lasted forty years—we should expect this end-time period to last forty years. If it continues longer, it will be for the sake of those being saved.

"For He will finish the work and
Cut it short in righteousness,
Because the LORD will make a
Short work upon the earth."
(Romans 9:28)

Chapter 4

THE MYSTERY OF THE GOSPEL OF GOD REVEALED

The Charge

> It is the glory of God to conceal a matter, But the
> glory of kings is to search out a matter. (Proverbs
> 25:2)

In the beginning, before anything was created that was created, God
the Father of us all, begot a Son. His Son was, in essence, identical
to Him. Nature teaches us that like begets like. Through God's
Son, He created everything that is seen and that is unseen. The
Father commanded, and His Son complied, so much so that He is
identified as the Word, the personification of God's command. All
things were created through Him, and for Him, and nothing was
created apart from Him. He is the sum total of all of creation.

What set John the Baptist apart from all of the other prophets
who came before him was that he recognized that the coming
Messiah had to be the Son of God. John witnessed that Jesus was
before John, but in physical terms, John was six months older than
Jesus.

Through signs and miracles, God witnessed to John the

Baptist—and to the disciples and apostles of Jesus—that Jesus of Nazareth is God's only begotten Son, the Christ. Salvation, as follows, can only happen if Jesus is the Christ, the only begotten Son of God. John the Baptist understood it cannot happen any other way, which will be shown in the entirety of this book.

One of the most important qualities of God is that He is just. He tempers justice with mercy, but He is—without parallel—just. The Old Testament writings introduce us to God's opinion of lawlessness. It also points out to humanity's inherent lawlessness. God cannot condone lawlessness. It would be diametrically opposed to His nature to do so.

Man was created in God's image with an ability to form a bond with God that transcends our current (after the "fall of humanity") human limitations. This bond was through God's Son, through whom He created the worlds and everything in them. The essence of the bond became incorporated into a binding contract or covenant, between Christ and mankind, comparable to an earthly marriage contract. The contract was perpetual, and it could only end by the death of one or both of the parties.

> So then, they are no longer two but one flesh.
> Therefore what God has joined together, let no man
> separate. (Matthew 19:6)

Lucifer and his legions were created to be ministering spirits to mankind, helps in their husbandry of the world.

Lucifer rebelled and incited humans to rebel with him. As the result of the rebellion, Lucifer—whose name was changed to Satan because of his rebellion—usurped God's authority and became the god of this world.

The penalty for rebellion is death.

God is just, merciful, and impartial.

God cannot condone rebellion.

Humanity was cursed with Lucifer.

Humanity immediately became alienated from God and would become subjected to a curse. In the first aspect of the curse, humanity was cursed, along with the world. The ground would no longer bear its fruit as designed, and humanity would be subjected to death. From the point of view of any legalistic claims, this curse was a permanent arrangement; in human terms, we became divorced from God.

In the second aspect of the curse, at the time of the deluge, at which time both the first and second aspects of the curse came into play, Satan and his legions were cast into hell, bound in eternal chains of darkness, and reserved for punishment until the coming Day of Judgment.

The third aspect of this curse is the coming Day of Judgment, in which the physical world and universe will be totally and completely annihilated, and the consequences of this curse are death and destruction upon humanity and this universe in various stages. Nothing can change this curse. It has been given to us by God in the form of a covenant or oath. It cannot be rescinded.

> Therefore what God has joined together, let not man separate. (Matthew 19:6)

God, in His mercy, was bound by His Nature to set things right. God's plan is alluded to in the book of Esther. At that time, King Ahasuerus was convinced to put the Jewish people under the curse of death by Haman, one of his high-ranking officials. King Ahasuerus was later convinced, by Queen Esther, of the injustice of his proclamation. Because King Ahasuerus had made an oath, that curse could not be rescinded (a physical representation of how God is bound by oaths.) In order to sidestep this order while at the same time upholding it, Ahasuerus made a second order that would permit;

> The Jews who were in every city to gather together and protect their lives—to destroy, kill, and annihilate all the forces of any people or province that would assault them, both little children and women, and to plunder their possessions. (Esther 8:11)

God designed a plan for humanity to escape the final enactment of the curse while at the same time allowing for the curse to be enacted. We cannot return to the Garden of Eden. That state of being can never again be realized. It was permanently lost due to humanity's rebellion. We can never get back to square one. Although that dream was lost, God has planned something better for humanity.

> But Joshua said to the people, "You cannot serve the LORD, for He is a holy God. He is a jealous God; He will not forgive your transgressions nor your sins." (Joshua 24:18)

God will not forgive our sins! God will destroy this body of sin. The soul who sins will die. God is the same yesterday, today and tomorrow. This is a fact. There is no amount of anything that can change this verdict. Even Christ's death on the cross does nothing to alter the verdict that was brought down upon humanity in the Garden of Eden.

> For there is no partiality with God. (Romans 2:11)

It's important to stress here that God is not capable of being partial. God cannot inflict judgment on Satan without inflicting judgment on humanity. This was demonstrated in the instance of the deluge or flood, which came down upon the world in ancient times. At that time, wrath was inflicted upon Satan, his angels, humanity, and the world. No one escaped except the eight persons in the ark, constructed by Noah and his sons. The flood represented baptism, the ark represented righteousness and the eight survivors represented the church. God's final wrath is now poised to shake the world again, and only those things that are unshakable will remain.

In these end-times, God is constructing for Himself an ark through His only begotten Son in the form of the church. The groundwork and foundation were completed in the first century AD.

The groundwork and foundation are as follows:

- God's Son had to give up His Godhead and become a man.
- In every aspect of a man, He needed to be found in the form of a man.
- Jesus referred to Himself as the Son of Man because, at that moment in time, He was completely, 100 percent man.
- In the form of a man, He was able to be tempted by evil just as every man who comes into the world is tempted by evil.
- He was declared to be innocent, having overcome all temptations.
- God the Father proclaimed His innocence by doing miracles through Him and by raising Him from the dead.
- He was obedient to the degree of allowing the authorities to crucify Him on the cross.
- Because He was found in the form of a man, He was subjected to the same curse that humanity was subjected to in the Garden of Eden.
- He suffered that curse by being hung on a tree and crucified.

  Christ has redeemed us from the curse of the law, having become a curse for us: (for it is written, "Cursed is everyone who hangs on a tree.") (Galatians 3:13)

Jesus was found by God to be obedient. He was judged to be innocent and because of a promise made to Christ by God, He was raised from the dead. Because He had been named an Heir by Him through whom the worlds were created, He received an inheritance. Because His death resulted in the end of His involvement in the covenant ordained in the Garden of Eden, He was entitled to enter into a New Covenant. That New Covenant is the promise that God had promised to Abraham after Abraham had proven his obedience and loyalty to God.

> But one testifies in a certain place, saying: "What is man that You are mindful of him, Or the son of man that You take care of him? You have made him a little lower than the angels; You have crowned him with glory and honor, And set him over the works of Your hands. You have put all things in subjection under his feet." (Hebrews 2:6–8)

Before Jesus's Crucifixion, God had Mary Magdalene anoint Jesus with oil, a physical representation of God anointing Jesus as High Priest forever, according to the order of Melchizedek. Just as Aaron was anointed high priest over the Levitical priesthood, by Moses, Jesus was figuratively anointed High Priest forever according to the order of Melchizedek by Mary Magdalene. And He received the Priesthood according to His inheritance.

> A woman came to Him having an alabaster flask of very costly fragrant oil, and she poured it on His head as He sat at the table. But when His disciples saw it, they were indignant, saying, "Why this waste? For this fragrant oil might have been sold for much and given to the poor." But when Jesus was aware of it, He said to them, "Why do you trouble the woman? For she has done a good work for Me. For you have the poor with you always, but Me you do not have always. For in pouring this fragrant oil

18

on My body, she did it for My burial. Assuredly, I
say to you, wherever this gospel is preached in the
whole world, what this woman has done will also
be told as a memorial to her." (Matthew 26:7–13)

Because Christ had died, He died to the covenant that He had
been bound to in the Garden of Eden. Jesus Christ is now sitting
at the right hand of God, waiting for God to put all of His enemies
beneath His feet and to bring about the figurative marriage between
Christ and His church.

Now—and only because Christ is the only begotten Son of God,
through whom all things were created—are we able to draw these
following conclusions: Because humanity had their origins in the
Son of God, because through Him all things were created, humanity
figuratively died through the death of Christ on the cross.

For in Him we live and move and have our being, as
also some of your poets have said, "For we are also
His offspring." (Acts 17:28)

Now if we died with Christ, we believe that we shall
also live with Him. (Romans 6:8)

There is no other person in creation who humanity could have
figuratively died through—except the One through whom we were
created. If we are to believe there is any hope for humanity, this
Gospel is our only saving grace. Because Christ was cursed—because
in Adam all people were cursed—then through the death of Christ,
humans figuratively suffered the curse that had been imposed upon
all of humanity.

In terms of covenants, mankind was unfaithful, broke their
covenant with Christ, and were deserving of death.

In human terms, we were betrothed to Christ. Joining Satan's
rebellion resulted in our breaking our covenant with Christ. The

breaking of this figurative marriage contract between Christ and humanity can be viewed as of a figurative form of adultery. In God's Law, the penalty for adultery is death. Because Christ died, He died to the covenant that bound Him with the adulterous humans in the Garden of Eden. Having died to the covenant, He has been freed from the consequences of that law or covenant.

> Or do you not know, brethren (for I speak to those
> who know the law), that the law has dominion over
> a man as long as he lives? (Romans 7:1)

Christ is now free to be bound in a new covenant, or in human terms, to be married to another. Because we have figuratively died to the covenant that we were bound to with Christ in the Garden of Eden, we are also free to be bound in a new covenant (or to be married to another).

Through our faith—that Christ is the only begotten Son of God, the Firstborn of creation, and that all things were created through Him, and that we have repented and become baptized—we are figuratively free to be raised with Jesus and seated with Him in His heavenly realm. We are free to be figuratively born again. We, Christ's church—or in human terms, Christ's bride—having been purified from past sins, are currently being prepared for the marriage feast that God is inviting us all to attend.

Although redemption has been provided to humanity through the Spirit, the physical world, including Satan, is still under the original curse. Christ provided aid to humanity but not to the angels. Redemption from this curse is only one aspect of the salvation plan that God has provided for us. In addition to our redemption from the curse, God has provided a New Covenant:

> But this is the covenant that I will make with the
> house of Israel after those days, says the LORD: "I
> will put My laws in their minds, and write them in

their hearts; and I will be their God and they shall be My people."

"No more shall every man teach his neighbour, and every man his brother, saying, 'Know the LORD,' for they all shall know Me, from the least of them to the greatest of them, says the LORD. For I will forgive their iniquity, and their sin I will remember no more." (Jeremiah 31:33–34)

We now have the opportunity to enter into a New Covenant with Christ. We now have the opportunity to be imprinted with the Spirit of Christ, to have Christ formed in us, and to be clothed with the Person of Christ.

The Old Covenant (Moses's Law) is becoming old and fading. In the Old Covenant, we had sacrifices and ceremonial washings to absolve us from the sins against the ordinances of the flesh. These were physical representations of the True, pointing to something better.

The entire Old Testament is a physical representation of the True, as Moses was instructed on the mount. The temple, the sacrifices, the service, as well as all of the prophets pointed to the True. All pointed to Christ so that He could be identified and believed in at His appearance.

And just as entrance into the holy of holies was only allowed once a year for sins committed in "ignorance" with the blood of bulls and goats, which cannot absolve the conscience of sin, today the curtain of the True Holy of Holies has been torn, as by Christ's flesh, and has given us a perpetual entrance into the presence of God.

Therefore, when He came into the world, He said: "Sacrifice and offering You did not desire, But a body You have prepared for Me. In burnt offerings and sacrifices for sin You had no pleasure. Then I said, 'Behold, I have come—In the volume of

> the book it is written of Me—To do Your will, O
> God.'" Previously saying, "Sacrifice and offering,
> burnt offerings, and offerings for sin You did not
> desire, nor had pleasure in them" (which are offered
> according to the law), then He said, "Behold, I have
> come to do Your will, O God." He takes away the
> first that He may establish the second. By that will
> we have been sanctified through the offering of the
> body of Jesus Christ once for all. (Hebrews 10:5–10)

The New Covenant is based on this concept: "Behold I have come to do Your will, O God."

Christ has been sacrificed once, making the Old Covenant obsolete and bringing into existence the New Covenant, which is the fulfillment of the promise. There is no longer a need for sacrifices and offerings. The New Covenant states emphatically that He will put His laws into our hearts and into our minds write them.

Once we have entered into this New Covenant, we are to do His will through Jesus's Spirit, which we receive at baptism. Once baptized, there is no longer a sacrifice for sin. You are commanded to be perfect even as your Father in heaven is perfect. It is now no longer us or Satan directing our lives; instead, the Spirit of Jesus Christ is working in us. We are no longer doing the work; Jesus Christ, in us, is doing the work until Christ is fully formed in us.

Christ in the Old Testament was the High Priest forever according to the order of Melchizedek. Moses anointed Aaron as high priest as a copy of the True High Priest. The purpose of the high priest was to make the people holy and acceptable to God. Aaron was a copy of the Christ. The term "Christ" or "Messiah" literally means "anointed one." Aaron was anointed as a direct imitation of the "Christ". The terms "Christ" and "Messiah" and the title "High Priest forever, according to the order of Melchizedek" can be used interchangeably.

There can only be One High Priest. In the Levitical priesthood which is a copy of the True, there can only be one high priest. It is only because of death that the high priest can be removed from his office.

The High Priest forever, according to the order of Melchizedek met Abraham after Abraham had defeated the kings, and Abraham gave the High Priest a tenth of all the spoils. This High Priest, whom Abraham met was the High Priest forever. For Jesus now to have been anointed High Priest forever, according to the order of Melchizedek, this High Priest who met Abraham needed to die.

It was Christ Who met Abraham in the Valley of the kings. It was Christ who walked with Adam and Eve in the Garden of Eden. It was Christ who created the worlds and everything in them, and it was Christ who was rejected and tortured and nailed to a cross in Jerusalem.

We will all stand before the judgment seat of Jesus Christ. Those who are judged worthy, by their patient continuance in doing good, who seek for glory, honor, and immortality, will receive the promise of eternal life. All others who have ignored the Gospel and continue in their worldly pursuits will receive their reward.

God is not partial; those who sin under the Law are just as guilty as those who sin without the Law, and those who sin after being baptized will be judged by the same impartial God. Even Satan and his angels believe that Jesus is the Christ and tremble. That knowledge avails them nothing. Anyone who believes the Gospel and ignores it will have the same fate as the rebellious. His one sacrifice has given us entrance into the body of Christ. We are figuratively raised with Him. The body of Christ is the manifestation of the New Covenant. The body of Christ is the union of the Spirit of Jesus Christ and the spirits of those baptized into His name. Those in the body of Christ are having Christ formed in them.

The church today is being prepared for the upcoming wedding feast. The church is described as a chaste virgin, pure and undefiled, being prepared for the wedding feast with Jesus Christ, who is Himself, pure and undefiled.

> Blessed are those who do His commandments, that
> they may have the right to the tree of life, and may
> enter through the gates into the city. But outside
> are dogs and sorcerers and sexually immoral and
> murderers and idolaters, and whoever loves and
> practices a lie. (Revelation 22:14–15)

God has given us witness through the things of creation, of the
majesty of His Person. From the witness that God has given to us
through creation, it is impossible for humanity to deny the existence
of God. It is impossible for humans to plead ignorance; they are
without excuse.

> God, who made the world and everything in it,
> since He is Lord of heaven and earth, does not dwell
> in temples made with hands. Nor is He worshipped
> with men's hands, as though He needed anything,
> since He gives to all life, breath, and all things.
> And He has made from one blood every nation
> of men to dwell on all the face of the earth, and
> has determined their pre-appointed times and the
> boundaries of their dwellings so that they should
> seek the Lord, in the hope that they might grope
> for Him and find Him, though He is not far from
> each one of us; for in Him we live and move and
> have our being, as also some of your own poets have
> said, "For we are also His offspring." Therefore,
> since we are the offspring of God, we ought not to
> think that the divine nature is like gold or silver or
> stone, something shaped by art and man's devising.
> Truly, these times of ignorance God overlooked,
> but now commands all men everywhere to repent,
> because He has appointed a day on which He will
> judge the world in righteousness by the Man whom

He has ordained. He has given assurance of this to all by raising Him from the dead. (Acts 17:24–31)

For the wrath of God is revealed from heaven against all ungodliness and unrighteousness of men, who suppress the truth in unrighteousness, because what may be known of God is manifest in them, for God has shown it to them. For since the creation of the world His invisible attributes are clearly seen, being understood by the things that are made, even His eternal power and Godhead, so that they are without excuse, because, although they knew God, they did not glorify Him as God, nor were thankful, but became futile in their thoughts, and their foolish hearts were darkened. (Romans 1:18–21)

And according to the law almost all things are purified with blood, and without shedding of blood there is no remission. (Hebrews 9:22)

According to the curse that was imposed upon the world in the Garden of Eden; he who breaks the law is cursed and the blood of him who is cursed must be shed.

For we must all appear before the judgment seat of Christ, that each one may receive the things done in the body, according to what he has done, whether good or bad. (2 Corinthians 5:10)

For the love of Christ compels us, because we judge thus: that if One died for all, then all died; and He died for all, that those who live should live no longer for themselves, but for Him who died for them and rose again. (2 Corinthians 5:14–15)

For He made Him who knew no sin to be sin for us, that we might become the righteousness of God in Him. (2 Corinthians 5:21)

Grace to you and peace from God the Father and our Lord Jesus Christ, who gave Himself for our sins, that He might deliver us from this present evil age, according to the will of our God and Father. (Galatians 1:3–4)

Christ has redeemed us from the curse of the law, having become a curse for us (for it is written, "Cursed is everyone who hangs on a tree,") that the blessing of Abraham might come upon the Gentiles in Christ Jesus, that we might receive the Spirit through faith. (Galatians 3:13–14)

But God forbid that I should boast except in the cross of our Lord Jesus Christ, by whom the world has been crucified to me, and I to the world. For in Christ Jesus neither circumcision nor uncircumcision avails anything, but a new creation. (Galatians 6:14–15)

The cross represents the deluge or flood, death, and repentance.

For there is one God and one Mediator between God and men, the Man Christ Jesus, who gave Himself a ransom for all. (1 Timothy 2:5–6)

Now all things are of God, who has reconciled us to Himself through Jesus Christ, and has given us the ministry of reconciliation, that is, that God was in Christ reconciling the world to Himself, not imputing their trespasses to them. (2 Corinthians 5:18–19)

And what agreement has the temple of God with idols? For you are the temple of the living God. As God has said: "I will dwell in them and walk among them. I will be their God, And they shall be My people." Therefore, "Come out from among them And be separated, says the Lord. Do not touch what is unclean, And I will receive you." "I will be a Father to you, And you shall be My sons and daughters, says the Lord Almighty." (2 Corinthians 6:16–18)

For I betrothed you to one husband, that I may present you as a chaste virgin to Christ. (2 Corinthians 11:2)

Paul, an apostle (not from men nor through man, but through Jesus Christ and God the Father who raised Him from the dead). (Galatians 1:1)

The entire Gospel of salvation is through Jesus Christ and God the Father who raised Him from the dead. Jesus is the Way, the Truth, and the Life. Christ came to the earth for the purpose of suffering and death. He suffered temptation so He would qualify to be the High Priest over us, cleansing us not just from past sins, but sins present.

God is not permissive. The ancient world was destroyed by the deluge. Sodom and Gomorrah were destroyed by fire and brimstone.

27

God does not change. He is the same yesterday, today, and tomorrow. The punishment for sin is still death.

> God shows personal favouritism to no man. (Galatians 2:6)

Jesus's death and resurrection were to institute a New Covenant, a covenant of the Spirit in which Christ is formed in us through His Holy Spirit. The law of ordinances pointed toward Christ. Sacrifices of bulls and goats and ceremonial washings do nothing to cleanse our consciences from sin.

> Brethren, I speak in the manner of men: Though it is only a man's covenant, yet if it is confirmed, no one annuls or adds to it. Now to Abraham and his Seed were the promises made, He does not say, "And to seeds," as of many, but as of one, "And to your Seed," who is Christ. And this I say, that the law, which was four hundred and thirty years later, cannot annul the covenant that was confirmed before by God in Christ, that it should make the promise of no effect. For if the inheritance is of the law, it is no longer of promise; but God gave it to Abraham by promise. (Galatians 3:15–18)

The covenant was confirmed before God in Christ 430 years before the law of Moses was instituted.

> Now I say that the heir, as long as he is a child, does not differ at all from a slave, though he is master of all, but is under guardians and stewards until the time appointed by the Father. Even so we, when we were children, were in bondage under the elements of the world. But when the fullness of

the time had come, God sent forth His Son, born
of a woman, born under the law, to redeem those
who were under the law, that we might receive the
adoption as sons. And because you are sons, God
has sent forth the Spirit of His Son into your hearts,
crying out, Abba, Father!" Therefore you are no
longer a slave but a son, and if a son, then an heir of
God through Christ. (Galatians 4:1–7)

We were slaves to the natural elements of the world, which dictated
our behaviors, which are defined by the Law. God has freed us
by sending the Spirit of Jesus Christ into our hearts in order to
transform us into children of God.

Now this is the main point of the things we are
saying: We have such a High Priest, who is seated
at the right hand of the throne of the Majesty in the
heavens, a Minister of the sanctuary and of the true
tabernacle which the Lord erected, and not man.
For every high priest is appointed to offer both gifts
and sacrifices. Therefore it is necessary that this
One also have something to offer. For if He were
on earth, He would not be a priest, since there are
priests who offer the gifts according to the law; who
serve the copy and shadow of the heavenly things,
as Moses was divinely instructed when he was about
to make the tabernacle. For He said, "See that you
make all things according to the pattern shown you
on the mountain." But now He has obtained a more
excellent ministry, inasmuch as He is also Mediator
of a better covenant, which was established on
better promises. For if that first covenant had been
faultless, then no place would have been sought for
a second. Because finding fault with them, He says:

"Behold, the days are coming, says the Lord, when I will make a new covenant with the house of Israel and with the house of Judah—"not according to the covenant that I made with their fathers in the day when I took them by the hand to lead them out of the land of Egypt; because they did not continue in My covenant, and I disregarded them, says the Lord. "For this is the covenant that I will make with the house of Israel after those days, says the Lord: I will put My laws in their mind and write them on their hearts; and I will be their God, and they shall be My people. "None of them shall teach his neighbour; and none his brother, saying, 'Know the Lord.' For all shall know Me, from the least of them to the greatest of them. "For I will be merciful to their unrighteousness, and their sins and their lawless deeds I will remember no more." In that He says, "A new covenant," He has made the first obsolete. Now what is becoming obsolete and growing old is ready to vanish away. (Hebrews 8:1–13)

Now when these things had been thus prepared, the priests always went into the first part of the tabernacle, performing the services. But into the second part the high priest went alone once a year, not without blood, which he offered for himself and for the people's sins committed in ignorance; the Holy Spirit indicating this, that the way into the Holiest of All was not yet made manifest while the first tabernacle was still standing. It was symbolic for the present time in which both gifts and sacrifices are offered which cannot make him who performed the service perfect in regard to the conscience—concerned only with foods and drinks, various washings, and fleshly ordinances imposed until the time of reformation.

But Christ came as High Priest of the good things to come, with the greater and more perfect tabernacle not made with hands, that is, not of this creation. Not with the blood of goats and calves, but with His own blood He entered the Most Holy Place once for all, having obtained eternal redemption. For if the blood of bulls and goats and the ashes of a heifer, sprinkling the unclean, sanctifies for the purifying of the flesh, how much more shall the blood of Christ, who through the eternal Spirit offered Himself without spot to God, cleanse your conscience from dead works to serve the living God? And for this reason He is the Mediator of the new covenant, by means of death, for the redemption of the transgressions under the first covenant, that those who are called may receive the promise of the eternal inheritance. For where there is a testament, there must be the death of the testator. For a testament is in force after men are dead, since it has no power at all while the testator lives. (Hebrews 9:6–17)

Through Jesus's death, the Old Covenant (Moses law) is fading. Through the New Testament, the inheritance was given. Once the inheritance was received, God fulfilled His promise and gave Jesus the authority to establish a New Covenant: "I will put My laws in their mind and write them in their hearts; and I will be their God, and they shall be My people."

Therefore it was necessary that the copies of the things in the heavens should be purified with these, but the heavenly things themselves with better sacrifices than these. For Christ has not entered the holy places made with hands, which are copies of the true, but into heaven itself, now to appear in the presence of God for us; not that He should offer Himself often, as the high priest enters the Most Holy Place every year with blood of another— He then would have had to suffer often since the foundation of the world; but now, once at the end of the ages, He has appeared to put away sin by the sacrifice of Himself. And as it is appointed for men to die once, but after this the judgment, so Christ was offered once to bear the sins of many. To those who eagerly wait for Him He will appear a second time, apart from sin, for salvation. (Hebrews 9:23–28)

Therefore if perfection were through the Levitical priesthood (for under it the people received the law), what further need was there that another priest should rise according to the order of Melchizedek, and not according to the order of Aaron? For the priesthood being changed, of necessity there is also a change of the law. (Hebrews 7:11–12)

Perfection could not be achieved through the Levitical priesthood.

And it is yet far more evident if, in the likeness of Melchizedek, there arises another priest who has come, not according to the law of a fleshly commandment but the power of an endless life. For He testifies: "You are a priest forever according to the order of Melchizedek." For on the one hand there is an annulling of the former commandment because of its weakness and unprofitableness, for the law made nothing perfect; on the other hand, there is the bringing in of a better hope, through which we draw near to God. (Hebrews 7:15–19)

The law made nothing perfect.

And inasmuch as He was not made priest without an oath (for they have become priests without an oath, but He with an oath by Him who said to Him: "The Lord has sworn And will not relent, 'You are a priest forever According to the order of Melchizedek'") by so much more Jesus has become a surety of a better covenant. Also there were many priests, because they were prevented by death from continuing. But He, because He continues forever, has an unchangeable priesthood. Therefore He is also able to save to the uttermost those who come to God through Him, since He always lives to make intercession for them. For such a High Priest was fitting for us, who is holy, harmless, undefiled, separate from sinners, and has become higher than the heavens; who does not need daily, as those high priests, to offer up sacrifices, first for His own sins and then for the people's, for this He did once for all when He offered up Himself. For the law appoints as high priest men who have weakness, but the word of the oath, which came after the law, appoints the Son who has been perfected forever. (Hebrews 7:20–28)

The flaw with the first covenant was that it did not make anything perfect. The promise made by God is that He would provide a better covenant and that better covenant would be overseen by someone with an endless life.

For the law, having a shadow of the good things to come, and not the very image of the things, can never with these same sacrifices, which they offer continually year by year, make those who approach perfect. For then would they not have ceased to be offered? For the worshipers, once purified, would have had no more conscience of sins. (Hebrews 10:1–2)

Therefore, with Jesus, we have no more conscience of sin. He doesn't just cancel the debt of sin owing; He has provided us a way to overcome sin in our present life, transforming us into children of God, making us perfect. Our surety comes from the realization that we have a strength other than ourselves to overcome sin in our daily lives. This is what gives us the confidence of our salvation, the token that we will redeem for eternal life when we stand before the judgment seat of Jesus Christ. There is no need for Christ to be sacrificed yearly because His one sacrifice perfects those who are being sanctified once and for all.

But in those sacrifices there is a reminder of sins every year. For it is not possible that the blood of bulls and goats could take away sins. Therefore, when He came into the world, He said: "Sacrifice and offering You did not desire, But a body You have prepared for Me. In burnt offerings and sacrifices for sin You had no pleasure. Then I said, 'Behold, I have come—In the volume of the book it is written of Me—To do Your will, O God,'" Previously saying, "Sacrifice and offering, burnt offerings, and offerings for sin You did not desire, nor had pleasure in them" (which are offered according to the law), then He said, "Behold, I have come to do Your will, O God." He takes away the first that He may establish the second. (Hebrews 10:3–9)

And why did He have a problem with the First Covenant? Because it did not make them perfect (Hebrews 7:19). He takes away the First Covenant, which was based on sacrifices for sin, in order to establish the Second Covenant which is based on "doing Your will, O God."

God is just. In the section of the Bible referred to as the Old Testament, God knew that humans were incapable of obeying Him, but He did not leave them without a witness. God directed that humans be given the Law in order to educate them about their sinful nature. Humanity had no idea how much further they had fallen from what had transpired in the Garden of Eden. Humanity did not just need to be educated about how far they had fallen. They needed to be educated about their complete inability to rise from their fallen state. That was the purpose of the Law. In addition, the Law was designed to teach us to be merciful as Jesus stated:

> "But go and learn what this means: 'I desire mercy and not sacrifice.' For I did not come to call the righteous, but sinners, to repentance." (Matthew 9:13)

The Ten Commandments focuses on the inherent nature of humanity. If human nature was good, there would be no need for the Ten Commandments. And even the Ten Commandments pointed to something much greater; they are just a shadow of what is expected from us. What is expected from us can be seen in the Sermon on the Mount.

Today, we have something completely new. Today, we have an opportunity to enter into a New Covenant. Entrance into that New Covenant requires a willingness to submit to Jesus Christ of Nazareth. Our submission will allow Him to intervene in each and every one of our personal lives and bring us to the obedience that God requires. Without that obedience, no one will see God.

> By that will we have been sanctified through the offering of the body of Jesus Christ once and for all. And every high priest stands ministering daily and offering repeatedly the same sacrifices, which can never take away sins. But this Man, after He had offered one sacrifice for sins forever, sat down at the right hand of God, from that time waiting till His enemies are made His footstool. For by one offering He has perfected forever those who are being sanctified. But the Holy Spirit also witnesses to us; for after He had said before, "This is the covenant that I will make with them after those days, says the Lord: I will put My laws into their hearts, and in their minds write them," then He adds, "Their sins and their lawless deeds I will remember no more." Now where there is remission of these, there is no longer an offering for sin. Therefore, brethren, having boldness to enter the Holiest by the blood of Jesus, by a new and living way which He consecrated for us, through the veil, that is, His flesh, and having a High Priest over the house of God, let us draw near with a true heart in full assurance of faith, having our hearts sprinkled from an evil conscience and our bodies washed with pure water. Let us hold fast the confession of hope without wavering, for He who promised is faithful. (Hebrews 10:10–23)

> For what is your life? It is even a vapour that appears for a little time and then vanishes away. (James 4:14)

He who believes in Him is not condemned; but he who does not believe is condemned already, because he has not believed in the name of the only begotten Son of God. (John 3:18)

He who loves his life will lose it, and he who hates his life in this world will keep it for eternal life. (John 12:25)

He who hates the works of the flesh and does everything through the name of Jesus Christ in order to resist and overcome those works will receive eternal life.

Enter by the narrow gate; for wide is the gate and broad is the way that leads to destruction, and there are many who go in by it. Because narrow is the gate and difficult is the way which leads to life, and there are few who find it. (Matthew 7:13–14)

Not everyone who says to Me, "Lord, Lord," shall enter the kingdom of heaven, but he who does the will of My Father in heaven. (Matthew 7:21)

But everyone who hears these sayings of Mine, and does not do them, will be like a foolish man who built his house on the sand: And the rain descended, the floods came, and the winds blew and beat on that house; and it fell. And great was its fall." (Matthew 7:26–27)

For the message of the cross is foolishness to those who are perishing, but to us who are being saved it is the power of God. For it is written: "I will destroy the wisdom of the wise, And bring to nothing the understanding of the prudent." (1 Corinthians 1:18–19)

For you see your calling, brethren, that not many wise according to the flesh, not many mighty, not many noble, are called. But God has chosen the foolish things of the world to put to shame the wise, and God has chosen the weak things of the world to put to shame the things which are mighty; and the base things of the world and the things which are despised God has chosen, and the things which are not, to bring to nothing the things that are, that no flesh should glory in His presence. (1 Corinthians 1:26–29)

Who has saved us and called us with a holy calling, not according to our works, but according to His own purpose and grace which was given to us in Christ Jesus before time began, but has now been revealed by the appearing of our Savior Jesus Christ, who has abolished death and brought life and immortality to light through the Gospel. (2 Timothy 1:9–10)

Chapter 5

THE MARRIAGE COVENANT AND AN UNCHANGEABLE PRIESTHOOD

God has chosen to reveal His design for humanity through the institutions in which we are familiar, so that we might have a better understanding of His ultimate plan for humanity. The institution of marriage is used throughout the Bible to describe God's relationship with humanity. In the ancient world, both bride and groom were to present themselves at their wedding ceremony pure and undefiled. The greatest of shame would be brought upon the family that presented an unchaste virgin to the marriage ceremony. This is a physical representation of the spiritual. Each and every member of Christ's body is to present themselves as chaste virgins, pure and undefiled by sin. Spiritual adultery, going after strange gods, is anathema to God's nature.

In the ancient world, a couple was engaged for one year before taking their wedding vows. Jesus's physical parents, Joseph and Mary, were engaged at the time of Mary's conception. Joseph considered divorcing Mary when she was found with child before their wedding. An angel informed Joseph of her immaculate conception.

In the Garden of Eden, Christ was, in essence, betrothed to humanity. Humanity committed adultery by rebelling with Lucifer.

Christ divorced humanity, but like Joseph, whose concern was for Mary, Christ and our Father God Almighty had concerns for the adulterous mankind.

The law states that a divorced couple cannot remarry. The verses that follow describe the relationship of Israel and Christ, metaphorically, through their tumultuous relationship.

These allegories are copies of the True. These allegories do not merely represent the spiritual condition of Israel and Judah. In these verses Israel and Judah are physical representations of the world's spiritual condition. This is the spiritual condition that the world was found in thousands of years ago. How much further have we sunk, and how much further still in this last generation?

> Therefore a man shall leave his father and mother and be joined to his wife, and they shall become one flesh. (Genesis 2:24)

> "For this reason a man shall leave his father and mother and be joined to his wife, and the two shall become one flesh." This is a great mystery, but I speak concerning Christ and the church. (Ephesians 5:31–32)

> The wife does not have authority over her own body, but the husband does. And likewise the husband does not have authority over his own body, but the wife does. (1 Corinthians 7:4)

Jesus Christ as our High Priest forever, has the authority over the church in order to cleanse her from all unrighteousness and to present her acceptable before God:

> A wife is bound by law as long as her husband lives; but if her husband dies, she is at liberty to be

married to whom she wishes, only in the Lord. (1 Corinthians 7:39)

Or do you not know, brethren (For I speak to those who know the law), that the law has dominion over a man as long as he lives? For the woman who has a husband is bound by the law to her husband as long as he lives. But if the husband dies, she is released from the law of her husband. So then if, while her husband lives, she marries another man, she will be called an adulteress; but if her husband dies, she is free from that law, so that she is no adulteress, though she has married another man. Therefore, my brethren, you also have become dead to the law through the body of Christ, that you may be married to another—to Him who was raised from the dead, that we should bear fruit to God. (Romans 7:1–4)

It is easier for heaven and earth to pass away than for one tittle of the law to fail. Whoever divorces his wife and marries another commits adultery; and whoever marries her who is divorced from her husband commits adultery. (Luke 16:17–18)

Or do you not know that he who is joined to a harlot is one body with her? For "the two," He says, "shall become one flesh." But he who is joined to the Lord is one spirit with Him. (1 Corinthians 6:16–17)

But I want you to know that the head of every man is Christ, the head of woman is man, and the head of Christ is God. (1 Corinthians 11:3)

Go and cry in the hearing of Jerusalem, saying, "Thus says the LORD: 'I remember you, the kindness of your youth, the love of your betrothal, when you went after Me in the wilderness, in a land not sown.'" (Jeremiah 2:2)

"Return, O backsliding children," says the LORD; "for I am married to you. I will take you, one from a city and two from a family, and I will bring you to Zion. (Jeremiah 3:14)

"Surely, as a wife treacherously departs from her husband, So have you dealt treacherously with Me, O house of Israel," says the LORD. (Jeremiah 3:20)

"How shall I pardon you for this? Your children have forsaken Me and sworn by those that are not gods. When I had fed them to the full, then they committed adultery and assembled themselves by troops in the harlots' houses. They were like well-fed lusty stallions; every one neighed after his neighbour's wife, shall I not punish them for these things?" says the LORD. "And shall I not avenge Myself on such a nation as this?" (Jeremiah 5:7–9)

I have seen your adulteries and your lustful neighings, the lewdness of your harlotry, your abominations on the hills in the fields. Woe to you, O Jerusalem! Will you still not be made clean? (Jeremiah 13:27)

Again the Word of the Lord came to me, saying, "Son of man, cause Jerusalem to know her abominations, and say, 'Thus says the LORD God to Jerusalem: "Your birth and your nativity are from the land of Canaan; your father was an Amorite and your mother a Hittite. As for your nativity, on the day you were born your navel cord was not cut, nor were you washed in water to cleanse you; you were not rubbed with salt nor wrapped in swaddling clothes. No eye pitied you, to do any of these things for you, to have compassion on you; but you were thrown out into the open field, when you yourself were loathed on the day you were born. And when I passed by you and saw you struggling in your own blood, I said to you in your blood, 'Live!' Yes, I said to you in your blood, 'Live!' I made you thrive like a plant in the field; and you grew, but you were naked and bare. When I passed by you again and looked upon you, indeed your time was the time of love; so I spread My wing over you and covered your nakedness. Yes, I swore an oath to you and entered into a covenant with you, and you became Mine," says the LORD God. "Then I washed you in water; yes, I thoroughly washed off your blood, and I anointed you with oil. I clothed you in embroidered cloth and gave you sandals of badger skin; I clothed you with fine linen and covered you with silk. I adorned you with ornaments, put bracelets on your wrists, and a chain on your neck. And I put a jewel in your nose, earrings in your ears, and a beautiful crown on your head. Thus you were adorned with gold and silver, and your clothing was of fine linen, silk, and embroidered cloth. You ate pastry of fine flour, honey, and oil. You were exceedingly beautiful, and succeeded to royalty. Your fame went out among the nations because of your beauty, for it was perfect through My splendour which I had bestowed on you," says the LORD God. "But you trusted in your own beauty, played the harlot because of your fame, and poured out your harlotry on everyone passing by who would have it. You took some of your garments and adorned multicoloured high places for yourself, and played the harlot on them. Such things should not happen, nor be. You have also taken your beautiful jewelry from My gold and My silver, which I had given you, and made for yourselves male images and played the harlot with them. You took your embroidered garments and covered them, and you set My oil and My incense before them. Also My food which I gave you—the pastry of fine flour, oil, and honey which I fed you—you set it before them as sweet incense; and so it was," says the LORD God. "Moreover you took your sons and your daughters, whom you bore to Me, and these you sacrificed to them to be devoured. Were your acts of harlotry a small matter, that you have slain My children and offered them up to them by causing them to pass through the fire? And in all your abominations and acts of harlotry you did not remember the days of your youth, when you were naked and bare, struggling in your blood. Then it was so, after all your wickedness—'Woe, woe to you!' says the LORD God—that you also built for yourself a shrine, and made a high place for yourself in every street. You built your high places at the head of every road, and made your beauty to be abhorred. You offered yourself to everyone who passed by, and multiplied your acts of harlotry. You also committed harlotry with the Egyptians, your very fleshly neighbours, and increased your acts of harlotry to provoke Me to anger. Behold, therefore, I stretched out My hand against you, diminished your allotment, and gave you up to the will of those who hate you, the daughters of the Philistines, who were ashamed of your lewd behaviour. You also played the harlot with the Assyrians, because you were insatiable; indeed you played the harlot with them and still were not satisfied. Moreover you multiplied your acts of harlotry as far as the land of the trader, Chaldea: and even then you were not satisfied. How degenerate is your heart!" Says the LORD God, "seeing you do all these things, the deeds of a brazen harlot. You erected your shrine at the head of every road, and built your high place in every street. Yet you were not like a harlot, because you scorned payment. You are an adulterous wife, who takes strangers instead of her husband. Men make payments to all harlots, but you made your payments to all your lovers, and hired them to come to you from all around for your harlotry. You are the opposite of other women in your harlotry, because no one solicited you to be a harlot. In that you gave payment but no payment was given you, therefore you are the opposite. Now then, O harlot, hear the Word of the LORD!" Thus says the LORD God: "Because your filthiness was poured out and your nakedness uncovered in your harlotry with your lovers, and with all your abominable idols, and because of the blood of your children which you gave to them, surely, therefore, I will gather all your lovers with whom you took pleasure, all those you loved, and all those you hated; I will gather them from all around against you and will uncover your nakedness to them, that they may see all your nakedness. And I will judge you as women who break wedlock or shed blood are judged; I will bring blood on you in fury and jealousy. I will also give you into their hand, and they shall throw down your shrines and break down your high places. They shall also strip you of your clothes, take your beautiful jewelry, and leave you naked and bare. They shall also bring up an assembly against you, and they shall stone you with stones and thrust you through with their swords. They shall burn your houses with fire, and execute judgments on you in the sight of many women; and I will make you cease playing the harlot, and you shall no longer hire lovers. So I will lay to rest My fury toward you, and My jealousy shall depart from you, I will be quiet, and be angry no more. Because you did not remember the days of your youth, but agitated Me with all these things, surely I will also recompense your deeds on your own head," says the LORD God. "And you shall not commit lewdness in addition to all your abominations. Indeed everyone who quotes proverbs will use this proverb against you: 'Like mother, like daughter!' You are your mother's daughter, loathing husband and children; and you are the sister of your sisters, who loathed their husbands and children; your mother was a Hittite and your father was an Amorite. Your eldest sister is Samaria, who dwells with her daughters to the north of you; and your younger sister, who dwells to the south of you, is Sodom and her daughters. You did not walk in their ways nor act according to their abominations; but, as if that were too little, you became more corrupt than they in all your ways. As I live," says the LORD God, "neither your sister Sodom nor her daughters have done as you and your daughters have done. Look, this was the iniquity of your sister Sodom: She and her daughter had pride, fullness of food, and abundance of idleness; neither did she strengthen the hand of the poor and needy. And they were haughty and committed abomination before Me; therefore I took them away as I saw fit. Samaria did not commit half of your sins; but you have multiplied your abominations more than they, and have justified your sisters by all the abominations which you have done. You who judge your sisters, bear your own shame also, because the sins which you committed were more abominable than theirs; they are more righteous than you. Yes, be disgraced also, and bear your own shame, because you justified your sisters. When I bring back their captives, the captives of Sodom and her daughters, and the captives of Samaria and her daughters, then I will also bring back the captives of your captivity among them, that you may bear your own shame and be disgraced by all that you did when you comforted them. When your sisters, Sodom and her daughters, return to their former state, and Samaria and her daughters return to their former state, then you and your daughters will return to your former state. For your sister Sodom was not a byword in your mouth in the days of your pride, before your wickedness was uncovered. It was like the time of the reproach of the daughters of Syria and all those around her, and of the daughters of the Philistines, who despise you everywhere. You have paid for your lewdness and your abominations." Says the LORD. 'For thus says the LORD God: "I will deal with you as you have done, who despised the oath by breaking the covenant. Nevertheless I will remember My covenant with you in the days of your youth, and I will establish an everlasting covenant with you. Then you will remember your ways and be ashamed, when you receive your older and younger sisters; for I will give them to you for daughters, but not because of My covenant with you. And I will establish My covenant with you. Then you shall know that I am the Lord, that you may remember and be ashamed, and never open your mouth anymore because of your shame, when I provide you an atonement for all you have done," says the LORD God.' (Ezekiel 16:1–63)

The Word of the Lord came again to me, saying: "Son of man, there were two women, the daughters of one mother. They committed harlotry in Egypt, they committed harlotry in their youth; their breasts were there embraced, their virgin bosom was there pressed. Their names: Oholah the elder and Oholibah her sister; they were Mine, and they bore sons and daughters. As for their names, Samaria is Oholah, and Jerusalem is Oholibah. Oholah played the harlot even though she was Mine; and she lusted for her lovers, the neighbouring Assyrians, who were clothed in purple, captains and rulers, all of them desirable young men, horsemen riding on horses. Thus she committed her harlotry with them, all of them choice men of Assyria; and with all for whom she lusted, with all their idols, she defiled herself. She has never given up her harlotry brought from Egypt, for in her youth they had lain with her, pressed her virgin bosom, and poured out their immorality upon her. Therefore I have delivered her into the hand of her lovers, into the hand of the Assyrians, for whom she lusted. They uncovered her nakedness, took away her sons and daughters, and slew her with the sword; she became a byword among women, for they had executed judgment on her. Now although her sister Oholibah saw this, she became more corrupt in her lust than she, and in her harlotry more corrupt than her sister's harlotry. She lusted for the neighbouring Assyrians, captains and rulers, clothed most gorgeously, horsemen riding on horses, all of them desirable young men. Then I saw that she was defiled; both took the same way. But she increased her harlotry; she looked at men portrayed on the wall, images of Chaldeans portrayed in vermillion, girded with belts around their waists, flowing turbans on their heads, all of them looking like captains, in the manner of the Babylonians of Chaldea. The land of their nativity. As soon as her eyes saw them, she lusted for them and sent messengers to them in Chaldea. Then the Babylonians came to her, into the bed of love, and they defiled her with their immorality; so she was defiled by them, and alienated herself from them. She revealed her harlotry and uncovered her nakedness. Then I alienated Myself from her, as I had alienated Myself from her sister. Yet she multiplied her harlotry in calling to remembrance the days of her youth, when she had played the harlot in the land of Egypt. For she lusted for her paramours, whose flesh is like the flesh of donkeys, and whose issue is like the issue of horses. Thus you called to remembrance the lewdness of your youth, when the Egyptians pressed your bosom because of your youthful breasts. Therefore, Oholibah, thus says the LORD God: "Behold, I will stir up your lovers against you, from whom you have alienated yourself, and I will bring them against you from every side: The Babylonians, all the Chaldeans, Pekod, Shoa, Koa, all the Assyrians with them, all of them desirable young men, governors and rulers, captains and men of renown, all of them riding on horses. And they shall come against you with chariots, wagons, and war-horses, with a horde of people. They shall array against you buckler, shield, and helmet all around. 'I will delegate judgment to them. And they shall judge you according to their judgments. I will set My jealousy against you, and they shall deal furiously with you; they shall remove your nose and your ears, and your remnant shall fall by the sword; they shall take your sons and your daughters, and your remnant shall be devoured by fire. They shall also strip you of your clothes And take away your beautiful jewelry. Thus I will make you cease your lewdness and your harlotry brought from the land of Egypt, so that you will not lift your eyes to them, nor remember Egypt anymore.' "For thus says the LORD God: 'Surely I will deliver you into the hand of those you hate, into the hand of those from whom you alienated yourself. They will deal hatefully with you, take away all you have worked for, and leave you naked and bare. The nakedness of your harlotry shall be uncovered, both your lewdness and your harlotry. I will do these things to you because you have gone as a harlot after the Gentiles, because you have become defiled by their idols. You have walked in the way of your sister; therefore I will put her cup in your hand.' Thus says the LORD God:

'You shall drink of your sister's cup, the deep and wide one; you shall be laughed to scorn and held in derision; it contains much. You will be filled with drunkenness and sorrow, the cup of horror and desolation, the cup of your sister Samaria. You shall drink and drain it, you shall break its shards, and tear at your own breasts; for I have spoken," says the LORD God. Therefore thus says the LORD God: "Because you have forgotten Me and cast Me behind your back, therefore you shall bear the penalty of your lewdness and your harlotry." The LORD also said to me: "Son of man, will you judge Oholah and Oholibah? Then declare to them their abominations. For they have committed adultery, and blood is on their hands. They have committed adultery with their idols, and even sacrificed their sons whom they bore to Me, passing them through the fire, to devour them. Moreover they have done this to Me: They have defiled My sanctuary on the same day and profaned My Sabbaths. For after they had slain their children for their idols, on the same day they came into My sanctuary to profane it; and indeed thus they have done in the midst of My house. Furthermore you sent for men to come from afar, to whom a messenger was sent; and there they came. And you washed yourself for them, painted your eyes, and adorned yourself with ornaments. You sat on a stately couch, with a table prepared before it, on which you had set My incense and My oil. The sound of a carefree multitude was with her, and Sabeans were brought from the wilderness with men of the common sort, who put bracelets on their wrists and beautiful crowns on their heads. Then I said concerning her who had grown old in adulteries, 'Will they commit harlotry with her now, and she with them?' Yet they went into her, as men go in to a woman who plays the harlot; thus they went into Oholah and Oholibah, the lewd women. But righteous men will judge them after the manner of adulteresses and after the manner of women who shed blood, because they are adulteresses, and blood is on their hands. For thus says the LORD God: 'Bring up an assembly against them, give them up to trouble and plunder. The assembly shall stone them with stones and execute them with swords; they shall slay their sons and their daughters, and burn their houses with fire. Thus I will cause lewdness to cease from the land, that all women may be taught not to practice lewdness. They shall repay you for your lewdness, and you shall pay for your idolatrous sins. Then you shall know that I am the LORD God.'" (Ezekiel 23:1–49)

Bring charges against your mother, bring charges; for she is not My wife, nor am I her husband! Let her put away her harlotries from her sight, and her adulteries from between her breasts; lest I strip her naked and expose her, as in the day she was born, and make her like a wilderness, and set her like a dry land, and slay her with thirst. I will not have mercy on her children, for they are the children of harlotry. For their mother has played the harlot; she who conceived them has behaved shamefully. For she said, "I will go after my lovers, who give me my bread and my water, my wool and my linen, my oil and my drink." (Hosea 2:2–5)

Do not rejoice, O Israel, with joy like other peoples, for you have played the harlot against your God. You have made love for hire on every threshing floor. (Hosea 9:1)

Thus says the LORD: "Where is the certificate of your mother's divorce, whom I have put away? Or which of My creditors is it to whom I have sold you? For your iniquities you have sold yourselves, And for your transgressions your mother has been put away." (Isaiah 50:1)

Then those of you who escape will remember Me among the nations where they are carried captive, because I was crushed by their adulterous heart which has departed from Me, and by their eyes which play the harlot after their idols; they will loathe themselves for the evils which they have committed in all their abominations. (Ezekiel 6:9)

Then I saw that for all the causes for which backsliding Israel had committed adultery, I had put her away and given her a certificate of divorce; yet her treacherous sister Judah did not fear, but went and played the harlot also. (Jeremiah 3:8)

They say, "If a man divorces his wife, and she goes from him and becomes another man's, may he return to her again?" Would not that land be greatly polluted? But you have played the harlot with many lovers yet return to Me," says the LORD. (Jeremiah 3:1)

Therefore I also have made you contemptible and base, before all the people, because you have not kept My ways but have shown partiality in the law. (Malachi 2:9)

And I took my staff, Beauty, and cut it in two, that I might break the covenant which I had made with all peoples. (Zechariah 11:10)

Behold, the days are coming, says the LORD, when I will make a new covenant with the house of Israel and with the house of Judah—not according to the covenant that I made with their fathers in the day that I took them by the hand to lead them out of the land of Egypt, My covenant which they broke, though I was a husband to them, says the LORD. "But this is the covenant that I will make with the house of Israel after those days," says the LORD: "I will put My law in their minds, and write it on their hearts; and I will be their God, and they shall be My people." No more shall every man teach his neighbour, and every man his brother, saying, "'Know the LORD,' for they all shall know Me, from the least of them to the greatest of them," says the LORD. "For I will forgive their iniquity, and their sin I will remember no more." (Jeremiah 31:31–34)

"Then I will give them one heart, and I will put a new spirit within them, and take the stony heart out of their flesh, and give them a heart of flesh, that they may walk in My statutes and keep My judgments and do them; and they shall be My people, and I will be their God. But as for those whose hearts follow the desire for their detestable things and their abominations, I will recompense their deeds on their own heads," says the LORD God. (Ezekiel 11:19–21)

"For the LORD God of Israel says that He hates divorce, for it covers one's garment with violence," says the LORD of hosts. "Therefore take heed to your spirit, That you do not deal treacherously." (Malachi 2:16)

"Hear, O Joshua, the high priest, you and your companions who sit before you, for they are a wondrous sign; for behold, I am bringing forth My Servant the Branch. For behold, the stone that I have laid before Joshua: Upon the stone are seven eyes. Behold, I will engrave its inscription," says the LORD of hosts, "and I will remove the iniquity of that land in one day. In that day," says the LORD of hosts, "everyone will invite his neighbour under his vine and under his fig tree." (Zechariah 3:8–10)

For I will take you from among the nations, gather you out of all countries, and bring you into your own land. Then I will sprinkle clean water on you, and you shall be clean; I will cleanse you from all your filthiness and from all your idols. I will give you a new heart and put a new spirit within you; I will take the heart of stone out of your flesh and give you a heart of flesh. I will put My Spirit within you and cause you to walk in My statutes, and you will keep My judgments and do them. Then you shall dwell in the land that I gave to your fathers;

you shall be My people, and I will be your God. (Ezekiel 36:24–28)

"And it shall be, in that day," says the LORD, "That you will call Me 'My Husband,' And no longer call Me 'My Master,' for I will take from her mouth the name of the Baals, and they shall be remembered by their name no more. In that day I will make a covenant for them with the beasts of the field, with the birds of the air, and with the creeping things of the ground. Bow and sword of battle I will shatter from earth, to make them lie down safely. I will betroth you to Me forever; yes, I will betroth you to me in righteousness and justice, in lovingkindness and mercy; I will betroth you to Me in faithfulness, And you shall know the LORD. It shall come to pass in that day That I will answer," says the LORD; "I will answer the heavens, and they shall answer the earth. The earth shall answer with grain, with new wine, and with oil; they shall answer Jezreel. Then I will sow her for Myself in the earth, and I will have mercy on her who had not obtained mercy; then I will say to those who were not My people, 'You are My people!' And they shall say, 'You are my God!'" (Hosea 2:16–23)

The Gentiles shall see your righteousness, and all kings your glory. You shall be called by a new name, which the mouth of the LORD will name. You shall also be a crown of glory in the hand of the LORD, and a royal diadem in the hand of your God. You shall no longer be termed forsaken, nor shall your land any more be termed desolate; but you shall be called Hephzibah, and your land Beulah. For the LORD delights in you, and your land shall be married. For as a young man marries a virgin, so shall your sons marry you, and as the bridegroom rejoices over the bride, so shall your God rejoice over you. (Isaiah 62:2–5)

Chapter 6

THE CARNAL MIND

One of the major hurdles that the ancients had with the prophets and those commissioned with the furtherance of the Gospel was of the prophets' complete and utter condemnation of human nature. Their testimony was diametrically at odds with the world's view of itself.

We are bombarded with the notion of how wonderful humans are, and we are all enticed into seeing the good in humanity, but God's appraisal of the matter is considerably different. Of course, all civilizations have the law, though justice can usually be found sitting on a park bench somewhere—quietly sobbing—human nature rarely rises above the mundane. God states that everyone has become corrupt. Jesus most aptly testified to the ruling class of the Jews during His ministry as follows:

> "Woe to you! For you build the tombs of the prophets, and it was your fathers who killed them."
> (Luke 11:47)

This is not at all to draw attention to the Jews. We have the same dynamic working in the current religious organizations of today. (Coincidentally, in the first part of the first century AD, the Jews were living what was believed to be the most religious of lives, and for the most part, they were trying to keep the Law to the letter of the Law.)

Today, laws are enacted in an effort to appease human nature. Morality takes a backseat to profit and contingency. Churches fail to provide the answers that people crave. Gangs run wild in the streets, and the only recourse for those who long for something better is to protest or support hospices.

The following scriptures testify to the true nature of humanity, which must be accepted in order to even begin to understand repentance.

> Then the LORD saw that the wickedness of man was great in the earth, and that every intent of the thoughts of his heart was only evil continually. (Genesis 6:5)

> Then the LORD said in His heart, "I will never again curse the ground for man's sake, although the imagination of man's heart is evil from his youth." (Genesis 8:21)

> Noah was a just man, perfect in his generations. Noah walked with God. (Genesis 6:9)

God is impartial, and He will not destroy the righteous with the wicked. Throughout the Old Testament, the righteous were those who believed in God and acted upon their belief. Noah's righteousness, which he professed by building an ark, enabled him to be recognized as "perfect in his generation."

> The LORD looks down from heaven upon the children of men, to see if there are any who understand, who seek God. They have all turned aside, they have together become corrupt; there is none who does good, no, not one. (Psalm 14:2–3)

If I regard iniquity in my heart, the LORD will not hear. (Psalm 66:18)

The LORD knows the thoughts of man, that they are futile. (Psalm 94:11)

But your iniquities have separated you from your God; and your sins have hidden His face from you, so that He will not hear. For your hands are defiled with blood, and your fingers with iniquity; your lips have spoken lies, your tongue has muttered perversity. No one calls for justice, nor does any plead for truth. They trust in empty words and speak lies, they conceive evil and bring forth iniquity. They hatch vipers' eggs and weave the spider's web; he who eats of their eggs dies, and from that which is crushed a viper breaks out. Their webs will not become garments, nor will they cover themselves with their works; their works are works of iniquity, and the act of violence is in their hands. Their feet run to evil, and they make haste to shed innocent blood; their thoughts are thoughts of iniquity; wasting and destruction are in their paths. The way of peace they have not known, and there is no justice in their ways; they have made themselves crooked paths; whoever takes that way shall not know peace. Therefore justice is far from us, nor does righteousness overtake us; we look for light, but there is darkness! For brightness, but we walk in blackness! We grope for the wall like the blind, and we grope as if we had no eyes; we stumble at noon day as at twilight; we are as dead men in desolate places. We all growl like bears, and moan sadly like doves; we look for justice, but there is none; for salvation, but it is far from us. For our transgressions are multiplied before You, and our sins testify against us; for our transgressions are with us, and as for our iniquities, we know them: in transgressing and lying against the LORD, and departing from our God, speaking oppression and revolt, conceiving and uttering from the heart words of falsehood. Justice is turned back, and righteousness stands afar off; for truth is fallen in the street, and equity cannot enter. So truth fails, and he who departs from evil makes himself a prey. (Isaiah 59:2–15)

For My people are foolish, they have not known Me. They are silly children, and they have no understanding. They are wise to do evil, but to do good they have no knowledge. (Jeremiah 4:22)

The heart is deceitful above all things, and desperately wicked; who can know it? (Jeremiah 17:9)

For out of the heart proceed evil thoughts, murders, adulteries, fornications, thefts, false witness, blasphemies. (Matthew 15:19)

And you have lifted yourself up against the Lord of heaven. They have brought the vessels of His house before you, and you and your lords, your wives and your concubines, have drunk wine from them. And you have praised the gods of silver and gold, bronze and iron, wood and stone, which do not see or hear or know; and the God who holds your breath in

His hand and owns all your ways, you have not
glorified. (Daniel 5:23)

You are of your father the devil. (John 8:44)

This condemnation was directed to the entire world because Satan
is the god of this world.

And He said, "What comes out of a man, that
defiles a man. For from within, out of the heart of
men, proceed evil thoughts, adulteries, fornication,
murders, thefts, covetousness, wickedness, deceit,
lewdness, an evil eye, blasphemy, pride, foolishness.
All these evil things come from within and defile a
man." (Mark 7:20–23)

These characteristics are the characteristics that are common to
humanity.

Be saved from this perverse generation. (Acts 2:40)

And even as they did not like to retain God in their
knowledge, God gave them over to a debased mind,
to do those things which are not fitting; being
filled with all unrighteousness, sexual immorality,
wickedness, covetousness, maliciousness; full of
envy, murder, strife, deceit, evil-mindedness; they
are whisperers, backbiters, haters of God, violent,
proud, boasters, inventors of evil things, disobedient
to parents, undiscerning, untrustworthy, unloving,
unforgiving, unmerciful; who, knowing the
righteous judgment of God, that those who practice
such things are deserving of death, not only do the

same but also approve of those who practice them. (Romans 1:28–32)

God gave them over to these debased things in order for humans to be repulsed with themselves, and as a result of that repulsion, that they should seek out the One and only True God. The wicked revel in their depravity and do not seek out the One and only True God.

And do you think this, O man, you who judge those practicing such things, and doing the same, that you will escaped the judgment of God? Or do you despise the riches of His goodness, forbearance, and long-suffering, not knowing that the goodness of God leads you to repentance? But in accordance with your hardness and your impenitent heart you are treasuring up for yourself wrath in the day of wrath and revelation of the righteous judgment of God, who "will render to each one according to his deeds": eternal life to those who by patient continuance in doing good seek for glory, honour, and immortality; but to those who are self-seeking and do not obey the truth, but obey unrighteousness—indignation and wrath, tribulation and anguish, on every soul of man who does evil, of the Jew first and also of the Greek; but glory, honour, and peace to everyone who works what is good, to the Jew first and also to the Greek. For there is no partiality with God. For as many as have sinned without law will also perish without law, and as many as have sinned in the law will be judged by the law (for not the hearers of the law are just in the sight of God, but the doers of the law will be justified). (Romans 2:3–13)

For to be carnally minded is death, but to be spiritually minded is life and peace. Because the carnal mind is enmity against God; for it is not subject to the law of God, nor indeed can be. So then, those who are in the flesh cannot please God. (Romans 8:6–8)

For you are still carnal. For where there are envy, strife, and divisions among you, are you not carnal and behaving like mere men? (1 Corinthians 3:3)

Let no one deceive himself. If anyone among you seems to be wise in this age, let him become a fool that he may become wise. For the wisdom of this world is foolishness with God. For it is written, "He catches the wise in their own craftiness"; and again, "The Lord knows the thoughts of the wise, that they are futile." (1 Corinthians 3:18–20)

Most assuredly, I say to you, whoever commits sin is a slave of sin. And a slave does not abide in the house forever, but a son abides forever. Therefore if the Son makes you free, you shall be free indeed. (John 8:34–36)

Do you not know the unrighteous will not inherit the kingdom of God? Do not be deceived. Neither fornicators, nor idolaters, nor adulterers, nor homosexuals, nor sodomites, nor thieves, nor covetous, nor drunkards, nor revilers, nor extortioners will inherit the kingdom of God. And such were some of you. But you were washed, but you were sanctified, but you were justified in the name of the Lord Jesus and by the Spirit of our God. (1 Corinthians 6:9–11)

But then, indeed, when you did not know God, you served those which by nature are not gods. (Galatians 4:8)

This I say, therefore, and testify in the Lord, that you should no longer walk as the rest of the Gentiles walk, in the futility of their mind, having their understanding darkened, being alienated from the life of God, because of the ignorance that is in them, because of the blindness of their heart; who, being past feeling, have given themselves over to lewdness, to work all uncleanness with greediness. (Ephesians 4:17–19)

And that they may come to their senses and escape the snare of the devil, having been taken captive by him to do his will. (2 Timothy 2:26)

Chapter 7

FOOD

Food has absolutely no bearing on our spiritual condition. Maintaining a particular diet does not purify the spirit or protect us from sin. There may be health-related advantages to pursuing a certain diet, but it will not make you a good person. If, on the other hand, your diet or behaviour is offensive to anyone, you should be reminded that anything that is not the specific will of God, and causes offense, is sin. Obviously, many people will take offense at hearing the Gospel. "I believed and therefore spoke."

> "Therefore I judge that we should not trouble those from among the Gentiles who are turning to God, but that we write to them to abstain from things polluted by idols, from sexual immorality, from things strangled, and from blood." (Acts 15:19–20)

> But food does not commend us to God; for neither if we eat are we the better, nor if we do not eat are we the worse. (1 Corinthians 8:8)

> Therefore, if food makes my brother stumble, I will never again eat meat, lest I make my brother stumble. (1 Corinthians 8:13)

Therefore, whether you eat or drink, or whatever you do, do all to the glory of God. (1 Corinthians 10:31)

In the meantime His disciples urged Him, saying, "Rabbi, eat." But He said to them, "I have food to eat of which you do not know." Therefore the disciples said to one another, "Has anyone brought Him anything to eat?" Jesus said to them, "My food is to do the will of Him who sent Me, and to finish His work." (John 4:31–34)

In the preceding verse Jesus speaks of the the True food. The True food is doing the will of our Sovereign LORD and Father Almighty God. There is only one True food and it is only through eating of this one True food that makes us capable of performing God's will. Jesus identifies the one True food:

Then Jesus said to them, "Most assuredly, I say to you, Moses did not give you the bread from heaven, but My Father gives you the true bread from heaven. For the bread of God is He who comes down from heaven and gives life to the world. Then they said to Him, "Lord, give us this bread always." And Jesus said to them, "I am the bread of life. He who comes to Me shall never hunger, and he who believes in Me shall never thirst. But I said to you that you have seen Me and yet do not believe. All that the Father gives Me will come to Me, and the one who comes to Me I will by no means cast out. For I have come down from heaven, not to do My own will, but the will of Him who sent Me. This is the will of the Father who sent Me, that of all He has given Me I should lose nothing, but should raise it up at the last day. And this is the will of Him who sent Me, that everyone who sees the Son and believes in Him may have everlasting life; and I will raise him up at the last day." (John 6:32–40)

Do not be carried about with various and strange doctrines. For it is good that the heart be established by grace, not with foods which have not profited those who have been occupied with them. We have an altar from which those who serve the tabernacle have no right to eat. For the bodies of those animals, whose blood is brought into the sanctuary by the high priest for sin, are burned outside the camp. Therefore Jesus also, that He might sanctify the people with His own blood, suffered outside the gate. Therefore let us go forth to Him, outside the camp, bearing His reproach. For here we have no continuing city, but we seek the one to come. Therefore by Him let us continually offer the sacrifice of praise to God, that is, the fruit of our lips, giving thanks to His name. (Hebrews 13:9–15)

Chapter 8

SIN

The earth mourns and fades away, the world languishes and fades away; the haughty people of the earth languish. The earth is also defiled under its

inhabitants, because they have transgressed the laws, changed the ordinance, broken the everlasting covenant. Therefore the curse has devoured the earth, And those who dwell in it are desolate. Therefore the inhabitants of the earth are burned And few men are left. (Isaiah 24:4–6)

Now therefore, do not be mockers, Lest your bonds be made strong; For I have heard from the LORD God of Hosts, A destruction determined even upon the whole earth. (Isaiah 28:22)

Now go, write it before them on a tablet, And note it on a scroll, That it may be for time to come, Forever and ever: That this is a rebellious people, Lying children, Children who will not hear the law of the LORD; Who say to the seers, "Do not see," And to the prophets, "Do not prophesy to us right things,

Speak to us smooth things, prophesy deceits, Get out of the way, Turn aside from the path, Cause the Holy One of Israel To cease from before us." Therefore thus says the Holy One of Israel: "Because you despise this word, And trust in oppression and perversity, And rely on them, Therefore this iniquity shall be to You Like a breach ready to fall, A bulge in a high wall, Whose breaking comes suddenly, in an instant. And He shall break it like the breaking of the potter's vessel, Which is broken in pieces; He shall not spare. So there shall not be found among its fragments A shard to take fire from the hearth, Or to take water from the cistern. (Isaiah 30:8–14)

Come near, you nations, to hear; And heed, you people! Let the earth hear, and all that is in it, The world and all things that come forth from it, For the indignation of the Lord is against all nations, And His fury against all their armies; He has utterly destroyed them, He has given them over to the slaughter. Also their slain shall be thrown out; Their stench shall rise from their corpses, And the mountains shall be melted with their blood. All the host of heaven shall be dissolved, And the heavens shall be rolled up like a scroll; All their hosts shall fall down As the leaf falls from the vine, And as fruit falling from a fig tree. (Isaiah 34:1–4)

For since the beginning of the world Men have not heard nor perceived by the ear, Nor has the eye seen any God besides You, Who acts for the one who waits for Him. You meet him who rejoices and does righteousness, Who remembers You in Your ways. You are indeed angry, for we have sinned—In these ways we continue; And we need to be saved. But we are all like an unclean thing, And all our righteousness are like filthy rags; We all fade as a leaf, And our iniquities, like the wind, Have taken us away. And there is no one who calls on Your name, Who stirs himself up to take hold of You; For You have hidden Your face from us, And have consumed us because of our iniquities. (Isaiah 64:4–7)

Behold, all souls are Mine; The soul of the father As well as the soul of the son is Mine; The soul who sins shall die. (Ezekiel 18:4)

And I gave them My statutes and showed them My judgments, "which, if a man does, he shall live by them." (Ezekiel 20:11)

And when He has come, He will convict the world of sin, and of righteousness, and of judgment: of sin, because they do not believe in Me. Of righteousness, because I go to My Father and you see Me no more. (John 16:8–10)

They don't believe that Christ is the only begotten Son of God, through whom God created the world.

They don't believe that through His death on the cross, He died to the First Covenant in the Garden of Eden, between Christ and man.

They don't believe that once God resurrected Jesus from the dead, He established the Second Covenant, through which humanity has the opportunity to be resurrected from sin.

Today we believe that Jesus is sitting at the right hand of Power and intervening in our lives. Today, the righteous have the same faith as the centurion:

> The centurion answered and said, "Lord, I am not worthy that You should come under my roof. But only speak a word, and my servant will be healed. For I also am a man under authority, having soldiers under me. And I say to this one, 'Go,' and he goes; and to another, 'Come,' and he comes; and to my servant, 'Do this,' and he does it." When Jesus heard it, He marvelled, and said to those who followed, "Assuredly, I say to you, I have not found such great faith, not even in Israel!" (Matthew 8:8–10)

With the same faith as the centurion, we must believe the Gospel and trust in Jesus to keep us from sin and make us an acceptable offering to God.

> Of judgment, because the ruler of this world is judged. (Matthew 8:11)

An avenue of escape has been provided to humanity so that the impending curse can be imposed upon Satan and all those who believe the lie.

> For we have previously charged both Jews and Greeks that they are all under sin. As it is written: "There is none righteous, no not one; There is none who understands; There is none who seeks after God. They have all turned aside; They have together become unprofitable; There is none who does good, no, not one. Their throat is an open tomb; With their tongues they have practiced

deceit; The poison of asps is under their lips, Whose mouth is full of cursing and bitterness. Their feet are swift to shed blood; Destruction and misery are in their ways; And the way of peace they have not known. There is no fear of God before their eyes." Now we know that whatever the law says, it says to those who are under the law, that every mouth may be stopped, and all the world may become guilty before God. Therefore by the deeds of the law no flesh will be justified in His sight, for by the law is the knowledge of sin. (Romans 3:9–20)

Therefore, just as through one man sin entered the world, and death through sin, and thus death spread to all men, because all sinned—(For until the law sin was in the world, but sin is not imputed when there is no law. Nevertheless death reigned from Adam to Moses, even over those who had not sinned according to the likeness of the transgression of Adam, who is a type of Him who was to come. But the free gift is not like the offence. For if by the one man's offence many died, much more the grace of God and the gift by the grace of the one Man, Jesus Christ, abounded to many. And the gift is not like that which came through the one who sinned. For the judgment which came from one offence resulted in condemnation, but the free gift which came from many offences resulted in justification. For if by one man's offence death reigned through the one, much more those who receive abundance of grace and of the gift of righteousness will reign in life through the One, Jesus Christ.) Therefore, as through one man's offence judgment came to all men, resulting in condemnation, even so through one Man's righteous act the free gift came to all men, resulting in justification of life. For as by one man's disobedience many were made sinners, so also by one Man's obedience many will be made righteous. Moreover the law entered that the offence might abound. But where sin abounded, grace abounded much more, so that as sin reigned in death, even so grace might reign through righteousness to eternal life through Jesus Christ our Lord. (Romans 5:12–21)

The Law was given to educate humans about sin and teach us that it is inherent in our nature. Though the world was condemned through Adam's rebellion, humans needed to be educated about the depths to which they had further sunk into sin.

For we know that the law is spiritual, but I am carnal, sold under sin. For what I am doing, I do not understand. For what I will to do, that I do not practice; but what I hate, that I do. If, then, I do what I will not to do, I agree with the law that it is good. But now, it is no longer I who do it, but sin that dwells in me. For I know that in me (that is, in my flesh) nothing good dwells; for to will is present with me, but how to perform what is good I do not find. For the good that I will to do, I do not do; but the evil I will not to do, that I practice. Now if I do what I will not to do, it is no longer I who do it, but sin that dwells in me. I find then a law, that evil is present with me, the one who wills to do good. For I delight in the law of God according to the inward man. (Romans 7:14–22)

The inward man—this is the spirit of a person that Jesus Christ joins with. Every other aspect of a person is destined for the fires of hell. Christ died in the flesh. We figuratively died with Him. Now we have the opportunity to be resurrected with Jesus in the Spirit. At Jesus Christ's appearance, when we are changed, we will shed this fleshly body of sin that figuratively died with Christ and be clothed with the same body as that of Jesus Christ. We shall be swallowed up by victory.

Death occurs when the spirit is separated from the body. When the body dies the spirit returns to God. "Then the dust will return to the earth as it was, And the spirit will return to God who gave it." (Ecclesiastes 12:7) "For the living know that they will die; But the dead know nothing, And they have no more reward, For the memory of them is forgotten. Also their love, their hatred, and their envy have now perished; Nevermore will they have a share In anything done under the sun." (Ecclesiastes 9:5–6)

Unless that inward man or spirit is joined to a body it does not have any self awareness. When humanity and the worlds find themselves thrown into the fires of hell the only chance of life is to be born again with a new body. Those who are deemed worthy will receive a new body like that of Jesus Christ once God's kingdom has been established.

> But I see another law in my members, warring against the law of my mind, and bringing me into captivity to the law of sin which is in my members. O wretched man that I am! Who will deliver me from this body of death? (Romans 7:23–24)

> But the Scripture has confined all under sin, that the promise by faith in Jesus Christ might be given to those who believe. But before faith came we were kept under guard by the law, kept for the faith which would afterward be revealed. Therefore the

> law was our tutor to bring us to Christ, that we
> might be justified by faith. (Galatians 3:22–24)

The Law taught us what was in human nature, tainted by rebellion
and the god of this world. We know that human nature cannot
please God. In order to please God, which is required in order not
to be condemned with the rest of the world, we need help. That help
is provided to us by Jesus Christ, by His Spirit. Through His Spirit,
we are able to overcome all temptation. This is the promise fulfilled,
the Spirit of Jesus Christ helping us. This is the guarantee. This is
the confidence that we hold to. This confidence, which we receive
once we begin to triumph over sin, is the token that God has given
us, which is to be redeemed at the return of Jesus Christ.

> But after faith has come, we are no longer under a
> tutor. For you are all sons of God through faith in
> Christ Jesus. (1 Corinthians 11:25–26)

The "tutor" is the Law and is specifically designed to teach us that
we are all sinners. Therefore the Law leads us to Christ. Once we
have received Christ we are no longer under the Law because Christ
is keeping us from sin.

> Therefore, as the Holy Spirit says: "Today, if you
> will hear His voice, Do not harden your hearts as
> in the rebellion, In the day of trial in the wilderness,
> Where your fathers tested Me, tried Me, And saw
> My works forty years. Therefore I was angry with
> that generation, And said, 'They always go astray
> in their heart, And they have not known My ways.'
> So I swore in My wrath, 'They shall not enter My
> rest.'" Beware, brethren, lest there be in any of you
> an evil heart of unbelief in departing from the living
> God; but exhort one another daily, while it is called

"Today," lest any of you be hardened through the deceitfulness of sin. For we have become partakers of Christ if we hold the beginning of our confidence steadfast to the end, while it is said: "Today, if you will hear His voice, Do not harden your hearts as in the rebellion." For who, having heard, rebelled? Indeed, was it not all who came out of Egypt, led by Moses? Now with whom was He angry forty years? Was it not with those who sinned, whose corpses fell in the wilderness? And to whom did He swear that they would not enter His rest, but to those who did not obey? So we see that they could not enter in because of unbelief. (Hebrews 3:7–19)

Remember that everything in the Old Testament was written as a copy of the True. Israel's departure from Egypt was allegorical to our departure from the world and from sin. Israel was baptized into Moses when they crossed the Red Sea just as we are baptized into Christ at our baptism. We have been saved from the avenging angel through Christ's death, just as the Israelites were saved by the Passover lamb. All of the struggles that Israel had in the wilderness for 40 years are synonymous with the struggles that we face after our conversion, repentance and baptism. Most of the adults escaping out of Egypt with Moses died in the wilderness. This is an admonition of just how dire our situation is.

Believing that Christ is God's only begotten Son, the first born of all creation, who existed prior to creation and through whom all things were created, is merely a starting point. One must repent. One must feel physical and emotional remorse for the sin in their lives. One must do everything physically possible in order to put an end to the sin in their lives. One must be baptized into the name of Jesus Christ of Nazareth and receive Jesus Christ's Holy Spirit. Then, one must embark on a Christian journey that is exemplified throughout the New Testament. Through Jesus's teachings and the teachings of Paul and the apostles in the letters of that same Testament, we are instructed and encouraged to live in the Spirit. Only then, and only if we can count ourselves victorious through Jesus Christ, do we stand the slightest chance of being presented acceptable before God. Remember Matthew 19:26, "But Jesus looked at them and said to them, 'With men this is impossible, but with God all things are possible.'"

Possibly the greatest apostle on record, Paul, years after His conversion wrote of his Christian journey;

> Yet indeed I also count all things loss for the excellence of the knowledge of Christ Jesus my Lord, for whom I suffered the loss of all things, and count them as rubbish, that I may gain Christ and be found in Him, not having my own righteousness, which is from the law, but that which is through faith in Christ, the righteousness which is from God by faith; that I may know Him and the power of His resurrection, and the fellowship of His sufferings, being conformed to His death, if, by any means, I may attain to the resurrection from the dead. Not that I have already attained, or am already perfected; but I press on, that I may lay hold of that for which Christ Jesus has also laid hold of me. Brethren, I do not count myself to have apprehended; but one thing I do, forgetting those things which are behind and reaching forward to those things which are ahead, I press toward the goal for the prize of the upward call of God in Christ Jesus.

If Paul, possibly the hardest working and most vocal of apostles, did not take for granted his salvation after years of subjecting himself to his Christian labours of love, how much more should we strive to be true to our faith, that we, with Paul and all of the apostles and saints, should be found worthy to stand before our Sovereign LORD and Father Almighty God.

> Therefore, since a promise remains of entering His rest, let us fear lest any of you seem to have come short of it. For indeed the gospel was preached to us as well as to them; but the word which they heard did not profit them, not being mixed with faith in those who heard it. (Hebrews 4:1–2)

> Let us therefore be diligent to enter that rest, lest anyone fall according to the same example of disobedience. For the word of God is living and powerful, and sharper than any two-edged sword, piercing even to the division of soul and spirit, and of joints and marrow, and is a discerner of the thoughts and intents of the heart. And there is no creature hidden from His sight, but all things are naked and open to the eyes of Him to whom we must give account. (Hebrews 4:11–13)

> If you really fulfill the royal law according to the Scripture, "You shall love your neighbour as yourself," you do well; but if you show partiality, you commit sin, and are convicted by the law as transgressors. For whoever shall keep the whole law, and yet stumble in one point, he is guilty of all. For He who said, "Do not commit adultery," also said, "Do not murder." Now if you do not commit adultery, but you do murder, you have become a transgressor of the law. So speak and so do as those who will be judged by the law of liberty. For judgment is without mercy to the one who has

shown no mercy. Mercy triumphs over judgment. (James 2:8–13)

Where do wars and fights come from among you? Do they not come from your desires for pleasure that war in your members? You lust and do not have. You murder and covet and cannot obtain. You fight and war. Yet you do not have because you do not ask. You ask and do not receive, because you ask amiss, that you may spend it on your pleasures. Adulterers and adulteresses! Do you not know that friendship with the world is enmity with God? Whoever therefore wants to be a friend of the world makes himself an enemy of God. Or do you think that the Scripture says in vain, "The Spirit who dwells in us yearns jealously"? But He gives more grace. Therefore He says: "God resists the proud, But gives grace to the humble." Therefore submit to God. Resist the devil and he will flee from you. Draw near to God and He will draw near to you. Cleanse your hands, you sinners; and purify your hearts, you double-minded. Lament and mourn and weep! Let your laughter be turned to mourning and your joy to gloom. Humble yourself in the sight of the Lord, and He will lift you up. Do not speak evil of one another, brethren. He who speaks evil of a brother and judges his brother, speaks evil of the law and judges the law. But if you judge the law, you are not a doer of the law but a judge. (James 4:1–11)

Chapter 9

REPENTANCE

That which is has already been, And what is to be has already been; And God requires an account of what is past. Moreover I saw under the sun: In the place of judgment, Wickedness was there; And in the place of righteousness, Iniquity was there. I said in my heart, "God shall judge the righteous and the wicked, For there is a time there for every purpose and for every work." (Ecclesiastes 3:15–17)

For there is not a just man on earth who does good And does not sin. (Ecclesiastes 7:20)

Truly, this only I have found: That God made man upright, But they have sought out many schemes. (Ecclesiastes 7:29)

"Come now, and let us reason together," says the LORD, "Though your sins are like scarlet, They shall be as white as snow; Though they are red like crimson, They shall be as wool." (Isaiah 1:18)

It may be that the house of Judah will hear all the adversities which I purpose to bring upon them, that everyone may turn from his evil way, that I may forgive their iniquity and their sin. (Jeremiah 36:3)

Thus says the LORD God: "Remove the turban, and take off the crown; Nothing shall remain the same. Exalt the humble, and humble the exalted. Overthrown, overthrown, I will make it overthrown! It shall be no longer, Until He comes whose right it is, And I will give it to Him.' (Ezekiel 21:26–27)

Say to them: "As I live," says the LORD God, "I have no pleasure in the death of the wicked, but that the wicked turn from his way and live. Turn, turn from your evil ways! For why should you die, O house of Israel?" Therefore you, O son of man, say to the children of your people: "The righteousness of the righteous man shall not deliver him in the day of his transgression; as for the wickedness of the wicked, he shall not fall because of it in the day that he turns from his wickedness; nor shall the righteous be able to live because of his righteousness in the day that he sins, When I say to the righteous that he shall surely live, but he trusts in his own righteousness and commits iniquity, none of his righteous works shall be remembered; but because of the iniquity that he has committed, he shall die." Again, when I say to the wicked, "You shall surely die," if he turns from his sin and does what is lawful and right, if the wicked restores the pledge, gives back what he has stolen, and walks in the statutes of life without committing iniquity, he shall surely live; he shall not die. None of his sins which he has committed shall be remembered against him; he has done what is lawful and right; he shall surely live." Yet the children of your people say, "The way of the LORD is not fair." But it is their way that is not fair! When the righteous turns from his righteousness and commits iniquity, he shall die because of it. But when the wicked turns form his wickedness and does what is lawful and right, he shall live because of it." Yet you say, "The way of the Lord is not fair." O house of Israel, I will judge every one of you according to his own ways. (Ezekiel 33:11–20)

When Jesus heard it, He said to them, "Those who are well have no need of a physician, but those who are sick. I did not come to call the righteous, but sinners, to repentance." (Mark 2:17)

Then Paul said, "John indeed baptized with a baptism of repentance, saying to the people that they should believe on Him who would come after him, that is, on Christ Jesus. (Acts 19:4)

How I kept nothing back that was helpful, but proclaimed it to you, and taught you publicly and from house to house, testifying to Jews, and also to Greeks, repentance toward God and faith toward our Lord Jesus Christ. (Acts 20:20–21)

When He had called the people to Himself, with His disciples also, He said to them, "Whoever desires to come after Me, let him deny himself, and take up his cross, and follow Me. For whoever desires to save his life will lose it, but whoever loses his life for My sake and the gospel's will save it. For what will it profit a man if he gains the whole world, and loses his own soul? Or what will a man give in exchange for his soul? For whoever is ashamed of Me and My words in this adulterous and sinful generation, of him the Son of Man also will be ashamed when He comes in the glory of His Father with the Holy angels." (Mark 8:34–38)

For Godly sorrow produces repentance leading to salvation, not to be regretted; but the sorrow of the world produces death. (2 Corinthians 7:10)

Chapter 10

CALCULATING THE APPEARANCE OF THE MESSIAH

This list shows the age of each individual when their heir was born and the years between major events that have been documented in the Bible;

Adam was 130 (Genesis 5:3)

Seth was 105 (Genesis 5:6)

Enosh was 90 (Genesis 5:9)

Cainan was 70 (Genesis 5:12)

Mahalalel was 65 (Genesis 5:15)

Jared was 162 (Genesis 5:18)

Enoch was 65 (Genesis 5:21)

Methuselah was 187 (Genesis 5:25)

Lamech was 182 (Genesis 5:28)

Noah was 500 (Genesis 5:32)

The flood took place when Noah was 600

in the year 1656 (Genesis 7:11)

Shem was 100 (Genesis 11:10)

Arphaxad was 35 (born 2 years after the flood) (Genesis 11:10–11)

Salah was 30 (Genesis 11:14)

Eber was 34 (Genesis 11:16)

Peleg was 30 (Genesis 11:18)
Reu was 32 (Genesis 11:20)
Serug was 30 (Genesis 11:22)
Nahor was 29 (Genesis 11:24)
Terah was 70 (Genesis 11:26)
Abraham was 100 (Genesis 21:5)
Isaac was 60 (Genesis 25:26)
Jacob was 130 when he and his family went into Egypt (Genesis 47:9)
Israel spent 430 years in Egypt (Genesis 12:40)
Solomon begins building the temple 480 years after Israel left
Egypt in the 4th year of his reign (1 Kings 6:1) in the year 3146
20 years to complete and consecrate the temple
(2 Chronicles 7:16), (Chronicles 8:1)
390 years from the consecration of the temple
to being led away captive into Babylon
70 years of Babylonian captivity
70 weeks equaling 490 years from the proclamation
by Cyrus to reconstruct the temple to the crucifixion
of the Messiah in order to make an end of sins

This list shows the reigns of the kings who reigned over the entirety of Israel and those who reigned over Judah after the kingdom was divided. The list shows the complete timeline from between the consecration of the temple and to being taken captive into Babylon.

Saul 3063–3102 (Acts 13:21), reigned over the entire Israel 40 years
King David 3103–3142 (1 Kings 2:11), (1 Chronicles
29:26–27), reigned over the entire Israel 40 years
Solomon 3143–3182 (1 Kings 11:42), (2 Chronicles
9:30), reigned over the entire Israel 40 years
The temple was consecrated in 3166 in
the 24th year of Solomon's reign
After the death of Solomon the kingdom was
divided between Israel and Judah

Rehoboam 3183–3199 (1 Kings 14:21), (2 Chronicles
12–13), reigned over Judah 17 years
Abijam (Abijah) 3200–3202 (1 Kings 15:1–
2), (2 Chronicles 13:1–2), 3 years
Asa 3203–3243 (1 Kings 15:9–10), (2 Chronicles 16:13), 41 years
Jehoshaphat 3244–3268 (1 Kings 22:42),
(2 Chronicles 20:31), 25 years
Jehoram 3269–3276 (2 Kings 8:16–17), (2 Chronicles 21:5), 8 years
Ahaziah 3277–3277 (2 Kings 8:26), (2 Chronicles 22:2), 1 year
Athaliah 3278–3283 (2 Kings 11:3), (2 Chronicles 22:12), 6 years
Joash 3284–3323 (2 Kings 12:1), (2 Chronicles 24:1), 40 years
Amaziah 3324–3352 (2 Kings 14:1–2), (2 Chronicles 25:1), 29 years
Azariah (Uzziah) 3353–3404 (2 Kings 15:1–
2), (2 Chronicles 26:3), 52 years
Jotham 3405–3420 (2 Kings 15:32–33), (2 Chronicles 27:1), 16 years
Ahaz 3421–3436 (2 Kings 16:2), (2 Chronicles 28:1), 16 years
Hezekiah 3437–3465 (2 Kings 18:1–2), (2 Chronicles 29:1), 29 years
Manasseh 3466–3520 (2 Kings 21:1), (2 Chronicles 33:1), 55 years
Amon 3521–3522 (2 Kings 21:19), (2 Chronicles 33:21), 2 years
Josiah 3523–3553 (2 Kings 22:1), (2 Chronicles 34:1), 31 years
Jehoahaz 3554–3554 (2 Kings 23:31), (2 Chronicle 36:2), 3 months
Jehoiakim 3554–3565 (2Kings 23:36), (2 Chronicles 36:5), 11 years
In the first year of Nebuchadnezzar's reign,
he took Jehoiakim captive to Babylon in 3556
(Dan.1:1, 2Kings 24:1), (2 Chronicles 36:6),
Therefore 3556 - 3166 = 390 years
Jehoiachin 3566–3566 (2 Kings 24:8), (2
Chronicles 36:9–10), 3 months
Zedekiah 3566–3577 (2 Kings 24:18), (2 Chronicles 36:11), 11 years

Therefore 3556 + 70 year captivity = the year 3626
In the year 3626 the proclamation went out from Cyrus king
of Persia to allow for the construction of the second temple.

To reconcile these dates with the Julian calendar, Ptolemy's canon and the tablet VAT4956 can be left for the scholars.

The purpose of this book is solely to identify the person of Jesus Christ and His gospel message. There are literally millions of people who worship Jesus but are completely ignorant of who He is and how is death and resurrection somehow exonerates those who believe in His name. The abilities to reconcile these dates with the various chronologies put together by man should in no way deter us one way or another from believing who Jesus is and what His message means.

Ezekiel prophesied that the time between the completion of Solomon's temple and the time that Judah would be taken into captivity and carried to Babylon was 390 years:

> For I have laid on you the years of their iniquity, according to the number of the days; three hundred and ninety days; so you shall bear the iniquity of the house of Israel. (Ezekiel 4:5)

The Babylonian captivity was to last seventy years.

> For thus says the Lord: After seventy years are completed at Babylon, I will visit you and perform My good word toward you, and cause you to return to this place. (Jeremiah 29:10)

The time between the return of the captivity to Jerusalem until the appearance of the Messiah was to be seventy weeks according to Daniel:

$$70 \text{ weeks} = 70 \times 7 = 490 \text{ years}$$

> Seventy weeks are determined for your people and for your holy city, to finish the transgression, to make an end of sins, to make reconciliation for

iniquity, to bring in everlasting righteousness, to seal up vision and prophecy, and to anoint the Most Holy. (Daniel 9:24)

Therefore, this is the calculation for the appearance of the Son of God in Jerusalem in the first century AD:

The consecration of Solomon's temple – 390 years (according to Ezekiel's prophecy) – 70 years of Judah's captivity – 490 years of Daniel's prophecy = the crucifixion of Christ.

The appearance of the Messiah was calculated by the wise men who brought gifts to Jesus in Bethlehem in a manger, and they looked for the appearance of the star as was prophesied by Moses.

"I see Him, but not now; I behold Him, but not near; A Star shall come out of Jacob; A Scepter shall rise out of Israel." (Numbers 24:17)

And the wise men were instructed that the child would be born in Bethlehem as prophesied by Micah.

But you, Bethlehem Ephrathah, Though you are little among the thousands of Judah, Yet out of you shall come forth to Me The One to be Ruler in Israel, Whose goings forth are from of old, From everlasting. (Micah 5:2)

Chapter 11

JOHN THE BAPTIST

Jesus declared that no one greater than John the Baptist had been born of man. His reasoning behind this proclamation was that John the Baptist recognized that the coming Messiah was actually the Son of God. It is possible that even Jesus's parents were unaware of His divinity. God, in times past, had intervened in the lives of those who believed in Him and given sons to barren wombs. The nation of Israel's forefather, Isaac, was born from Sarah, Abraham's wife, when she was ninety years old. Samuel and others were born from barren women.

John himself was born of a barren woman, past her physiological childbearing age. The Spirit of God revealed to John the divinity of the Christ, and because John was the son of a priest, he was able to sift through scriptures and confirm the True being of the Messiah. He also was given direction in baptism.

The baptism that John and his disciples performed was a baptism of repentance. John was fully aware that the baptism that he baptized with was merely a recognition of the sinfulness of human nature. When Jesus approached John in order to be baptized, John immediately hesitated and exclaimed that he needed to be baptized by Jesus. John's baptism was a copy of the baptism that would be offered once Jesus had been raised from the dead and had received the promise. It was also performed in order to identify the Messiah.

John was informed by the Spirit that the person whom the Spirit descended upon in the form of a dove was the Son of God. When Jesus was baptized, a voice was heard from heaven, claiming, "This is My beloved Son, in whom I am well pleased." And Jesus was filled with the Holy Spirit and was led into the wilderness where He was tempted by the devil.

These same scriptures that John poured over are still available to us today. Scripture showed without a doubt that humans were incapable of lifting themselves out of the muck of their existence. The angels could not be trusted. There was only One person in heaven or earth who could be trusted to perform the task that was required of Him, remembering too that He was the only person other than God Himself who was the sum total of all of creation.

> How then can man be righteous before God? Or how can he be pure who is born of a women? If even the moon does not shine, And the stars are not pure in His sight, How much less man, who is a maggot, And a son of man, who is a worm? (Job 25:4–6)

> I will declare the decree: "The LORD has said to Me, 'You are My Son, Today I have begotten You. Ask of Me, and I will give You The nations for Your inheritance, And the ends of the earth for Your possession. You shall break them with a rod of iron; You shall dash them to pieces like a potter's vessel.'" (Psalm 2:7–9)

> Kiss the Son, lest He be angry, And you perish in the way, When His wrath is kindled but a little. Blessed are all those who put their trust in Him. (Psalm 2:12)

Hear the Word of the LORD You rulers of Sodom; Give ear to the law of our God, You people of Gomorrah: "To what purpose is the multitude of your sacrifices to Me?" Says the LORD. "I have had enough of burnt offerings of rams And the fat of fed cattle. I do not delight in the blood of bulls, Or of lambs or goats. When you come to appear before Me, Who has required this from your hand, To trample My courts? Bring no more futile sacrifices; Incense is an abomination to Me. The New Moons, the Sabbaths, and the calling of assemblies—I cannot endure iniquity and the sacred meeting. Your New Moons and your appointed feasts My soul hates; They are a trouble to Me, I am weary of bearing them. When you spread out your hands, I will hide My eyes from you; Even though you make many prayers, I will not hear. Your hands are full of blood. Wash yourself, make yourselves clean; Put away the evil of your doings from before My eyes. Cease to do evil, Learn to do good; Seek justice, Rebuke the oppressor; Defend the fatherless, Plead for the widow." (Isaiah 1:10–17)

The LORD testifies to His abhorrence of sacrifices and sacred assemblies. He calls for those who would worship Him to turn from their evil ways and to make themselves clean, which signifies a need for repentance and baptism.

The voice of one crying in the wilderness: "Prepare the way of the Lord; Make strait in the desert A highway for our God. Every valley shall be exalted And every mountain and hill brought low; The crooked places shall be made straight And the rough places smooth; The glory of the LORD shall be

> revealed, And all flesh shall see it together; For the
> mouth of the LORD has spoken." (Isaiah 40:3–5)

> I even I, am He who blots out your transgressions
> for My own sake; And I will not remember your
> sins. (Isaiah 43:25)

It is only God who can remove sin. Man is incapable of lifting himself from the mire of sin that is drowning him. John knew—as the wise men from the east as well as Jewish scholars—that the Messiah was prophesied to appear on the scene in the very near future. As was stated in Old Testament writings, it was necessary to prepare oneself for that appearance. Even in the first century, as in our current century, there was and is a specific time when He can be found. Remember the parable of the virgins with their oil lamps in Matthew 25:1–13.

> Seek the LORD while He may be found, Call upon
> Him while He is near. Let the wicked forsake his
> way, And the unrighteous man his thoughts; Let
> him return to the LORD, And He will have mercy
> on him; And to our God, For He will abundantly
> pardon. (Isaiah 55:6–7)

> O Jerusalem, wash your heart from wickedness,
> That you may be saved. How long shall your evil
> thoughts lodge within you? (Jeremiah 4:14)

As Jesus pointed out in the Sermon on the Mount, it wasn't just the action that was sin; the very thought of transgressing the law was sin. It is the same way we are taught to think by the world. From a very early age, children are taught about vengeance, revenge, rebelliousness, and the myriads of methods to seduce and exploit. Who doesn't idolize the rebel who stands up against impossible odds or the young starlet in a skimpy costume? Ask any Hollywood producer what sells. Sin sells, and the masses crave it. Hollywood crafts the youngsters mind to crave power, prestige, sex, and money. Hollywood sits on the largest superpower and economy the world has ever seen. It has the greatest influence of any nation. All the nations of the world have subjected themselves to her.

> Then those of you who escape will remember Me among the nations where they are carried captive, because I was crushed by their adulterous heart which has departed from Me, and by their eyes which play the harlot after their idols; they will loathe themselves for the evils which they committed in all their abominations. (Ezekiel 6:9)

> Son of man, cause Jerusalem to know her abominations. (Ezekiel 16:2)

> "Nevertheless I will remember My covenant with you in the days of your youth, and I will establish an everlasting covenant with you. Then you will remember your ways and be ashamed, when you receive your older and your younger sisters; for I will give them to you for daughters, but not because of My covenant with you. And I will establish My covenant with you. Then you shall know that I am the LORD, that you may remember and be ashamed, and never open your mouth anymore because of your shame, when I provide you an atonement for all you have done," says the LORD God. (Ezekiel 16:60–63)

> Cast away from you all the transgressions which you have committed, and get yourselves a new heart and

a new spirit. For why should you die, O house of Israel? (Ezekiel 18:31)

John knew that his baptism of repentance was merely a copy of the True baptism that the Messiah would perform when He baptized with the Holy Spirit:

I indeed baptize you with water unto repentance: but he who is coming after me is mightier than I, whose sandals I am not worthy to carry. He will baptize you with the Holy Spirit and fire. (Matthew 3:11)

Then I will sprinkle clean water on you, and you shall be clean; I will cleanse you from all your filthiness and from all your idols. (Ezekiel 36:25)

For I desire mercy and not sacrifice, And the knowledge of God more than burnt offerings. (Hosea 6:6)

So rend your heart, and not your garments; Return to the LORD your God, For He is gracious and merciful, Slow to anger, and of great kindness; And He relents from doing harm. (Joel 2:13)

He will again have compassion on us, And will subdue our iniquities. You will cast all our sins into the depths of the sea. (Micah 7:19)

Throughout the Bible, water has been symbolic for cleansing, rejuvenation, and death. Today, being baptized into the body of Jesus Christ signifies the dying of the old man, our old way of life, and our old way of thinking. We are being resurrected with Jesus, we are putting on Jesus—being clothed with His person—so that we might be made righteous members of God's household.

> "Behold, I send My messenger, And he will prepare the way before Me. And the Lord, whom you seek, Will suddenly come to His temple, Even the Messenger of the covenant, In whom you delight. Behold, He is coming," says the LORD of hosts. (Malachi 3:1)

> "Behold, I will send you Elijah the prophet Before the coming of the great and dreadful day of the LORD. And he will turn The hearts of the fathers to the children, And the hearts of the children to their fathers, Lest I come and strike the earth with a curse." (Malachi 4:5–6)

Chapter 12

CHRIST IS THE ONLY BEGOTTEN SON OF GOD

Christ is the Firstborn of all of creation, the only begotten Son of God. Christ is the personification of God's Word. God spoke, and the Word, Christ, complied. Christ is the only Person who shares in the divine nature with the Father because He is the only begotten Son of God.

Through Christ, the worlds, both physical and spiritual, were created. Everything that was created was created through Him. All things were created through Him and for Him. Christ can be described as the True Witness of God. In the Old Testament, Christ as God's True Witness testified of the Father; in the New Testament, the Father testified of the Son.

> I of Myself can do nothing. As I hear, I judge; and My judgment is righteous, because I do not seek My own will but the will of the Father who sent Me. If I bear witness of Myself, My witness is not true. There is another who bears witness of Me, and I know that the witness which He witnesses of Me is true. (John 5:30–32)

God witnessed to humanity to the fact that Jesus is the Christ by doing miracles through Him, giving legitimacy to His claim that He is the Son of God, the Firstborn of creation. Jesus received His inheritance after proving His obedience by dying on the cross. Christ became a man for the purpose of suffering and death. Suffering, that He may suffer temptation, and dying, that He may put an end to the Old Covenant and be raised in order to establish a New Covenant. Prior to becoming a man, Christ shared in the divine nature because He was the only begotten Son of the Father. It wasn't possible for the Son of God to be tempted prior to Him becoming a man.

> Let no one say when he is tempted, "I am tempted by God"; for God cannot be tempted by evil, nor does He Himself tempt anyone. (James 1:13)

The facts state that someone who is in possession of the divine nature cannot be tempted by evil, nor can they tempt anyone. Drawing on this fact we can conclude that because the angels were obviously tempted to rebel against God and actually tempted Adam and Eve to rebel with them, against God; the angels were not and are not in possession of the divine nature. Eve who also was tempted and who succumbed to that temptation, and later tempted Adam to rebel with her, was not and is not in possession of the divine nature. It is only our Sovereign LORD and Father Almighty God and His only begotten Son, the High Priest forever, according to the order of Melchizedek, the Christ, who have ever been in the possession of, or who are currently in possession of, the divine nature. The divine nature is represented as the Tree of Life .

> So He drove out the man; and He placed cherubim at the east of the Garden of Eden, and a flaming sword which turned every way, to guard the way to the tree of life. (Genesis 3:24)

And just as is described in the preceding passage, immediately after the rebellion, access to the Tree of Life was cut off. Until the second Adam was born into the world no one had access to the Tree of Life. Jesus had never eaten from the Tree of the Knowledge of Good and Evil, and therefore had never lost access to the Tree of Life.

The first century church has had the divine nature developed in them, but they have not yet been raised as sons and daughters to God and brothers and sisters to Christ. They will not be made perfect apart from us.

Therefore, there are only two persons in all of creation who have the ability to share in the divine nature. There are only two persons in all of creation who can offer us, humanity, something other than the insanity that is currently running and operating this world.

Through the death and resurrection of Jesus Christ, we enter into that grace that God has prepared for us since the beginning of time. The only temptation left on the table for those who have been baptized into the body of Jesus Christ and who have received His Holy Spirit, is the temptation not to call on Jesus's name.

The works have been completed. We do not have to personally struggle and defeat temptation on our own resources. We don't have to do anything other than call on the name of Jesus Christ of Nazareth and enter into His rest. And just as Christ took on the form of a man for the purpose of temptation and death, humanity now has the opportunity to take on the form of the resurrected Son of God for the purpose of obtaining victory over temptation and death. We are now able to put on the Lord Jesus Christ.

In what is commonly referred to as the Old Testament section of the Bible, God the Father, as He does today, held total and complete authority over all of creation. All things were created through God's only begotten Son. All have their being in Christ because, through Him, everything was created, and because all have their being in Christ, through faith, all have died through Christ's death.

In the first week of creation, Christ—through whom all things were created—made a last Will and Testament for those who would be His heirs. In order to leave something to an heir, it must first be in the power of the testator to bequeath the inheritance. Christ now, having been the Testator, has died, putting an end to His participation in the Covenant that was made in the Garden of Eden and any arrangements He had prior to His death.

Now that Jesus has been raised from the dead, He has received His part in the inheritance. His inheritance, which is to be shared with those who reap eternal life with Him, includes all of the power and authority that He held prior to His death. In addition to this inheritance, He has received an entitlement to establish a New Covenant with humanity. Currently, He is seated at the right hand of God, waiting for the final defeat of all of His enemies and the realization of those who will share in His inheritance with Him— at the Wedding Feast.

In the first week of creation the Son of God made a last Will and Testament. As in every will, an heir or heirs need to be appointed. In the making of His Will it was necessary for the Son of God to appoint those who would be His beneficiaries. Being the Son of God and thereby, being beyond reproach in regards to His conduct, it was necessary for Him to make a list of requirements that must be met before someone could lay claim to His inheritance. The powers and authorities that the Son of God held were beyond anything that humanity could comprehend. The responsibilities required to wield these powers and authorities is unfathomable. The task of appointing heirs was formidable. Not only was the list of the requirements which were needed to be met by a beneficiary long, the task of ensuring that the requirements were met had to be overseen by someone who would ensure that all of the instructions of the Will would be followed. God the Father was the only Person that the Son of God could responsibly appoint to be the Executor of His Will.

After the death and resurrection of Jesus, it was necessary for Jesus to face judgement. Just as the Scriptures declare that Christ has the Pre-eminence in all things, it was necessary for Christ to face judgement just as all of humanity will face judgement. There was a process to be followed and a judgement to be made. Jesus was determined to be the Heir of the Son of God's estate and on the Day of Pentecost Jesus received God's Promise.

Jesus was only One of a list of possible heirs who could possibly lay claim to the only begotten Son of God's estate. Jesus being the First, received the lions share of the inheritance. Those who would come after Jesus would face the same judgement as did Jesus. The only beings that were listed as possible heirs to the Son of God were humans.

Even though humans were later cursed and would be incapable of being raised from the dead, the Son of God acting under the Father's direction made a last Will and Testament specifically naming humans as His heirs.

Therefore, because the Son of God was in possession of eternal life, the only reason that He could possibly have for making a Testament was because our Sovereign LORD and Father Almighty God had the precognition of what would transpire in the Garden of Eden between Adam and Eve and Satan.

Now even though humans have been specifically named as possible heirs of the Son of God's estate, they, just as did Jesus, needed to be raised from the dead, and face judgement.

For one to be found innocent and become entitled to a portion of the inheritance offered to us by the only begotten Son of God should be our main goal while we still have time to pursue it.

> And for this reason He is the Mediator of the new covenant, by means of death, for the redemption of the transgressions under the First Covenant, that those who are called may receive the promise of the eternal inheritance. For where there is a testament, there must also of necessity be the death of the testator. For a testament is in force after men are dead, since it has no power at all while the testator lives. (Hebrews 9:15–17)

The First Covenant enacted by Moses was a copy of the True Covenant. Moses's covenant was established by the blood of bulls and goats. It signified that it was necessary that One had to die in order to bring a new covenant into force. It was necessary that someone had to die in order to put an end to the covenant that had been enacted in the Garden of Eden.

The One who had to die had to be someone specific. For a man or an angel to die, would have absolutely no relevance on the overall affect of the covenant. Because all have partaken of the same nature, then all are guilty. The only part that they had left in the covenant was death. Christ was and is innocent. Christ was not deserving of death. Christ chose to follow His Father's directions and subject Himself to death. Even Christ's death had no overall affect on the covenant that He died to. Christ's death eliminated the power that the covenant held over Him. That covenant is still in force.

If a man divorces his wife and marries another, he shall be declared to be an adulterer. Remember after your spouse dies you are free to marry whomever you will. Christ's death entitled Him the opportunity to be remarried, He would no longer be considered divorced. He would no longer need to wait for the death of His spouse in order to remarry because He has died. And if we believe that we have our existence in Christ, in that Christ actually created us, then through our faith that we can be baptized into his death, God will account that faith to us as righteousness and declare that we have died with Christ and are now free to be married to another, even Jesus Christ our Lord and Saviour, Amen.

Aaron, the temple, and the sacrifices were copies of the True. Aaron was a type of the Jesus who was to come—as well as the type of the Christ who was in the Garden of Eden. In the Garden of Eden, Christ was the image of the ideal (the divine nature). Prior to the fall of mankind, there was no need for Christ to give aid to those who were being tempted other than to continually share in the divine nature with them. The defence that Adam and Eve had against Satan in the Garden of Eden was their faith. They needed to believe God. Remember the first commandment, "Thou shalt love the Lord thy God with all thy heart, and with all thy soul, and with all thy mind." If Eve had followed the first commandment and believed God, she could not have been tempted. She would not have succumbed to Satan's deception and she would not have allowed Satan to bring about her fall through her senses and emotions.

That First Covenant enacted by Moses cannot be considered a testament. No one died, and nothing was inherited. Obviously, the blood of bulls and goats can do nothing to end the covenant that was in force in the Garden of Eden. Therefore, Moses' covenant was merely a reflection of what was, and a copy of what was promised. The blood of bulls and goats can do nothing to bring about enforcement of a covenant or put an end to humanity's rebellious nature. Sacrifices and ceremonial washings pointed to humanity's need for purification.

The washing of organs before burning them on the altar signified man's need to have his inner man cleansed of past and present sins. All were physical representations of the Spiritual, all pointed toward Christ.

Although God the Father held complete authority over all of creation, angels and spirits were given free will, as were humans. Satan had free will. He chose to rebel against God. There were two trees in the Garden of Eden: the Tree of Life and the Tree of the Knowledge of Good and Evil. The first tree represented obedience, and the second tree represented rebellion.

Humanity was betrothed to the Son of God in the Garden of Eden. Adam and Eve had the opportunity to believe and be obedient to God, but they chose not to believe God and succumbed to Satan's temptation and rebelled with Him. Their choice resulted in their expulsion from the Garden of Eden and the revocation of their rights to eat from the Tree of Life. In human terms, they were divorced from God.

The Tree of the Knowledge of Good and Evil was presented to Eve by Satan as a means of becoming like God, a means of gaining possession of His power and authority. Satan told Eve that in the day that you eat of it, your eyes will be opened, and you will be like God, knowing good and evil. It was obviously a lie, but it is still held to be true by many.

> Then God saw everything that He had made, and indeed it was very good. So the evening and the morning were the sixth day. (Genesis 1:31)

> But of the fruit of the tree which is in the midst of the garden, God has said, "You shall not eat it, nor shall you touch it, lest you die." Then the serpent said to the woman, "You will not surely die." (Genesis 3:3–4)

By extension of Satan's deception in the Garden of Eden, the Law was given to man by angels. And again, Satan presented his way—humanity could develop the nature of God simply by adhering to a number of statutes. Again, mankind could usurp God's authority and become like God. According to the Law, humanity did not need God, they could get along quite well without Him. Many are the arguments made today where people justify their actions by their perceived adherence to the laws of man.

> "Who have received the law by the direction of angels and have not kept it." (Acts 7:53)

> But if the ministry of death, written and engraved on stones, was glorious, so that the children of Israel could not look steadily at the face of Moses because of the glory of his countenance, which glory was passing away, how will the ministry of the Spirit not be more glorious? For if the ministry of condemnation had glory, the ministry

of righteousness exceeds much more in glory. For even what was made glorious had no glory in this respect, because of the glory that excels. For if what is passing away was glorious, what remains is much more glorious. Therefore, since we have such hope, we use great boldness of speech—unlike Moses, who put a veil over his face so that the children of Israel could not look steadily at the end of what was passing away. But their minds were blinded. For until this day the same veil remains unlifted in the reading of the Old Testament, because the veil is taken away in Christ. But even to this day, when Moses is read, a veil lies on their heart. Nevertheless when one turns to the Lord, the veil is taken away. Now the Lord is the Spirit; and where the Spirit of the Lord is, there is liberty. But we all, with unveiled face, beholding as in a mirror the glory of the Lord, are being transformed into the same image from glory to glory, just as by the Spirit of the Lord. (2 Corinthians 3:7–18)

As stated in the preceding passage, there was a veil placed over the scriptures that prevented anyone from understanding the True Gospel. Understanding of the Gospel and all of the Scriptures becomes possible once one has come to the knowledge of the True identity of Jesus Christ. Once someone comes to the full understanding of the identity of the Person of Jesus of Nazareth, one invariably has the veil that has been blinding mankind for thousands of years removed. The True identity of Jesus of Nazareth is that He is the only begotten Son of God, the first born of all creation, through whom all things were created, the Christ, the High Priest forever, according to the order of Melchizedek. Once one comes to that complete understanding, one invariably has the veil removed.

In spite of their rebellion, God—in His mercy and long-suffering, had already designed a plan of salvation to rescue humanity from their ultimate destiny. God is just, but He is also impartial. God cannot condemn Satan without condemning humanity. As described, humanity has been held captive since the Garden of Eden. Had the rulers of this world known God's design, they would not have crucified the Prince of Peace.

> Therefore, as through one man's offense judgment came to all men, resulting in condemnation, even so through one Man's righteous act the free gift came to all men, resulting in justification of life. For as by one man's disobedience many were made sinners, so also by one Man's obedience many will be made righteous. Moreover the law entered that the offense might abound. But where sin abounded, grace abounded much more, so that as sin reigned in death, even so grace might reign through righteousness to eternal life through Jesus Christ our Lord. (Romans 5:18–21)

> But we speak the wisdom of God in a mystery, the hidden wisdom which God ordained before the ages for our glory, which none of the rulers of this age knew; for had they known, they would not have crucified the Lord of glory. (1 Corinthians 2:7–8)

Satan was unaware that the way in which Satan treated Jesus was exactly the way that Jesus needed to be treated in order to fulfill God's salvation plan. Satan did everything in his power to destroy Jesus through fierce temptations and the most violent of tortures and executions.

Even though Satan is the god of this world and has been wreaking havoc throughout history, God uses Satan's evil intent upon humanity to bring God's chosen ones closer to God. The book of Job illustrates how God allowed Satan to torment Job in order to bring Job closer to God and afford Job a better understanding of God—all for the glory of God and the betterment of those being saved.

In the section of the Bible referred to as the Old Testament, the Law was given to humans through the agency of angels. The law dealt with sin and the consequences of sin, which is death. Those who sin will die. (A reflection of the Law that was in force in the Garden of Eden.) In the New Testament, God's divine nature was revealed to us through Jesus Christ. This Gospel—or the good news of the divine nature that is being offered to humanity—is summed up in the Sermon on the Mount. It is through the development of this divine nature in us through the workings of Jesus Christ that once again grants us access to the Tree of Life. (Matthew 5–7)

Because Jesus was under the curse that had been imposed upon humanity, God could not intervene in His brutal torture and execution. Remember what Jesus was reported to have said as that torturous time slowly came to a close on the cross:

My God, My God, why have You forsaken Me?
(Mark 15:34)

The only thing Jesus had in His arsenal to fight against Satan was His faith, hope, and love. He believed God, He believed in God's purpose for Him, and He believed in all the scriptures that testified to His sufferings, crucifixion, and resurrection. He had the hope that God would not leave His body in Hades. His love for humanity spurred Him to despise the humiliation of the cross and led Him to victory. His faith, hope and love were dynamic. They were the strength that Jesus drew on.

What puts this all into perspective is that Jesus could have at any time stopped His torture and execution. Remember, Jesus had not yet died. During Jesus's time on the earth, He was still in possession of the name that is above every other name. He still commanded the authority that He had prior to becoming a man. He still was the 'I am'. Therefore, Jesus, while still holding the authority that He was in possession of prior to becoming a man; allowed the authorities to wrongfully accuse Him, to wrongfully arrest Him, to wrongfully convict Him, to wrongfully sentence Him to death and to wrongfully torture and execute Him. Obedience has never been so intensely defined.

> But Jesus said to Him, "Put your sword in its place, for all who take the sword will perish by the sword. Or do you not think that I cannot now pray to My Father, and He will provide Me with more than twelve legions of angels? How then could the Scriptures be fulfilled, that it must happen thus?" (Matthew 26:52–54)

After a beating, disfigurement, and scourging, Satan had Jesus nailed to a cross. Throughout this intense suffering and humiliation, God hid His face from the brutality, considering it a small price to pay in order to save humanity from the ultimate destruction that is to rain down upon Satan and this physical universe, while bringing us into our ultimate inheritance.

Throughout the Old Testament, Christ was the True Witness of God, reiterating again and again to God's omnipotence. If God is for you, who can be against you? No one can stand before God. All of the character traits and power that were attributed to God in the Old Testament were to call to mind God's Omnipotence and give us an appreciation of the Power that was upholding Jesus. God the Father still remains omnipotent, just as Pharaoh remained Pharaoh after he appointed Joseph absolute ruler over all of Egypt:

> Then Pharaoh said to Joseph, "Inasmuch as God has shown you all this, there is no one as discerning and wise as you. You shall be over my house, and all

my people shall be ruled according to your word; only in regard to the throne will I be greater than you." And Pharaoh said to Joseph, "See, I have set you over all the land of Egypt." Then Pharaoh took his signet ring off his hand and put it on Joseph's hand; and he clothed him in garments of fine linen and put a gold chain around his neck. And he had him ride in the second chariot which he had; and they cried out before him, "Bow the knee!" So he set him over all the land of Egypt. Pharaoh also said to Joseph, "I am Pharaoh, and without your consent no man may lift his hand or foot in all of Egypt." (Genesis 41:39–44)

The description of this relationship between God and Christ in the Old Testament is referenced to throughout the Bible, remembering that the things that were enacted in the Old Testament were copies of the True.

And see to it that you make them according to the pattern which was shown to you on the mountain. (Exodus 25:40)

Now you shall speak to him and put words in his mouth. And I will be with your mouth and with his mouth, and I will teach you what you shall do. So he shall be your spokesman to the people. And he himself shall be a mouth for you, and you shall be to him as God. (Exodus 4:15–16)

So the Lord said to Moses: "See, I have made you as God to Pharaoh, and Aaron your brother shall be your prophet." (Exodus 7:1)

No man has seen God at any time. The only begotten Son, who is in the bosom of the Father, He has declared Him. (John 1:18)

And they saw the God of Israel. And there was under His feet as it were a paved work of sapphire stone, and it was like the very heavens in its clarity. But on the nobles of the children of Israel He did not lay His hand. So they saw God, and they ate and drank. (Exodus 24:10–11)

So the Lord spoke to Moses face to face, as a man speaks to his friend. (Exodus 33:11)

Then He said, "Hear now My words: If there is a prophet among you, I, the Lord, make Myself known to him in a vision; I speak to him in a dream. Not so with My servant Moses; He is faithful in all My house. I speak to him face to face, Even plainly, and not in dark sayings; And he sees the form of the Lord. Why then were you not afraid To speak against My servant Moses?" (Numbers 12:6–8)

And God said to Moses, "I Am Who I Am." And He said, "Thus you shall say to the children of Israel, 'I Am has sent me to you." (Exodus 3:14)

Jesus said to them, "Most assuredly, I say to you, before Abraham was, I Am." Then they took up stones to throw at Him; but Jesus hid Himself and went out of the temple, going through the midst of them, and so passed by. (John 8:58–59)

The Pharisees were witnesses to John's testimony that Jesus

was the promised Messiah, the only begotten Son of God. Their reaction to Jesus's claim that He was the "I Am" who existed prior to Abraham was an attempt to stone Him for blasphemy. There was absolutely no doubt in the Pharisees' minds who He was claiming to be. In John 1:18, Jesus emphatically states that no one has ever seen God, and it is the only begotten Son who has proclaimed Him. Jesus went on to say that if you don't believe Me, believe then the miracles that I do in My Father's name. The Pharisees witnessed that God does not answer the prayers of a sinner. God would not honor someone who was committing blasphemy by doing miracles through Him.

The analogy is made between Jesus and Joseph. Joseph, in his coat of many colors, went out from the presence of his father Jacob to minister to his brothers tending sheep. And just as Joseph's brothers threw Joseph into the pit and sold him into slavery, Jesus's brothers, Israel, crucified Him, and threw Him into the pit.

And just as Joseph was raised up to become the ruler over all of Egypt, Jesus has also been raised up to become the ruler over all of creation. As the True Witness of God, Jesus proclaimed the utterances of God and continued to be the Word of God, the personification of God's Word and command.

Humanity did not recognize the divine nature of Jesus. They hated Him without a cause because He was innocent. He testified that their works were evil. In the flesh, Jesus was not much different than the first Adam. The creation story describes the creation of Adam by the Holy Spirit. The Gospels describe the creation of Jesus in the flesh by the Holy Spirit. Jesus was declared to be the Son of David, according to the flesh, and He was proclaimed to be the Son of God, according to the resurrection from the dead.

Man could not be resurrected from the dead to face judgement. Man had already been judged and sentenced to death. The individuals that Jesus raised from the dead were just raised that they may die again. (A copy of the coming judgement day.) Jesus was raised from the dead by a promise made to Him by God.

> For You will not leave my soul in Hades, Nor will
> You allow Your Holy One to see corruption. (Acts
> 2:27)

Before the Covenant that was made in the Garden of Eden, God the Father Almighty, made a promise to Christ. On the seventh day of creation when Christ made out His Last Will and Testament, God the Father Almighty promised to Christ that He would not leave His Soul in Hades. The promise made by God superseded the covenant that was made between Christ and mankind in the Garden of Eden.

> And this I say, that the law, which was four hundred
> and thirty years later, cannot annul the covenant
> that was confirmed before by God in Christ, that
> it should make the promise of no effect. (Galatians
> 3:17)

This is a copy of the True. This is the Gospel. This is our salvation. Jesus Christ is the only Person that God the Father promised to raise from the dead. Jesus Christ is the only Person that has been raised from the dead. It is now only through Jesus's resurrection that humanity will be raised from the dead.

Christ gave up His Godhead in order to be made flesh. Christ was the express image of God the Father. They share the same Spirit. We, in the flesh, have the opportunity to be joined with Jesus through His Spirit—through our inner person. Jesus, the second Adam, fulfilled what the first Adam failed to do in the Garden of Eden: triumph over temptation.

Living the perfect spiritual life that is demanded by God can only be accomplished with the aid of Jesus Christ's Holy Spirit, which allows us to overcome temptation in our daily lives. We are commanded to be perfect—even as our Father in heaven is perfect. We now have the opportunity of accepting Jesus Christ as our High

Priest, and we must allow Him to consecrate us in order to become sons and daughters of God and brothers and sisters of Christ.

Although there is one Spirit—Christ—it is said that the Father and the Son shall come and make their home in us. Jesus's victory over temptation added a new dimension to His Spirit. Jesus's Spirit represents victory over sin and death, and God's Spirit represents the divine nature. Victory over sin does not equate to perfection. Jesus's Spirit becomes the Way, or the Sheep's Gate, to God's Holy Spirit. Once we've become victorious over sin, God is able to create the divine nature in us through the Spirit of His only begotten Son. Our only battle is in choosing to call on the name of Jesus Christ of Nazareth the moment we are tempted.

> And God made the beast of the earth according to its kind, cattle according to its kind, and everything that creeps on the earth according to its kind. And God saw that it was good. Then God said, "Let Us make man in Our image, according to Our likeness; let them have dominion over the fish of the sea, over the birds of the air, and over the cattle, and over all the earth and every creeping thing that creeps on the earth." (Genesis 1:25–26)

In this passage, God illustrates that everything that reproduces does so after its kind. When God begat a Son, He was born in the similitude of God after the God kind. During the period that is commonly referred to as the Old Testament, the Christ was the True Witness of God, the Servant of God, the Commander of the hosts of heaven, and High Priest forever, according to the Order of Melchizedek.

In the New Testament, Jesus inherited a name above every other name. God the Father still reigns supreme, and Jesus has received the inheritance of the priesthood with all of its powers and authorities. In addition to His inheritance, He received the rights to establish a

New Covenant. This New Covenant actually defines the scope of the Priesthood. This New Covenant has now been established: "I will put My law in their minds, and write it on their hearts; and I will be their God, and they shall be My people."

Jesus has the power and authority over all of the spirits and angels—and the entirety of creation—and there is nothing that is not subjected to Jesus except for the Father Himself. Today, the name of Jesus Christ gives us victory over all of temptations. Spirit denotes emotion. Through the name of Jesus Christ of Nazareth, a person can have the strength to overcome negative emotions, fears, angers, and lusts.

Satan is still Satan. Satan is still the rebel. Satan will continue to do what he has always done and more so as he sees his time coming to an end. Jesus, through His victory over temptation affords us the Spirit of victory over temptation. Jesus's Holy Spirit in us, affords us, the power to overcome all temptations and therefore empowers us to become victorious over sin.

The final power that Jesus will exact upon Satan and all those who wish to believe the lie will be realized once our Sovereign Lord and Father Almighty God establishes His Kingdom beneath Jesus's feet.

> The LORD your God will raise up for you a Prophet like me from your midst, from your brethren, Him you shall hear. (Deuteronomy 18:15)

> I will raise up for them a Prophet like you from among their brethren, and will put My words in His mouth, and He shall speak to them all that I command Him. And it shall be that whoever will not hear My words, which He speaks in My name, I will require it of him. (Deuteronomy 18:18–19)

And it came to pass, when Joshua was by Jericho, that he lifted his eyes and looked, and behold, a Man stood opposite him with His sword drawn in His hand. And Joshua went to Him and said to Him, "Are You for us or for our adversaries?" So He said, "No, but as Commander of the army of the LORD I have now come." And Joshua fell on his face to the earth and worshipped and said to Him, "What does my Lord say to His servant?" Then the Commander of the LORD's army said to Joshua, "Take your sandal off your foot, for the place where you stand is holy." And Joshua did so. (Joshua 5:13–15)

We are only allowed to worship God. Christ, in His portrayal as the Commander of the LORD's army, was the Emissary of God as well as Israel's Spouse. As Sarah honored Abraham by calling him lord, Joshua honored the Commander of the LORD's army by worshipping Him.

When your days are fulfilled and you rest with your fathers, I will set up your seed after you, who will come from your body, and I will establish his kingdom. He shall build a house for My name, and I will establish the throne of his kingdom forever. I will be his Father, and he shall be My son. If he commits iniquity, I will chasten him with the rod of men and with the blows of the sons of men. But My mercy shall not depart from him, as I took it from Saul, whom I removed from before you. And your house and your kingdom shall be established forever. (2 Samuel 7:12–16)

I tell you that the LORD will build you a house, And it shall be, when your days are fulfilled, when you must go to be with your fathers, that I will set up your seed after you, who will be of your sons; and I will establish His kingdom. He shall build Me a house, and I will establish his throne forever. I will be His Father, and He shall be My son; and I will not take My mercy away from him, as I took it from him who was before you. And I will establish him in My house and in My kingdom forever; and his throne shall be established forever. (1 Chronicles 17:10–14)

Behold, a son shall be born to you, who shall be a man of rest; and I will give him rest from all his enemies all around. His name shall be Solomon, for I will give peace and quietness to Israel in his days. He will build a house for My name, and he shall be My son, and I will be his Father; and I will establish the throne of his kingdom over Israel forever. (1 Chronicles 22:9–10)

Solomon means peace. Solomon was another type of Jesus. Jesus is often referred to as David. In this instance, the reference to Solomon points towards the peace that God is providing to humanity through our Lord and Saviour Jesus Christ of Nazareth.

After some time, when he returned to get her, he turned aside to see the carcass of the lion. And behold, a swarm of bees and honey were in the carcass of the lion. (Judges 14:8)

The Messiah would come out of Judah, represented as a lion.

Then Samson said, "Let me die with the Philistines!" And he pushed with all his might, and the temple fell on the lords and all the people who were in it. So the dead he killed at his death were more than he had killed in his life. (Judges 16:30)

Jesus would bring judgment down upon Satan and this physical world, as well as death and destruction down upon death and destruction themselves.

If He puts no trust in His servants, If He charges His angels with error, How much more those who dwell in houses of clay, Whose foundation is the dust, Who are crushed before a moth? (Job 4:18–19)

Jesus could not simply be a man or an angel.

What is man, that he could be pure? And he who is born of a woman, that he could be righteous? If God puts no trust in His saints, And the heavens are not pure in His sight, How much less man, who is abominable and filthy, Who drinks iniquity like water! (Job 15:14–16)

For I know that my Redeemer lives, And He shall stand at last on the earth; And after my skin is destroyed, this I know, That in my flesh I shall see God, (Job 19:25–26)

My Redeemer was alive before He stood on the earth:

"Behold, the days are coming," says the LORD, "when I will make a new covenant with the house of Israel and with the house of Judah—not according to the covenant that I made with their fathers in the day that I took them by the hand to lead them out of the land of Egypt, My covenant which they broke, though I was a husband to them," says the LORD. "But this is the covenant that I will make with the house of Israel after those days," says the LORD: "I will put My law in their minds, and write it on their hearts; and I will be their God, and they shall be My people. No more shall every man teach his neighbour, and every man his brother, saying, 'Know the LORD,' for they all shall know Me, from the least of them to the greatest of them," says the LORD. "For I will forgive their iniquity, and their sin I will remember no more." (Jeremiah 31:31–34)

For You will not leave my soul in Sheol, Nor will You allow Your Holy One to see corruption. (Psalm 16:10)

For You meet him with the blessings of goodness; You set a crown of pure gold upon his head. He asked life from You, and You gave it to him— Length of days forever and ever. His glory is great in Your salvation; Honor and majesty You have placed upon him. For You have made him most blessed forever. (Psalm 21:3–6)

For dogs have surrounded Me; The congregation of the wicked has enclosed Me. They pierced My hands and My feet; I can count all My bones. They look and stare at Me. They divide My garments among them, And for My clothing they cast lots. (Psalm 22:16–18)

He guards all his bones; Not one of them is broken. (Psalm 34:20)

Your throne, O God, is forever and ever; A scepter of righteousness is the scepter of Your kingdom. You love righteousness and hate wickedness; Therefore God, Your God, has anointed You With the oil of gladness more than Your companions. All Your garments are scented with myrrh and aloes and cassia, Out of the ivory palaces, by which they have made You glad. Kings' daughters are among Your honorable woman; At Your right hand stands the queen in gold from Ophir. (Psalm 45:6–9)

You have ascended on high, You have led captivity captive; You have received gifts among men. (Psalm 68:18)

Because for Your sake I have borne reproach; Shame has covered my face. I have become a stranger to my brothers, And an alien to my mother's children; Because zeal for Your house has eaten me up, And the reproaches of those who reproach You have fallen on me. (Psalm 69:7–9)

Give the king Your judgments, O God, And Your righteousness to the king's Son. He will judge Your people with righteousness, And Your poor with justice. The mountains will bring peace to the people, And the little hills, by righteousness. He will bring justice to the poor of the people; He will save the children of the needy, And will break in pieces the oppressor. They shall fear You As long as the sun and moon endure, Throughout all generations.

He shall come down like rain upon the grass before mowing, Like showers that water the earth. In His days the righteous shall flourish, And abundance of peace, Until the moon is no more. He shall have dominion also from sea to sea, And from the River to the ends of the earth. Those who dwell in the wilderness will bow before Him, And His enemies will lick the dust. The kings of Tarshish and of the isles Will bring presents; The kings of Sheba and Seba Will offer gifts. Yes, all kings will fall down before Him; All nations shall serve Him. For He will deliver the needy when he cries, The poor also, and him who has no helper. He will redeem their life from oppression and violence; And precious shall be their blood in His sight. And He shall live; And the gold of Sheba will be given to Him; Prayer also will be made for Him continually, And daily He shall be praised. There will be an abundance of grain in the earth, On the top of the mountains; Its fruit shall wave like Lebanon; And those of the city shall flourish like grass of the earth. His name shall endure forever; His name shall continue as long as the sun. And men shall be blessed in Him; All nations shall call Him blessed. Blessed be the LORD God, the God of Israel, Who only does wondrous things! And blessed be His glorious name forever! And let the whole earth be filled with His glory. Amen and Amen. (Psalm 72:1–19)

I will open my mouth in a parable. (Psalm 78:2)

David was actually a copy of the True. After David's death, references made to David were actually referencing the Messiah and that the Messiah would be a descendant of David in terms of physical lineage, but, as David states, "The LORD said to My Lord, 'Sit at My right hand, Till I make Your enemies Your footstool'? If David then calls Him 'Lord,' how is He his Son?" (Matthew 22:44–45), signifying that according to the Spirit, the Messiah was the only begotten Son of God.

> I have found My servant David; With My holy oil I have anointed him, With whom My hand shall be established; Also My arm shall strengthen him. The enemy shall not outwit him, Nor the son of wickedness afflict him. I will beat down his foes before his face, And plague those who hate him. But My faithfulness and My mercy shall be with him, And in My name his horn shall be exalted. Also I will set his hand over the sea, And his right hand over the rivers. He shall cry to Me, "You are my Father, My God, and the rock of my salvation." Also I will make him My firstborn, The highest of the kings of the earth. My mercy I will keep for him forever, And My covenant shall stand firm with him. His seed also I will make to endure forever, And his throne as the days of heaven. (Psalm 89:20–29)

> He weakens my strength in the way; He shortened my days. I said, "O my God, Do not take me away in the midst of my days; Your years are throughout all generations. Of old You laid the foundation of the earth, And the heavens are the work of Your hands. They will perish, but You will endure; Yes, they will all grow old like a garment; Like a cloak You will change them, And they will be changed. But You are the same, And Your years will have no end. The children of Your servants will continue,

And their descendants will be established before
You." (Psalm 102:23–28)

Moses was another copy of the True. Moses stood between God and
Israel to plead Israel's cause. That instance was a copy of how the
Messiah would stand between humanity and God, acting as High
Priest forever and sanctifying the ungodly.

> Therefore He said that He would destroy them,
> Had not Moses His chosen one stood before Him in
> the breach, To turn away His wrath, lest He destroy
> them. (Psalm 106:23)

> The Lord said to my Lord, "Sit at My right hand,
> Till I make Your enemies Your footstool." The Lord
> shall send the rod of Your strength out of Zion.
> Rule in the midst of Your enemies! Your people
> shall be volunteers In the day of Your power; In the
> beauties of holiness, from the womb of the morning,
> You have the dew of Your youth. The Lord has
> sworn And will not relent, "You are a priest forever
> According to the order of Melchizedek." The Lord
> is at Your right hand; He shall execute kings in the
> day of His wrath. He shall judge among the nations,
> He shall fill the places with dead bodies, He shall
> execute the heads of many countries. He shall drink
> of the brook by the wayside; Therefore He shall lift
> up the head. (Psalm 110:1–7)

> The stone which the builders rejected Has become
> the chief cornerstone. This was the Lord's doing; It
> is marvellous in our eyes. (Psalm 118:22–23)

Who has ascended into heaven, or descended? Who has gathered the wind in His fists? Who has bound the waters in a garment? Who has established all the ends of the earth? What is His name, and what is His Son's name, If you know? (Proverbs 30:4)

Therefore the Lord Himself will give you a sign: Behold, the virgin shall conceive and bear a Son, and shall call His name Immanuel. (Isaiah 7:14)

If Jesus was not the Son of God, the Firstborn of all creation, there would be no need for this immaculate conception. The virgin was to be impregnated with the pre-existing Son of God. Immanuel literally means "God with us".

He will be as a sanctuary, But a stone of stumbling and a rock of offence To both the houses of Israel, As a trap and a snare to the inhabitants of Jerusalem. And many among them shall stumble; They shall fall and be broken, Be snared and taken." Bind up the testimony, Seal the law among My disciples. And I will wait on the LORD, Who hides his face from the house of Jacob; And I will hope in Him. Here am I and the children whom the LORD has given me! We are for signs and wonders in Israel From the LORD of hosts, Who dwells in Mount Zion. (Isaiah 8:14–18)

Nevertheless the gloom will not be upon her who is distressed, As when at first He lightly esteemed The land of Zebulun and the land of Naphtali, And afterward more heavily oppressed her, By the way of the sea, beyond the Jordan, In Galilee of the Gentiles. The people who walked in darkness Have

seen a great light; Those who dwelt in the land of
the shadow of death, Upon them a light has shined.
(Isaiah 9:1–2)

For unto us a Child is born, Unto us a Child is given;
And the government will be upon His shoulder.
And His name will be called Wonderful, Counselor,
Mighty God, Everlasting Father, Prince of Peace.
Of the increase of His government and peace There
will be no end, Upon the throne of David and over
His kingdom, To order it and establish it with
judgment and justice From that time forward, even
forever. The zeal of the LORD of hosts will perform
this. (Isaiah 9:6–7)

God the Father had the section of the Bible that is commonly
referred to as the Old Testament written for the express purpose of
witnessing to God's ultimate plan of how He would work out His
saving grace. God left nothing to the imagination. He explained
creation, the rebellion, the consequential fall of humanity, and His
plan of salvation. He explained who He is and what His Spiritual
makeup is like.

It was necessary for God to explain His personal character traits
because they are completely alien to humanity. Honesty, loyalty,
fidelity, justice, mercy, and long-suffering are concepts that are
diametrically opposed to everything humanity holds dear. Although,
the Law has always been viewed as a rudimentary description of
the way God behaves, from a humanitarian perspective, the law is
needed in order to put a check on humanities' behaviour. Allowed
to run unchecked, humanity's behaviour always gravitates to the
worst. Throughout history, unrestrained power always gives rise to
despots. Lawlessness always breeds dictatorship. Left unaccountable,
humanity will always unleash hell upon the world.

Jesus, during His ministry, preached the kingdom of God. The kingdom of God that Jesus preached is God's divine nature. The Sermon on the Mount (Matthew 5–7) is actually a picture postcard of the Kingdom of God or God's divine nature. This is the nature that is to be cultivated in each and every Christian individual with the help of the Spirit of Jesus Christ of Nazareth.

Jesus's Spirit enables us to overcome sin and places us in a state of spiritual purity—so that we can be transformed by God's Holy Spirit into children of the Most High God. God's saving plan for humanity was summed up by the Messiah. In the Old Testament, the Spirit of Christ witnessed to what was required in order to accomplish salvation—and that there was only One in all of existence who could perform this salvation plan.

Throughout the Old Testament the Spirit of Christ witnessed to the prophets of the coming of the Glorious One, and how this Glorious One would be subjected to rejection, humiliation, suffering and death. He also testified to the promise that God made that He would not leave Christ's soul in Hades but would rather raise Him from the dead.

> There shall come forth a Rod from the stem of Jesse, And a Branch shall grow out of his roots. The Spirit of the LORD shall rest upon Him, The Spirit of wisdom and understanding, The Spirit of counsel and might, The Spirit of knowledge and of the fear of the LORD. His delight is in the fear of the LORD, And He shall not judge by the sight of His eyes, Nor decide by the hearing of His ears; But with righteousness He shall judge the poor, And decide with equity for the meek of the earth; He shall strike the earth with the rod of His mouth, And with the breath of His lips He shall slay the wicked. Righteousness shall be the belt of His loins, And faithfulness the belt of His waist. The wolf also shall dwell with the lamb, The leopard shall lie

down with the young goat, The calf and the young lion and the fatling together; And a little child shall lead them. The cow and the bear shall graze; Their young ones shall lie down together; And the lion shall eat straw like the ox. The nursing child shall play by the cobra's hole, And the weaned child shall put his hand in the viper's den. They shall not hurt or destroy in all My holy mountain, For the earth shall be full of the knowledge of the LORD As the waters cover the sea. And in that day there shall be a Root of Jesse, Who shall stand as a banner to the people; For the Gentiles shall seek Him, And His resting place shall be glorious. It shall come to pass in that day That the Lord shall set His hand again the second time To recover the remnant of His people who are left. From Assyria and Egypt, From Pathros and Cush, From Elam and Shinar, From Hamath and the islands of the sea. He will set up a banner for the nations, And will assemble the outcasts of Israel, And gather together the dispersed of Judah From the four corners of the earth. Also the envy of Ephraim shall depart, And the adversaries of Judah shall be cut off; Ephraim shall not envy Judah, And Judah shall not harass Ephraim. But they shall fly down upon the shoulder of the Philistines toward the west; Together they shall plunder the people of the East; They shall lay their hand on Edom and Moab; And the people of Ammon shall obey them. The LORD will utterly destroy the tongue of the Sea of Egypt; With His mighty wing He will shake His fist over the River, And strike it in the seven streams, And make men cross over dry-shod. There will be a highway for the remnant of His people Who will be left from

Assyria, As it was for Israel In the day that he came up from the land of Egypt. (Isaiah 11:1–16)

I will clothe him with your robe And strengthen him with your belt; I will commit your responsibility into his hand. He shall be a father to the inhabitants of Jerusalem And to the house of Judah. The key of the house of David I will lay on his shoulder; So he shall open, and no one shall shut; And he shall shut, and no one shall open. I will fasten him as a peg in a secure place, And he will become a glorious throne to his father's house. (Isaiah 22:21–23)

He will feed His flock like a shepherd; He will gather the lambs with His arm, And carry them in His bosom, And gently lead those who are with young. (Isaiah 40:11)

"Behold! My Servant whom I uphold, My Elect One in whom My soul delights! I have put My Spirit upon Him; He will bring forth justice to the Gentiles. He will not cry out, nor raise His voice, Nor cause His voice to be heard in the street. A bruised reed He will not break, And smoking flax He will not quench; He will bring forth justice for truth. He will not fail nor be discouraged, Till He has established justice in the earth; And the coastlands shall wait for His law." Thus says God the LORD, Who created the heavens and stretched them out, Who spread forth the earth and that which comes from it, Who gives breath to the people on it: "I, the LORD, have called You in righteousness, And will hold Your hand; I will keep You and give You as a covenant to the people,

As a light to the Gentiles, To open blind eyes, To bring out prisoners from the prison, Those who sit in darkness from the prison house. I am the LORD, that is My name; And My glory I will not give to another, Nor My praise to carved images. Behold the former things have come to pass, And new things I declare; Before they spring forth I tell you of them." (Isaiah 42:1–9)

Listen, O coastlands, to Me, And take heed, you peoples from afar! The LORD has called Me from the womb; From the matrix of My mother He has made mention of My name. And He has made My mouth like a sharp sword; In the shadow of His hand He has hidden Me, And made Me a polished shaft; In His quiver He has hidden Me. And He said to me, "You are My servant, O Israel, In whom I will be glorified." Then I said, "I have laboured in vain, I have spent my strength for nothing and in vain; Yet surely my just reward is with the LORD, And my work with my God." And now the LORD says, "Who formed Me from the womb to be His Servant, To bring Jacob back to Him, So that Israel is gathered to Him (For I shall be glorious in the eyes of the LORD, And My God shall be My strength)." Indeed He says, "It is too small a thing that You should be My Servant To raise up the tribes of Jacob, And to restore the preserved ones of Israel; I will also give you as a light to the Gentiles, That You should be My salvation to the ends of the earth.'" Thus says the LORD, The Redeemer of Israel, their Holy One, To Him whom man despises, To Him whom the nation abhors, To the Servant of rulers: "Kings shall see and arise, Princes also shall worship, Because of the LORD who is faithful, The Holy One of Israel; And He has chosen You." Thus says the LORD: "In an acceptable time I have heard You, And in the day of salvation I have helped You; I will preserve You and give You As a covenant to the people, To restore the earth, To cause them to inherit the desolate heritages; That You may say to the prisoners, Go forth," To those who are in darkness, "Show yourselves." They shall feed along the roads, And their pastures shall be on all desolate heights They shall neither hunger or thirst, Neither heat nor sun shall strike them; For He who has mercy on them will lead them, Even by the springs of water He will guide them. (Isaiah 49:1–10)

The LORD God has given Me The tongue of the learned, That I should know how to speak A word in season to him who is weary. He awakens Me morning by morning, He awakens My ear To hear as the learned. The Lord God has opened My ear; And I was not rebellious, Nor did I turn away. I gave My back to those who struck Me, And My cheeks to those who plucked out My beard; I did not hide My face from shame and spitting. (Isaiah 50:4–6)

Behold My Servant shall deal prudently; He shall be exalted and extolled and be very high. Just as many were astonished at you, So His visage was marred more than any man, And His form more than the sons of men; So shall He sprinkle many nations. Kings shall shut their mouths at Him; For what had not been told them they shall see, And what they had not heard they shall consider. (Isaiah 52:13–15)

Who has believed our report? And to whom has the arm of the LORD been revealed? For he shall grow up before Him as a tender plant, And as a root out of dry ground. He has no form or comeliness; And when we see Him, There is no beauty that we should desire Him. He is despised and rejected by men, A Man of sorrows and acquainted with grief. And we hid, as it were, our faces from Him; He was despised, and we did not esteem Him. Surely He has borne our griefs And carried our sorrows; Yet we esteemed Him stricken, Smitten by God, and afflicted. But He was wounded for our transgressions, He was bruised for our iniquities; The chastisement for our peace was upon Him, And by His stripes we were healed. All we like sheep have gone astray; We have turned, every one, to his own way; And the LORD has laid on Him the iniquity of us all. He was oppressed and He was afflicted, Yet He opened not His mouth; He was led as a lamb to the slaughter, And as a sheep before its shearers is silent, So He opened not His mouth. He was taken from prison and from judgment, And who will declare His generation? For He was cut off from the land of the living; For the transgressions of My people He was stricken. And they made His grave with the wicked—But with the rich at His death, Because He had done no violence, Nor was any deceit in His mouth. Yet it pleased the LORD to bruise Him; He has put Him to grief. When You make His soul an offering for sin, He shall see His seed, He shall prolong His days, And the pleasure of the LORD shall prosper in His hand. He shall see the labour of His soul, and be satisfied. By His knowledge My righteous Servant shall justify many,

For He shall bear their iniquities. Therefore I will divide Him a portion with the great, And He shall divide the spoil with the strong, Because He poured out His soul unto death, And He was numbered with the transgressors, And He bore the sin of many, And made intercession for the transgressors. (Isaiah 53:1–12)

The Spirit of the LORD God is upon Me, Because the LORD has anointed Me To preach good tidings to the poor; He has sent Me to heal the brokenhearted, To proclaim liberty to the captives, And the opening of the prison to those who are bound; To proclaim the acceptable year of the LORD, And the day of vengeance of our God; To comfort all who mourn, To console those who mourn in Zion, To give them beauty for ashes, The oil of joy for mourning, The garment of praise for the spirit of heaviness; That they may be called trees of righteousness, The planting of the LORD, that He may be glorified. (Isaiah 61:1–3)

I looked, but there was no one to help, And I wondered That there was no one to uphold; Therefore My own arm brought salvation for Me; And My own fury, it sustained Me. (Isaiah 63:5)

Before she was in labor, she gave birth; Before her pain came, She delivered a male child. Who has heard such a thing? Who has seen such things? Shall the earth be made to give birth in one day? Or shall a nation be born at once? For as soon as Zion was in labor, She gave birth to her children. (Isaiah 66:7–8)

For behold, the LORD will come with fire And with His chariots, like a whirlwind, To render His anger with fury, And His rebuke with flames of fire. For by fire and by His sword The LORD will judge all flesh; And the slain of the LORD shall be many. (Isaiah 66:15–16)

"Behold, the days are coming," says the LORD, "That I will raise to David a Branch of righteousness; A King shall reign and prosper, And execute judgment and righteousness in the earth. In His days Judah will be saved, And Israel will dwell safely; Now this is His name by which He will be called: the LORD our Righteousness. Therefore, behold, the days are coming," says the LORD, "that they shall no longer say, 'As the LORD lives who brought up the children of Israel from the land of Egypt,' but, 'As the LORD lives who brought up and led the descendants of the house of Israel from the north country and from all the countries where I had driven them.' And they shall dwell in their own land." (Jeremiah 23:5–8)

But they shall serve the LORD their God, And David their king, Whom I will raise up for them. (Jeremiah 30:9)

In those days and at that time I will cause to grow up to David a branch of righteousness; He shall execute judgment and righteousness in the earth. In those days Judah will be saved, And Jerusalem will dwell safely. And this is the name by which she will be called: the LORD our Righteousness. (Jeremiah 33:15–16)

This preceding passage is especially interesting because it claims that Jerusalem itself will be called "the LORD our Righteousness." If the city of Jerusalem will be called after the LORD, how much more so will Jesus? In the physical, Jesus at times is referred to as Israel, the Root of Jesse, The Branch, David, etc. He is also referenced at times as the LORD and Father because, as Jesus stated, He was the express image of God our Father.

> I will establish one Shepherd over them, and he shall feed them—My servant David. He shall feed them and be their shepherd. And I, the LORD, will be their God, and My servant David a prince among them; I, the LORD have spoken. (Ezekiel 34:23–24)

> And I will make them one nation in the land, on the mountains of Israel; and one king over them all; they shall no longer be two nations, nor shall they ever be divided into two kingdoms again. They shall not defile themselves anymore with their idols, nor with their detestable things, nor with any of their transgressions; but I will deliver them from all their dwelling places in which they have sinned, and will cleanse them. Then they shall be My people, and I will be their God. David, My servant, shall be king over them, and they shall all have one Shepard; they shall also walk in My judgments and observe My statutes, and do them. Then they shall dwell in the land that I have given to Jacob My servant, where your fathers dwelt; and they shall dwell there, they, their children, and their children's children, forever; and My servant David shall be their prince forever. Moreover I will make a covenant of peace with them, and it shall be an everlasting covenant with

them; I will establish them and multiply them, and I will set My sanctuary in their midst forevermore. My tabernacle also shall be with them; indeed I will be their God, and they shall be My people. The nations also will know that I, the LORD, sanctify Israel, when My sanctuary is in their midst forevermore. (Ezekiel 37:22–28)

Then Nebuchadnezzar was full of fury, and the expression on his face changed toward Shadrach, Meshach, and Abed-Nego. He spoke and commanded that they heat the furnace seven times more than it was usually heated. And he commanded certain mighty men of valor who were in his army to bind Shadrach, Meshach, and Abed-Nego, and cast them into the burning fiery furnace. Then these men were bound in their coats, their trousers, their turbans, and their other garments, and were cast into the midst of the burning fiery furnace. Therefore, because the king's command was urgent, and the furnace exceedingly hot, the flame of the fire killed those men who took up Shadrach, Meshach, and Abed-Nego. And these three men, Shadrach, Meshach, and Abed-Nego, fell down bound into the midst of the burning fiery furnace. Then King Nebuchadnezzar was astonished; and he rose in haste and spoke, saying to his councillors, "Did we not cast three men bound into the midst of the fire?" They answered and said to the king, "True, O king." "Look!" He answered, "I see four men loose, walking in the midst of the fire; and they are not hurt, and the form of the fourth is like the Son of God." (Daniel 3:19–25)

I was watching in the night visions, And behold, One like the Son of Man, Coming with the clouds of heaven! He came to the Ancient of Days, And they brought Him near before Him. Then to Him was given dominion and glory and a kingdom, That all peoples, nations, and languages should serve Him. His dominion is an everlasting dominion, Which shall not pass away, And His kingdom the one Which shall not be destroyed. (Daniel 7:13–14)

When Israel was a child, I loved him, And out of Egypt I called My son. (Hosea 11:1)

Now the Lord had prepared a great fish to swallow Jonah. And Jonah was in the belly of the fish three days and three nights. (Jonah 1:17)

And just as Jonah spent three days and three nights in the belly of the whale, Jesus would spend three days and three nights in the belly of the grave. Contrary to popular myth, Jesus was crucified at the time in which the Passover lamb was killed. Jesus died at the commencement of the Passover, which coincidentally fell on the same day in 2023 as it did in the year that Jesus was crucified.

Jesus was resurrected three days and three nights later. He was actually resurrected on Saturday before sunset. His resurrection was witnessed to on Sunday morning when certain women went to His grave. The timeline is as follows: Once crucified, Jesus died at approximately three o'clock on Wednesday afternoon. After His death, Joseph, a Pharisee, received permission from Pilate to retrieve Jesus's body and bury Him. Joseph and Nicodemus then practiced the Jewish custom of burial by wrapping Jesus's body in strips of linen soaked in a mixture of myrrh and aloes.

Once Jesus's body had been properly prepared, He was laid in a grave just before sunset, which was witnessed to by Mary

Magdalene and Jesus's mother, Mary. Thursday was the Passover, a High Sabbath in which no work could be done. The chief priests went to Pilate and received permission to have guards stationed on Jesus's grave so that no one could steal the body.

On Friday, the women busied themselves buying and mixing spices in order to anoint Jesus in His burial shroud on Sunday, the first day of the week. Saturday was the weekly Sabbath, and no work could be done. Jesus rose from the dead before sunset on Saturday evening.

Early on Sunday morning, Mary Magdalene, Jesus's mother, and Jesus's sister Salome went to Jesus's grave to perform their customary anointing and found the grave empty (Mark 16:1–2). They immediately ran back to Jesus's disciples and told them that someone had rolled back the stone and removed Jesus's body from the grave. John and Peter immediately ran to the grave and found it just as the women had said. Mary Magdalene again went to the grave, and the resurrected Jesus revealed Himself to her.

> I went down to the moorings of the mountains;
> The earth with its bars closed behind me forever;
> Yet You have brought up my life from the pit, O
> LORD, my God. (Jonah 2:6)

> Now gather yourself in troops, O daughter of
> troops; He has laid siege against us; They will
> strike the judge of Israel with a rod on the cheek.
> But you, Bethlehem Ephrathah, Though you are
> little among the thousands of Judah, Yet out of you
> shall come forth to Me The One to be Ruler in
> Israel, Whose goings forth are from of old, From
> everlasting. (Micah 5:1–2)

It is said that this Ruler, who would come out of Bethlehem "whose goings forth are from of old, from everlasting," existed before creation.

> Then speak to him, saying, "Thus says the LORD of hosts, saying: 'Behold, the Man whose name is the Branch! From His place He shall branch out, And He shall build the temple of the LORD; Yes, He shall build the temple of the LORD. He shall bear the glory, And shall sit and rule on His throne; So He shall be a priest on His throne, And the council of peace shall be between them both.'" (Zechariah 6:12–13)

> Rejoice greatly, O daughter of Zion! Shout, O daughter of Jerusalem! Behold, your King is coming to you; He is just and having salvation, Lowly and riding on a donkey, A colt, the foal of a donkey. (Zechariah 9:9)

> My anger is kindled against the shepherds, And I will punish the goatherds. For the LORD of hosts will visit His flock, The house of Judah, And will make them as His royal horse in the battle. From him comes the cornerstone, From him the tent peg, From him the battle bow, From him every ruler together. (Zechariah 10:3–4)

> Then I said to them, "If it is agreeable to you, give me my wages; and if not, refrain: so they weighed out for my wages thirty pieces of silver. And the LORD said to me, 'Throw it to the potter'—that princely price they set on me. So I took the thirty

pieces of silver and threw them into the house of the LORD for the potter." (Zechariah 11:12–13)

And I will pour on the house of David and on the inhabitants of Jerusalem the Spirit of grace and supplication; then they will look on Me whom they pierced. Yes, they will mourn for Him as one mourns for his only son, and grieve for Him as one grieves for a firstborn. (Zechariah 12:10)

And one will say to him, "What are these wounds between your arms?" Then he will answer, "Those with which I was wounded in the house of my friends. Awake, O sword, against My Shepherd, Against the Man who is My companion," says the LORD of hosts. "Strike the Shepherd, And the sheep will be scattered; Then I will turn My hand against the little ones." (Zechariah 13:6–7)

"Behold, I send My messenger, And he will prepare the way before Me. And the LORD, whom you seek, Will suddenly come to His temple, Even the Messenger of the covenant, In whom you delight. Behold, He is coming," says the LORD of hosts. (Malachi 3:1)

"And I will come near you for judgment; I will be a swift witness Against sorcerers, Against adulterers, Against perjurers, Against those who exploit wage earners and widows and orphans, And against those who turn away an alien—Because they do not fear Me," says the LORD of hosts. "For I am the LORD, I do not change. (Malachi 3:5–6)

In the beginning was the Word, and the Word was with God, and the Word was God. He was in the beginning with God. All things were made through Him, and without Him nothing was made that was made. In Him was life, and the life was the light of men. And the light shines in the darkness, and the darkness did not comprehend it. (John 1:1–5)

He was in the world, and the world was made through Him, and the world did not know Him. He came to His own, and His own did not receive Him. (John 1:10–11)

And the Word became flesh and dwelt among us, and we beheld His glory as of the only begotten of the Father, full of grace and truth. (John 1:14)

No one has ascended to heaven but He who came down from heaven, that is, the Son of Man who is in heaven. (John 3:13)

For God so loved the world that He gave His only begotten Son, that whoever believes in Him should not perish but have everlasting life. For God did not send His Son into the world to condemn the world, but that the world through Him might be saved. He who believes in Him is not condemned; but he who does not believe is condemned already, because he has not believed in the name of the only begotten Son of God. (John 3:16–18)

The Father loves the Son, and has given all things into His hand. He who believes in the Son has everlasting life; and he who does not believe the

Son shall not see life, but the wrath of God abides on him. (John 3:35–36)

But Jesus answered them, "My Father has been working until now, and I have been working." Therefore the Jews sought all the more to kill Him, because He not only broke the Sabbath, but also said that God was His Father, making Himself equal with God. (John 5:17–18)

For as the Father raises the dead and gives life to them, even so the Son gives life to whom He will. For the Father judges no one, but has committed all judgment to the Son, that all should honour the Son just as they honour the Father. He who does not honour the Son does not honour the Father who sent Him. For as the Father has life in Himself, so He has granted the Son to have life in Himself and has given Him authority to execute judgment also, because He is the Son of Man. (John 5:21–27)

For if you believed Moses, you would believe Me, for he wrote about Me. (John 5:46)

I am One who bears witness of Myself, and the Father who sent Me bears witness of Me. (John 8:18)

For if you do not believe that I am He, you will die in your sins (John 8:24)

And that I do nothing of Myself; but as My Father taught Me, I speak these things. (John 8:28)

For I proceeded forth and came from God. (John 8:42)

Jesus said to them, "Most assuredly, I say to you, before Abraham was, I Am." (John 8:58)

Do you say of Him whom the Father sanctified and sent into the world, "You are blaspheming," because I said, "I am the Son of God"? If I do not do the works of My Father, do not believe Me; but if I do, though you do not believe Me, believe the works, that you may know and believe that the Father is in Me, and I in Him." (John 10:36–38)

Jesus said to her, "I am the resurrection and the life. He who believes in Me, though he may die, he shall live. And whoever lives and believes in Me shall never die. Do you believe this?" She said to Him, "Yes, Lord, I believe that you are the Christ, the Son of God, who is to come into the world." (John 11:25–27)

While the Pharisees were gathered together, Jesus asked them, saying, "What do you think about the Christ? Whose Son is He?" They said to Him, "The Son of David," He said to them, "How then does David in the spirit call Him 'Lord, saying: "The LORD said to my Lord, 'Sit at My right hand, Till I make Your enemies Your footstool'"? "If David then calls Him 'Lord,' how is He his Son?" (Matthew 22:41–45)

But Jesus kept silent. And the high priest answered and said to Him, "I put You under oath by the living

God: Tell us if You are the Christ, the Son of God!" Jesus said to him, "It is as you said. Nevertheless, I say to you, hereafter you will see the Son of Man sitting at the right hand of the Power, and coming on the clouds of heaven." (Matthew 26:63–64)

For the Father Himself loves you, because you have loved Me, and have believed that I came forth from God. I came forth from the Father, and have come into the world. Again, I leave the world and go to the Father. (John 16:27–28)

Father, the hour has come. Glorify Your Son, that Your Son also may glorify You, as You have given Him authority over all flesh, that He should give eternal life to as many as You have given Him. And this is eternal life, that they may know You, the only true God, and Jesus Christ whom You have sent. I have glorified You on the earth. I have finished the work which You have given Me to do And now, O Father, glorify Me together with Yourself, with the glory which I had with You before the world was. (John 17:1–5)

Father, I desire that they also whom You gave Me may be with Me where I am, that they may behold My glory which You have given Me; for You loved Me before the foundation of the world. (John 17:24)

And the eunuch said, "See, here is water. What hinders me from being baptized?" Then Philip said, "If you believe with all your heart, you may." And he answered and said, "I believe that Jesus Christ is the Son of God." (Acts 8:36–37)

As it is written in the second psalm: "You are My Son, Today I have begotten You." (Acts 13:33)

Paul, a bondservant of Jesus Christ, called to be an apostle, separated to the gospel of God which He promised before through His prophets in the Holy Scriptures, concerning His Son Jesus Christ our Lord, who was born of the seed of David according to the flesh, and declared to be the Son of God with power according to the Spirit of holiness, by the resurrection of the dead. (Romans 1:1–4)

For no other foundation can anyone lay than that which is laid, which is Jesus Christ. (1 Corinthians 3:11)

Yet for us there is one God, the Father, of whom are all things, and we for Him; and one Lord Jesus Christ, through whom are all things, and through whom we live. (1 Corinthians 8:6)

For you know the grace of our Lord Jesus Christ, that though He was rich, yet for your sakes He became poor, that you through His poverty might become rich. (2 Corinthians 8:9)

"He became poor." He gave up His Godhead and became a man.

Now I, Paul, myself am pleading with you by the meekness and gentleness of Christ. (2 Corinthians 10:1)

And to make all see what is the fellowship of the mystery, which from the beginning of the ages has been hidden in God who created all things through Jesus Christ; to the intent that now the manifold wisdom of God might be made known by the church to the principalities and powers in the heavenly places, according to the eternal purpose which He accomplished in Christ Jesus our Lord. (Ephesians 3:9–11)

But to each one of us grace was given according to the measure of Christ's gift. Therefore He says: "When He ascended on high, He led captivity captive, And gave gifts to men." (Ephesians 4:7–8)

"He led captivity captive." He led Satan captive who has been holding humanity hostage.

In order to understand how Satan has been holding humanity hostage, one must first understand the mechanics of a person and the elements that go into making a person a person. A person is comprised of 3 elements, the body, the soul and the spirit as is testified to in the following scripture.

Now may the God of peace Himself sanctify you completely; and may your whole spirit, soul, and body be preserved blameless at the coming of our Lord Jesus Christ. (1 Thessalonians 5:23)

In the Garden of Eden, Christ as the High Priest forever, according to the order of Melchizedek had a bond with Adam and Eve that allowed Him to share the divine nature with them. That bond was through man's "soul." Christ in the time of the Garden of Eden was able to share with Adam and Eve the divine nature through their senses and emotions, through their physical surroundings. Christ was able to interact with Adam and Eve in the same way that we interact with our physical world on a daily basis.

They communicated freely, just as we freely communicate with our friends and neighbours.

Being incited by Satan, Adam and Eve rebelled and as a consequence of that rebellion became subject to death and were literally cut off from the bond through which Christ was able to share the divine nature with them. Through Adam and Eve's rebellion they became filled with sin, became alienated from God and could no longer share in the divine nature with God. You cannot serve God and mammon.

> The soul who sins shall die. (Ezekiel 18:20)

> Then the dust will return to the earth as it was,
> And the spirit will return to God who gave it.
> (Ecclesiastes 12:7)

> For the living know that they will die; But the dead know nothing, And they have no more reward, For the memory of them is forgotten. Also their love, their hatred, and their envy have now perished; Nevermore will they have a share In anything done under the sun. (Ecclesiastes 9:5–6)

The body cannot exist apart from the human spirit, nor the spirit apart from the body. As the consequences of the rebellion, the soul and the body will die and the spirit will return to God. The spirit gives animation to the body and cannot exist apart from the body.

As the result of the rebellion in the Garden of Eden humanity became mortal and lost their inheritance. Humanity was originally designed to rule over the world. That rule included every creature on the earth including Lucifer and his angels. That rule gave humanity the right to judge Satan and his angels. God must follow the rule of Law.

> But I want you to know that the head of every man
> is Christ, the head of woman is man, and the head
> of Christ is God. (1Corinthians 11:3)

The hierarchy that God designed is that God is the head of all and then Christ and afterwards humanity. Satan is considered as a beast of the field.

> So the LORD God said to the serpent: "Because
> you have done this, You are cursed more than all
> cattle, And more than every beast of the field; On
> your belly you shall go, And you shall eat dust All
> the days of your life." (Genesis 3:14)

Because humanity lost their inheritance through the rebellion, that hierarchy was reduced to God and Christ. Therefore because humanity has lost their ability to manage the world, a void has been established leaving Satan bereft of a judge. Satan has been free to continue in his rebellion because of humanities malfeasance.

Christ has now come in the flesh. He has endured the trials and temptations that only Satan could devise. He has not succumbed to one of the temptations inflicted upon Him. He has been proven to have maintained His innocence. Because Jesus maintained His innocence throughout the period of time that He was in the form of a man, He has received an entitlement that the first Adam gave up through his lost inheritance, the entitlement to judge the worlds. Jesus through His obedience qualified to be appointed Judge of the universe. Having by necessity been born into this world, He needed to suffer the same condemnation that had been imposed upon all of humanity. He suffered that condemnation by being nailed to a cross and crucified.

Because of God's promise that He would not leave Christ's soul in Hades, He raised Him from the dead. Now that He has been raised from the dead, God has given Christ a new body.

> Therefore, if anyone is in Christ, he is a new creation; old things have passed away; behold, all things have become new. (2 Corinthians 5:17)

Jesus has inherited all of the Authorities and Powers that He held prior to His death. In addition to having received His inheritance He has been granted the rights to establish a New Covenant. And in addition to being granted the rights to establish a New Covenant, He has received a new body. This is the new body that we shall be clothed with when Christ Jesus returns to the earth. The only thing that remains of Christ is His Spirit, all other things have become new.

> For our citizenship is in heaven, from which we also eagerly wait for the Savior, the Lord Jesus Christ, who will transform our lowly body that it may be conformed to His glorious body, according to the working by which He is able even to subdue all things to Himself. (Philippians 3:20–21)

Because we have lost our inheritance, God is having Christ share His inheritance with us as is described in the parable of the prodigal son, Luke 15:11–32. And the prodigal son went out from his father and wasted all of his inheritance with prodigal living. And once this prodigal son came to his senses he returned to his father. And just as the father welcomed him back and presented him with the best robe and a ring for his finger, we, the prodigal sons, have returned home after having wasted all of our inheritance, and God has met us and given us a share in the inheritance of His obedient Son.

Now, although we have completely destroyed and brought to a miserable end, every aspect of our inheritance, God, beyond anything that can be conceived by the human mind is offering us the opportunity to share with Christ, His inheritance, the Kingdom of God.

Christ having become a man, has triumphed over temptation, has suffered the curse that had been imposed upon mankind and has been raised to Glory. He has been found worthy to Judge the living and the dead, and He has been found worthy to open the scroll that has been sealed with the seven seals and usher in the Kingdom of God.

> And I saw in the right hand of Him who sat on the throne a scroll written inside and on the back, sealed with seven seals. Then I saw a strong angel proclaiming with a loud voice, "Who is worthy to open the scroll and to loose its seals?" And no one in heaven or on the earth or under the earth was able to open the scroll, or to look at it. So I wept much, because no one was found worthy to open and read the scroll, or to look at it. But one of the elders said to me, "Do not weep, the Root of David, has prevailed to open the scroll and to loose its seven seals." And I looked and behold, in the midst of the throne and of the four living creatures, and in the midst of the elders, stood a Lamb as though it had been slain, having seven horns and seven eyes, which are the seven Spirits of God sent out into all the earth. Then He came and took the scroll out of the right hand of Him who sat on the throne. Now when He had taken the scroll, the four living creatures and twenty-four elders fell down before the Lamb, each having a harp, and golden bowls full of incense, which are the prayers of the saints. And they sang a new song, saying:

> "You are worthy to take the scroll,
> And to open its seals;
> For You were slain,

And have redeemed us to God
By your blood
Out of every tribe and tongue and
People and nation,
And have made us kings and priests to our God;
And we shall reign on the
Earth."
(Revelations 5:1–10)

Now that we have lost our inheritance through the flesh we have the opportunity of receiving a greater inheritance through the Spirit.

Now this, "He ascended"—what does it mean but that He also first descended into the lower parts of the earth? He who descended is also the One who ascended far above all the heavens, that He might fill all things. (Ephesians 4:9–10)

He descended from heaven to the earth and was given the form of a man.

Let this mind be in you which was also in Christ Jesus, who, being in the form of God, did not consider it robbery to be equal with God, but made Himself of no reputation, taking the form of a bondservant, and coming in the likeness of men. And being found in appearance as a man, He humbled Himself and became obedient to the point of death, even death of the cross. Therefore God also has highly exalted Him and given Him the name which is above every name, that at the name of Jesus every knee should bow, of those in heaven, and of those on earth, and of those under the earth, and that every tongue should confess that

149

Jesus Christ is Lord, to the glory of God the Father. (Philippians 2:5–11)

He has delivered us from the power of darkness and conveyed us into the kingdom of the Son of His love, in whom we have redemption through His blood, the forgiveness of sins. He is the image of the invisible God, the firstborn over all creation. For by Him all things were created that are in heaven and that are on earth, visible and invisible, whether thrones or powers. All things were created through Him and for Him. And He is before all things, and in Him all things consist. And He is the head of the body, the church, who is the beginning, the firstborn from the dead, that in all things He may have the pre-eminence. For it pleased the Father that in Him all the fullness should dwell, and by Him to reconcile all things to Himself, by Him, whether things on earth or things in heaven, having made peace through the blood of His cross. And you, who once were alienated and enemies in your mind by wicked works, yet now He has reconciled in the body of His flesh through death, to present you holy, and blameless, and above reproach in His sight—if indeed you continue in the faith, grounded and steadfast, and are not moved away from the hope of the gospel which you heard, which was preached to every creature under heaven, of which I Paul, became a minister. (Colossians 1:13–23)

This is a faithful saying and worthy of all acceptance, that Christ Jesus came into the world to save sinners, of whom I am chief. (1 Timothy 1:15)

> I urge you in the sight of God who gives life to all things, and before Christ Jesus who witnessed the good confession before Pontius Pilate. (1 Timothy 6:13)

Jesus confessed to Pontius Pilate as He did to the high priest, that He was the Son of God and they naturally believed that to mean that He had His origins in heaven. Those are the grounds that were used to crucify Him.

> Do not think that I came to bring peace on earth, I did not come to bring peace but a sword. For I have come to set a man against his father, a daughter against her mother, and a daughter-in-law against her mother-in-law; and a man's enemies will be those of his own household. He who loves father or mother more than Me is not worthy of Me. And he who loves son or daughter more than Me is not worthy of Me. And he who does not take his cross and follow after Me is not worthy of Me. He who finds his life will lose it, and he who loses his life for My sake will find it. He who receives you receives Me, and he who receives Me receives Him who sent Me. (Matthew 10:34–40)

Jesus had a very different idea about peace on earth and goodwill toward man. As is repeatedly stated throughout this book, Jesus is the Way, the Truth, and the Life, and no one comes to the Father except through Him. The consequences of sin is death, and no one who sins can see God—period. The emphasis here is that *the person who sins will die.*

We are commanded to be perfect even as our Father in heaven is perfect, and perfection can only be achieved through the Spirit of Jesus Christ living in us, keeping us from sin and creating the divine nature in us. The peace that God speaks of in the Bible is in regard to the peace that God is offering to us through His plan of salvation through Jesus Christ.

There is a curse on the world, which is about to be realized in the very near future. God's offering of peace—and the only way out of this coming cataclysmic event—is by His Holy Spirit, which is being made available to us through Jesus Christ, His only begotten Son, the Firstborn of creation.

Just as death to all of humanity came through the one man Adam, the resurrection of the dead of all of humanity has come by the One Man Jesus Christ. There will be a resurrection of the just and the unjust. All in their own time. Prior to Jesus's death and resurrection humanity was void of hope. There was nothing that could rescue humanity from the death that every person has experienced since the beginning of time. All that have died are dead and have ceased to exist. They have no more consciousness, no more memory, no more nothing. For the most part, it is only God and of course Jesus Christ who have any remembrance of them. The facts are as follows; because all have their being in Christ, then through Christ's resurrection in the flesh, all will be raised from the dead in the flesh. All of humanity who were condemned to death through Adam will now be raised to judgement through Christ. Again, God is not partial, He cannot raise some and not others. Everyone will be raised from the dead to face judgement. To stand before Jesus Christ in judgement will be a terrifying experience for those being saved; for those who have blatantly rejected God and His saving grace, the terror that awaits cannot be imagined. The curse will be completed once God's final judgement has been made. Even the resurrection of the dead is a copy of the True. The True resurrection is reserved for those who have had Christ's Spirit fully formed in them.

> "There will be weeping and gnashing of teeth,
> when you see Abraham and Isaac and Jacob and all

the prophets in the kingdom of God, and yourself thrust out." (Luke 13:28)

(But the free gift is not like the offence. For if by the one man's offence many died, much more the grace of God and the gift by the grace of the one Man, Jesus Christ, abounded to many. And the gift is not like that which came through the one who sinned. For the judgement which came from one offence resulted in condemnation, but the free gift which came from many offences resulted in justification. For if by one man's offence death reigned through the one, much more those who receive abundance of grace and of the gift of righteousness will reign in life through the One, Jesus Christ) Therefore, as through one man's offence judgement came to all men, resulting in condemnation, even so through one Man's righteous act the free gift came to all men, resulting in justification of life. (Romans 5:16–18)

For since by man came death, by Man also came the resurrection of the dead. For as in Adam all die, even so in Christ all shall be made alive. But each one in his own order: Christ the firstfruits, afterward those who are Christ's at His coming. Then comes the end, when He delivers the kingdom to God the Father, when He puts an end to all rule and all authority and power. (1 Corinthians 15:21–24)

"I have hope in God, which they themselves also accept, that there will be a resurrection of the dead, both of the just and the unjust. This being so, I myself always strive to have a conscience without offence toward God and men." (Acts 24:15–16)

God, who at various times and in various ways spoke in time past to the fathers by the prophets, has in these last days spoken to us by His Son, whom He has appointed heir of all things, through whom also He made the worlds; who being the brightness of His glory and the express image of His person, and upholding all things by the word of His power, when He had by Himself purged our sins, sat down at the right hand of the Majesty on high, having become so much better than the angels, as He has by inheritance obtained a more excellent name than they. For to which of the angels did He ever say: "You are My Son, Today I have begotten You"? And again: "I will be to Him a Father, And He shall be to Me a Son"? But when He again brings the Firstborn into the world, He says: "Let all the angels of God worship Him." (Hebrews 1:1–6)

We are commanded that only God can be worshipped.

And of the angels He says: "Who makes His angels spirits And His ministers a flame of fire," But to the Son He says: "Your throne, O God, is forever and ever; A sceptre of righteousness is the sceptre of Your kingdom. You have loved righteousness and hated lawlessness: Therefore God, Your God, has anointed You With the oil of gladness more than Your companions." And: "You, Lord, in the beginning laid the foundation of the earth, And the heavens are the work of Your hands. They will perish, but You remain; And they will all grow old like a garment: Like a cloak You will fold them up, And they will be changed. But You are the same, And Your years will not fail." But to which of the angels has He ever said: "Sit at My right hand, Till I make Your enemies Your footstool"? Are they not all ministering spirits sent forth to minister for those who will inherit salvation? (Hebrews 1:7–14)

For He has not put the world to come, of which we speak, in subjection to angels. But one testified in a certain place, saying: "What is man that You are mindful of Him, Or the son of man that You take care of him? You made him a little lower than the angels; You have crowned him with glory and honor, And set him over the works of Your hands. You have put all things in subjection under his feet." For in that He put all in subjection under him, He left nothing that is not put under him. But now we do not yet see all things put under him. (Hebrews 2:5–8)

Today's world is under the subjection of angels. God is certainly not the God of this world. "He left nothing that is not put under Him." Our inheritance is to rule over all of creation with Jesus. Our inheritance is to be realized once Christ returns, sets up God's Kingdom and brings into existence a new world.

But we see Jesus, who was made a little lower than the angels, for the suffering of death, crowned with glory and honour, that He, by the grace of God, might taste death for everyone. For it was fitting for Him, for whom are all things and by whom are all things, in bringing many sons to glory, to make the captain of their salvation perfect through sufferings, For both He who sanctifies and those who are being sanctified are all of one, for which reason He is not ashamed to call them brethren, saying: "I will declare Your name to My brethren; In the midst of the assembly I will sing praise to you." And again: "I will put My trust in Him." And again: "Here am I and the children whom God has given Me." Inasmuch then as the children have partaken of flesh and blood, He Himself likewise shared in the same, that through death He might destroy him who had the power of death, that is, the devil, and release those who through fear of death were all their lifetime subject to bondage. For indeed He does not give aid to angels, but He does give aid to the seed of Abraham. Therefore, in all things He had to be made like His brethren, that He might be a merciful and faithful High Priest in things pertaining to God, to make propitiation for the sins of the people. For in that He Himself has suffered, being tempted, He is able to aid those who are tempted. (Hebrews 2:9–18)

Jesus Christ is the same yesterday, today, and tomorrow. (Hebrews 13:8)

Simon Peter, a bondservant and apostle of Jesus Christ, To those who have obtained like precious faith with us by the righteousness of our God and Savior Jesus Christ: Grace and peace be multiplied to you in the knowledge of God and of Jesus our Lord, as His divine power has given to us all things that pertain to life and godliness, through the knowledge of Him who called us by glory and virtue, by which have been given to us exceedingly great and precious promises, that through these you may be partakers of the divine nature, having escaped the corruption that is in the world through lust. (2 Peter 1:1–4)

For He received from God the Father honor and glory when such a voice came to Him from the Excellent Glory: "This is My beloved Son, in whom I am well pleased." And we heard this voice which came from heaven when we were with Him on the holy mountain. (2 Peter 1:17–18)

That which was from the beginning, which we have heard, which we have seen with our eyes, which we have looked upon, and our hands have handled, concerning the Word of life. (1 John 1:1)

"Word" is the personification of God's command, complete and utter obedience, and submission.

The life was manifested, and we have seen, and bear witness, and declare to you that eternal life which was with the Father and was manifested to us—that which we have seen and heard we declare to you, that you also may have fellowship with the Father and with His Son Jesus Christ. And these things we write to you that your joy may be full. This is the message which we have heard from Him and declare to you, that God is light and in Him is no darkness at all. If we say that we have fellowship with Him, and walk in darkness, we lie and do not practice the truth. But if we walk in the light as He is in the light, we have fellowship with one another,

> and the blood of Jesus Christ His Son cleanses us
> from all sin. (1 John 1:2–7)

The blood of Jesus cleanses us from all sin because it puts an end to
the Old Covenant and allows the New Covenant to be established.
(Without blood, there can be no forgiveness of sin. You have a choice
of who's blood it will be to make atonement for your sins, Jesus's or
your own). The Old Covenant, which was based on laws and rituals,
has ended, and we are no longer bound by it. The New Covenant
states, "I will put My laws into their hearts and in their minds write
them, and I will be to them a God and they shall be My people."
That is the doctrine that now dictates our lives. It is necessary
to believe that Jesus Christ is the only begotten Son of God, the
Firstborn of creation and repent and be baptized into His Body.

> If we say that we have no sin, we deceive ourselves,
> and the truth is not in us. If we confess our sins,
> He is faithful and just to forgive us our sins and to
> cleanse us from all unrighteousness. If we say that
> we have not sinned, we make Him a liar, and His
> word is not in us. (1 John 1:8–10)

> My little children, these things I write to you,
> so that you may not sin. And if anyone sins, we
> have an Advocate with the Father, Jesus Christ the
> righteous. And He Himself is the propitiation for
> our sins, and not our sins only but also for the whole
> world. Now by this we know that we know Him, if
> we keep His commandments. (1 John 2:1–3)

We know we know Him because we're able to overcome temptations
and keep His commandments. This is the guarantee. This is the token
that is redeemable when Christ Jesus returns. Those who triumph
over sin through Jesus Christ will share eternal life with Him.

> He who says, "I know Him," and does not keep His
> commandments, is a liar, and the truth is not in
> him. But whoever keeps His word, truly the love of
> God is perfected in him. By this we know that we
> are in Him. He who says he abides in Him ought
> himself also to walk just as He walked. (1 John
> 2:4–6)

> Who is a liar but he who denies that Jesus is the
> Christ? He is antichrist who denies the Father and
> the Son. (1 John 2:22)

The Father and the Son—two separate persons, both being Spirit
and sharing the same Spirit (just as all of humanity shares in the
same spirit with all of humanity). And now we have the opportunity
to share in God's Spirit.

> Whoever denies the Son does not have the Father
> either; he who acknowledges the Son has the Father
> also. (1 John 2:23)

> By this you know the Spirit of God: Every spirit that
> confesses that Jesus Christ has come in the flesh is
> of God. and every spirit that does not confess that
> Jesus Christ has come in the flesh is not of God.
> And this is the spirit of the Antichrist, which you
> have heard was coming, and is now already in the
> world. (1 John 4:2–3)

"Jesus Christ *has come* in the flesh." This implies that He was
somewhere before He got to where He is. He existed prior to coming
in the flesh. He existed as the only begotten Son of God, a person
unique from the Father. And every spirit that does not believe that

Jesus Christ has come in the flesh and is a completely separate entity from God the Father is the spirit of the antichrist.

> In this the love of God was manifested toward us, that God has sent His only begotten Son into the world, that we might live through Him. (1 John 4:9)

He "sent His only begotten Son into the world." When His only begotten Son was not in the world, He sent Him into the world.

> In this is love, not that we loved God, but that He loved us and sent His Son to be the propitiation for our sins. Beloved, if God so loved us, we also ought to love one another. No one has seen God at any time. If we love one another, God abides in us, and His love has been perfected in us. By this we know that we abide in Him, and He in us, because He has given us of His Spirit. And we have seen and testify that the Father has sent the Son as Savior of the world. Whoever confesses that Jesus is the Son of God, God abides in him, and he in God. (1 John 4:10–15)

> Whoever believes that Jesus is the Christ is born of God, and everyone who loves Him who begot also loves him who is begotten of Him. By this we know that we love the children of God, when we love God and keep His commandments. For this is the love of God, that we keep His commandments. And His commandments are not burdensome. For whatever is born of God overcomes the world. And this is the victory that has overcome the world—our faith. (1 John 5:1–4)

"Our faith." Jesus is being formed in us—perfect, harmless, and undefiled, through our faith in His name—the name of the only begotten Son of God. Our faith gives us the assurance that when we are tempted and call on His name, He will give us the strength to overcome.

> Who is he who overcomes the world, but he who believes that Jesus is the Son of God? This is He who came by water and blood—Jesus Christ; not only by water, but by water and blood. And it is the Spirit who bears witness because the Spirit is truth. (1 John 5:5–6)

"Overcomes the world." The world is sin. The Spirit bears witness by allowing us to overcome sin in our lives. If you sin, then you are none of His. We know that we are His because His Spirit keeps us from sin.

> Then Jesus cried out, as He taught in the temple, saying, "You both know Me, and you know where I am from; and I have not come of Myself, but He who sent Me is true, whom you do not know. But I know Him, for I am from Him, and He sent Me." (John 7:28–29)

"I am from Him, and He sent Me." Jesus was originally with His Father, God, and His Father sent Him.

> Abide in Me, and I in you. As the branch cannot bear fruit of itself, unless it abides in the vine, neither can you, unless you abide in Me. (John 15:4)

Sharing with Jesus the divine nature and the ability to overcome sin through faith in His name.

> If we receive the witness of men, the witness of God is greater; for this is the witness of God which He has testified of His Son. He who believes in the Son of God has the witness in himself; he who does not believe God has made Him a liar, because he has not believed the testimony that God has given of His Son. (1 John 5:9–10)

"The witness in himself." The witness we have in ourselves is the Spirit that keeps us from sin.

> And this is the testimony: that God has given us eternal life, and this life is in His Son. He who has the Son has life; he who does not have the Son of God does not have life. These things I have written to you who believe in the name of the Son of God, that you may know that you have eternal life, and that you may continue to believe in the name of the Son of God. Now this is the confidence that we have in Him, that if we ask anything according to His will, He hears us. (1 John 5:11–14)

> The Christ is God's Son,
> The High Priest forever
> According to the order of Melchizedek,
> The only begotten of God,
> Born before time began,
> This Jesus whom we preach
> Is the Christ.

Chapter 13

THE JEWS' REACTION TO JESUS

The Jews were stoked by jealousy toward Jesus. Jesus performed never-before-seen-before miracles. There are documented reports of Jesus raising the dead. At one point, the Jews actually conspired to kill Lazarus after Jesus raised Him from the dead four days after his internment. Because of these unbelievable miracles, Jesus amassed a huge following. It wasn't because of the Gospel that Jesus preached that the crowds followed Him. They followed Him because of the miracles that God was doing through Him.

Because the crowds esteemed Jesus to be some kind of new revivalist, the Jews feared that their coveted position as Israel's priestly leaders was coming under attack. Jesus's habit was to preach to the crowds that followed Him. It immediately became apparent that there was a huge conflict between the doctrine that Jesus preached and the doctrine held by the Jews. This schism between Jesus's doctrine and the Jews' doctrine eventually led to Jesus's crucifixion.

Jesus preached the truth about human nature. Jesus preached that humanity's thoughts were continuously bent on evil from His youth. This offended the Jews since they thought of themselves as righteous. In addition, and for the precise grounds on which Jesus was crucified, He claimed that He was the Son of God, the prophesied Messiah of whom John the Baptist testified.

The Jews answered Him, saying, "For a good work we do not stone You, but for blasphemy, and because You, being a Man, make Yourself God." (John 10:33)

Then the chief priests and the Pharisees gathered a council and said, "What shall we do? For this Man works many signs. If we let Him alone like this, everyone will believe in Him, and the Romans will come and take away both our place and nation." And one of them, Caiaphas, being high priest that year, said to them, "You know nothing at all, nor do you consider that it is expedient for us that one man should die for the people, and not that the whole nation should perish." Now this he did not say on his own authority; but being high priest that year he prophesied that Jesus would die for the nation. (John 11:47–51)

The Jews answered him, "We have a law, and according to our law He ought to die, because He made Himself the Son of God." (John 19:7)

"He made Himself the Son of God." There were instances in the Bible where God divinely intervened in women's lives and caused them to conceive. God had Abraham's wife, Sarah, miraculously conceive Isaac. Samuel's mother, Hannah, was another who conceived with the aid of the Spirit of God. Elijah prayed, and the Shunammite woman conceived a child. Even Eve was formed when Adam was put into a deep sleep, and the Spirit of God formed Eve from one of Adam's ribs. Were they all begotten of God? The Spirit of God came over them all, but none were begotten of God.

The Pharisees and Sadducees were not accusing Jesus of claiming that His birth was a miracle of divine intervention. They were accusing Him of claiming to be the only begotten Son of God, the Messiah. These leaders of the people debated the preposterous and threatening idea that this unassuming, harmless, quiet individual could somehow begin a movement that could attempt to institute a new world government. They assumed amongst themselves that the Romans would quickly get wind of this "conspiracy," destroy their country, and remove them from their leadership roles. They reasoned that it would be better for a single man to die than for their nation to be destroyed.

Chapter 14

GOD'S WITNESS THAT JESUS IS THE CHRIST

God the Father was witnessed to throughout the Old Testament. We learn, in the New Testament, that a witness of oneself is not considered legitimate. God the Father did not witness of Himself. It was actually the Christ who testified of God the Father in the Old Testament.

As we read in the New Testament, angels and spirits could not be trusted to give an accurate and honest witness. Satan is actually identified as the father of lies. When the various attributes of God the Father were given in the Old Testament—some of which included testimonies to His mercy, justice, loyalty, fidelity, and forgiveness—they were witnessed to by the True Witness of God, the man we have come to know as Jesus Christ.

Jesus reflected the express image of God, and all of God's attributes could all be found in the person of Jesus Christ. In order for Jesus to be raised from the dead and receive His inheritance, these attributes had to be tested and proven in Jesus through an agonizing torture and ultimate death by crucifixion.

Jesus lived an exemplary life that was completely free from sin. This was witnessed to by God the Father through various miracles, culminating in Him resurrecting Jesus from the dead. Although

Jesus did agree with God the Father's witness, it was the Father who witnessed of His only begotten Son throughout the New Testament using the same logic previously described: that it was necessary for someone other than the recipient of praise to give praise to the recipient.

> "You are My witnesses," says the LORD, "And My servant whom I have chosen, That you may know and believe Me, And understand that I am He. Before Me there was no God formed, Nor shall there be after Me. I, even I, am the LORD, And besides Me there is no savior. I have declared and saved, I have proclaimed, And there was no foreign god among you; Therefore you are My witnesses," says the LORD, "that I am God. Indeed before the day was, I am He; And there is no one who can deliver out of My hand; I work, and who will reverse it?" (Isaiah 43:10–13)

> I am the LORD, your Holy One, the Creator of Israel, your King. (Isaiah 43:15)

> Thus says the LORD, the King of Israel, And his Redeemer, the LORD of hosts: "I am the First and the Last; Besides Me there is no God. And who can proclaim as I do? Then let him declare it and set it in order for Me, Since I appointed the ancient people. And the things that are coming and shall come, Let them show these to them. Do not fear, nor be afraid; Have I not told you from that time, and declared it? You are My witnesses. Is there a God besides Me? Indeed there is no other Rock; I know not one." (Isaiah 44:6–8)

"Besides Me, there is no God." One of the main character traits of God is His humility. Christ being the True Witness of God was proclaiming the omnipotence of God, and even though He is God's only begotten Son, humility prevented Him from claiming that someone could consider Him to be on the same plane as God. Of course, all authority and power ultimately begins and ends with God the Father.

> That they may know from the rising of the sun to its setting That there is none besides Me. I am the LORD, and there is no other. (Isaiah 45:6)

> For thus says the LORD, Who created the heavens, Who is God, Who formed the earth and made it, Who has established it, Who did not create it in vain, Who formed it to be inhabited: "I am the LORD, and there is no other. I have not spoken in secret, In a dark place of the earth; I did not say to the seed of Jacob, Seek Me in vain; I, the LORD, speak righteousness, I declare things that are right." (Isaiah 45:18–19)

> Tell and bring forth your case; Yes, let them take counsel together. Who has declared this from ancient time? Who has told it from that time? Have not I, the LORD? And there is no other God besides Me, A just God and a Saviour; There is none besides Me. (Isaiah 45:21)

> To whom will you liken Me, and make Me equal And compare Me, that we should be alike? (Isaiah 46:5)

Remember the former things of old, For I am God, and there is no other; I am God, and there is none like Me, Declaring the end from the beginning, And from ancient times things that are not yet done, Saying, "My counsel shall stand, And I will do all My pleasure." (Isaiah 46:9–10)

As for our Redeemer, the LORD of hosts is His name, The Holy One of Israel. (Isaiah 47:4)

Listen to Me, O Jacob, And Israel, My called: I am He, I am the First, I am also the Last. Indeed My hand has laid the foundation of the earth, And My right hand has stretched out the heavens; When I call to them, They stand up together. (Isaiah 48:12–13)

Yet I am the LORD your God Ever since the land of Egypt, And you shall know no God but Me. (Hosea 13:4)

"Father, glorify Your name." Then a voice came from heaven, saying, "I have both glorified it and will glorify it again." Therefore the people who stood by and heard it said that it had thundered. Others said, "An angel has spoken to Him." (John 12:28–29)

"Father, glorify Your name." Who was being glorified? Was it not for the people's sake who were with Jesus that this happened? God was glorifying the name of Jesus so that the people around Him would know that God had set His seal on Him. And through all the wondrous deeds that God has done through Jesus, God has been glorified.

I am the true vine, and My Father is the vinedresser.
Every branch in Me that does not bear fruit He
takes away; and every branch that bears fruit He
prunes, that it bears more fruit. (John 15:1–2)

Chapter 15

MIRACLES

Now we know that God does not hear sinners; but if anyone is a worshiper of God and does His will, He hears him. Since the world began it has been unheard of that anyone opened the eyes of one who was born blind. If this Man were not from God He could do nothing. (John 9:31–33)

Others said, "These are not the words of one who has a demon. Can a demon open the eyes of the blind?" (John 10:21)

Jesus answered them, "I told you, and you do not believe. The works that I do in My Father's name, they bear witness of Me." (John 10:25)

They bear witness to who Jesus is. They bear witness that Jesus is the Christ. They bear witness that the name that the Father has ordained is Jesus Christ of Nazareth.

Then some of the scribes and Pharisees answered, saying, "Teacher, we want to see a sign from You." But He answered and said to them, "An evil and

> adulterous generation seeks after a sign, and no sign
> will be given to it except the sign of the prophet
> Jonah. For as Jonah was three days and three nights
> in the belly of the great fish, so will the Son of Man
> be three days and three nights in the heart of the
> earth." (Matthew 12:38–40)

All the miracles and signs that have been appointed for this
generation were performed in the first century AD, some 2,000 years
ago. The miracles that Jesus and His disciples performed were well
documented and could not and were not disputed by anyone. All the
signs and wonders were witnessed to and carefully documented. All
were done as were all the events in the Old Testament as a witness to
our generation. We are living in the time that has been prophesied
throughout the entire Bible. We are now entering into the time that
will culminate in the return of Jesus Christ and the establishment
of the Kingdom of God. No sign will be given to this adulterous
generation that has not already been given.

> Now when Jesus had entered Capernaum, a
> centurion came to Him, pleading with Him, saying,
> "Lord, my servant is lying at home paralyzed,
> dreadfully tormented." And Jesus said to him, "I
> will come and heal him." The centurion answered
> and said, "Lord, I am not worthy that You should
> come under my roof. But only speak a word, and
> my servant will be healed. For I also am a man
> under authority, having soldiers under me. And I
> say to this one, 'Go,' and he goes; and to another,
> 'Come,' and he comes; and to my servant, 'Do this,'
> and he does it." When Jesus heard it, He marvelled,
> and said to those who followed, "Assuredly, I say to
> you, I have not found such great faith, not even in
> Israel! And I say to you that many will come from

east and west, and sit down with Abraham, Isaac, and Jacob in the kingdom of heaven. But the sons of the kingdom will be cast out into outer darkness. There will be weeping and gnashing of teeth." Then Jesus said to the centurion, "Go your way; and as you have believed, so let it be done for you." And his servant was healed that same hour. (Matthew 8:5–13)

Today, those of this generation who are to be found worthy to stand pure and undefiled before the judgement seat of Jesus Christ are those who will be found standing in the same faith as the centurion. Today, we don't look for the physical miracles to sooth our earthly appetites; today, we look to the spiritual miracles that sooth and nurture our broken spirits and contrite hearts.

Then He said to Thomas, "Reach your finger here, and look at My hands; and reach your hand here, and put it into My side. Do not be unbelieving, but believing." And Thomas answered and said to Him, "My Lord and my God!" Jesus said to him, "Thomas, because you have seen Me, you have believed. Blessed are those who have not seen and yet have believed." (John 20:27–29)

In the preceding verse, Thomas an apostle of Jesus had missed out on seeing an appearance of the resurrected Jesus. Having not witnessed the resurrection himself, Thomas refused to believe. At the next appearance of the resurrected Jesus, Thomas is admonished and given undeniable proof of Jesus's resurrection. Blessed are those who continue in the faith that Thomas lacked. Blessed are those who's proof is found in their hearts and not in someone's miracles.

Chapter 16

THE SPIRITUAL MIND

LORD, who may abide in Your tabernacle? Who may dwell in Your holy hill? He who walks uprightly, And works righteousness, And speaks the truth in his heart; He who does not backbite with his tongue, Nor does evil to his neighbour, Nor does he take up a reproach against his friend; In whose eyes a vile person is despised, But he honours those who fear the LORD; He who swears to his own hurt and does not change; He who does not put out his money at usury, He who does these things shall never be moved. (Psalm 15:1–5)

Whoever offers praise glorifies Me; And to him who orders his conduct aright I will show the salvation of God. (Psalm 50:23)

He has shown you, O man, what is good; And what does the LORD require of you But to do justly, To love mercy, And to walk humbly with your God? (Micah 6:8)

Thus says the LORD of hosts: "Execute true justice, Show mercy and compassion Everyone to his brother. Do not oppress the widow or the fatherless, The alien or the poor. Let none of you plan evil in his heart Against his brother." (Zechariah 7:9–10)

Thus says the LORD; "Heaven is My throne, And earth is My footstool. Where is the house that you will build Me? And where is the place of My rest? For all those things My hand has made, And all those things exist," says the LORD. "But on this one will I look: On him who is poor and of a contrite spirit, And who trembles at My word." (Isaiah 66:1–2)

For I did not speak to your fathers, or command them in the day that I brought them out of the land of Egypt, concerning burnt offerings or sacrifices. But this is what I commanded them, saying, "Obey My voice, and I will be your God, and you shall be My people. And walk in all the ways that I have commanded you, that it may be well with you." (Jeremiah 7:22–23)

The Nature of God or Divine Nature

Jesus preached the kingdom of God or, more specifically the divine nature. He taught about the Spirit of God. Jesus did not condemn anyone. Those who did not believe who He was or His Gospel message were condemned already. The people who followed Him took great delight in Jesus testifying that the Pharisees and Sadducees were sinners. Jesus put the rulers of the people on the same footing as the poor, the prostitutes, and the outcasts. The people who followed Him believed John the Baptist and were baptized by John, acknowledging their sinful natures. The Pharisees and Sadducees refused John's baptism, were self-righteous, and believed practicing the ordinances of the law made them righteous.

> "Teacher, which is the great commandment in the law?" Jesus said to him, "'You shall love the Lord your God with all your heart, with all your soul, and with all your mind.' This is the first and great commandment. And the second is like it: 'You shall love your neighbour as yourself.' On these two commandments hang all the Law and the Prophets." (Matthew 22:36–40)

> And why do you look at the speck in your brother's eye, but do not perceive the plank in your own eye? Or how can you say to your brother, "Brother, let me remove the speck that is in your eye," when you yourself do not see the plank that is in your own eye? Hypocrite! First remove the plank from your own eye, and then you will see clearly to remove the spec that is in your brother's eye. (Luke 6:41–42)

> He who is of God hears God's words. (John 8:47)

> A new commandment I give to you, that you love one another; as I have loved you, that you also love one another. By this all will know that you are My disciples, if you have love for one another. (John 13:34–35)

> My little children, for whom I laboured in birth again until Christ is formed in you. (Galatians 4:19)

Chapter 17

THE RESURRECTION

Men of Israel, hear these words: Jesus of Nazareth, a Man attested by God to you by miracles, wonders, and signs which God did through Him in your midst, as you yourself also know—Him, being delivered by the determined purpose and foreknowledge of God, you have taken by lawless hands, have crucified, and put to death; whom God raised up, having loosed the pains of death, because it was not possible that He should be held by it. For David says concerning Him: "I foresaw the LORD always before my face, For He is at My right hand, that I may not be shaken. Therefore my heart rejoiced, and my tongue was glad; Moreover my flesh also will rest in hope. For You will not leave my soul in Hades. Nor will You allow Your Holy One to see corruption. You have made known to me the ways of life; You will make me full of joy in Your presence." (Acts 2:22–28)

This Jesus God has raised up, of which we are all witnesses. (Acts 2:32)

But in every nation whoever fears Him and works righteousness is accepted by Him. The word which God sent to the children of Israel, preaching peace through Jesus Christ—He is Lord of all—that word you know, which was proclaimed throughout all Judea, and began from Galilee after the baptism which John preached: how God anointed Jesus of Nazareth with the Holy Spirit and with power, who went about doing good and healing all who were oppressed by the devil, for God was with Him. And we are witnesses of all things which He did both in the land of the Jews and in Jerusalem, whom they killed by hanging on a tree. Him God raised up on the third day, and showed Him openly. (Acts 10:35–40)

Therefore He also says in another Psalm: "You will not allow Your Holy One to see corruption." (Acts 13:35)

Chapter 18

PROMISE AND OATH

1) The promise to Abraham that through his Seed he would inherit the world.

2) The promise to David that his Heir would be a Savior to all of those who would call upon His name.

3) The promise of the Holy Spirit: "I will put My law in their minds, and write it on their hearts; and I will be their God, and they shall be My people."

4) The promise that God would not allow His Holy One to see corruption.

> And Abram said, "Look, You have given me no offspring; indeed one born in my house is my heir!" And behold, the word of the LORD came to him, saying, "This one shall not be your heir, but one who will come from your own body shall be your heir." Then He brought him outside and said, "Look now toward heaven, and count the stars if you are able to number them." And He said to him, "So shall your descendants be." And he believed in the LORD, and He accounted it to him for righteousness. (Genesis 15:3–6)

As will be focused on in the next chapter, the promises made by God in the Old Testament had a twofold meaning; there were physical components and spiritual components to those promises. In the Old Testament, God's promises elicited an immediate physical response, while at the same time, they pointed to an ultimate spiritual fulfillment of those same promises.

God has repeatedly emphasized the fact that humanity's flawed nature prevents us from achieving the excellence that is required of us in order to inherit the eternal blessings that God has continually offered to Israel. In the preceding verse, God promises Abram an heir. On one level, the promise is realized in the physical birth of Isaac. The physical fulfillment of the promise was a direct copy of God's ultimate plan.

Once Isaac grew up, God directed Abraham to sacrifice Isaac on the Mount of Moriah. Again, this is a copy of the True. God would raise up to Abraham an Heir, and that Heir would be sacrificed on the Mount of Moriah, and as a result of His obedience to God's will, the second part of that promise would be fulfilled: "Look now toward heaven, and count the stars if you are able to number them." And He said to him, "So shall your descendants be."

> And Abraham called the name of the place, The-LORD-Will-Provide; as it is said to this day, "In the Mount of the LORD it shall be provided." Then the Angel of the LORD called to Abraham a second time out of heaven, and said: "By Myself I have sworn, says the LORD, because you have done this thing, and have not withheld your son, your only son— Blessing I will bless you, and multiplying I will multiply your descendants as the stars of the heaven and as the sand which is on the seashore; and your descendants shall possess the gate of their enemies. In your seed all the nations of the earth

shall be blessed, because you have obeyed My voice."
(Genesis 22:14–18)

Then Isaac trembled exceedingly, and said, "Who?
Where is the one who hunted game and brought
it to me? I ate all of it before you came, and I have
blessed him—and indeed he shall be blessed."
(Genesis 27:33)

Even though Jacob behaved deceitfully and stole the blessing that
Isaac had designed for Esau, the blessing held. Esau was deprived of
the birthright even though Jacob had obtained it by deceit. This is
an example of how binding an oath is in the eyes of God.

You yourselves write a decree concerning the Jews,
as you please, in the king's name, and seal it with
the king's signet ring; for whatever is written in the
king's name and sealed with the king's signet ring
no one can revoke. (Esther 8:8)

"Since he despised the oath by breaking the
covenant, and in fact gave his hand and still did all
these things, he shall not escape." Therefore thus
says the Lord God: "As I live, surely My oath which
he despised, and My covenant which he broke, I will
recompense on his own head." (Ezekiel 17:18–19)

Now, O king, establish the decree and sign the
writing, so that it cannot be changed, according to
the law of the Medes and Persians, which does not
alter. (Daniel 6:8)

And they went before the king, and spoke
concerning the king's decree: "Have you not signed

a decree that every man who petitions any god or man within thirty days, except you, O king, shall be cast in the den of lions?" The king answered and said, "The thing is true, according to the law of the Medes and Persians, which does not alter." (Daniel 6:12)

And the king, when he heard these words, was greatly displeased with himself, and set his heart on Daniel to deliver him; and he laboured till the going down of the sun to deliver him. Then these men approached the king, and said to the king, "Know, O king, that it is the law of the Medes and Persians that no decree or statute which the king establishes may be changed." So the king gave the command, and they brought Daniel and cast him into the den of lions. But the king spoke, saying to Daniel, "Your God, whom you serve continually, He will deliver you." (Daniel 6:14–16)

(This allegory of Daniel in the lions' den is another copy of the True—it alludes to Jesus being rescued from the pit and resuming His former position in heaven.)

The king was duped into enacting a law in which certain conspirators devised a scheme that would result in Daniel, the king's most honored statesman and friend, to be removed from his seat of power and be executed by being thrown into the den of lions. The king searched every means possible, but in the end, he could not revoke the indictment. The charge held, and Daniel was thrown into the den of lions. If humans are bound to oaths to their own hurt, how much more so than is God? In the New Testament, we are advised to confirm a confirmation with a yes, to oppose a confirmation with a no, and to prevent ourselves from making oaths.

It's likely that Lucifer actually incited Christ to enact the covenant that was put into force in the Garden of Eden which resulted in the fall of mankind. Daniel 6:4–16, describes the situation where King Darius's governors and officials banded together and conspired to bring about the demise of Daniel. This then being a copy of the True, portrays Lucifer as having played a much larger role than the simple protagonist in a tragic story. It appears as though Lucifer himself was the actual author and director of this tragedy.

This being the scenario, we see the consequences and judgement made against Satan in Bible verse. Satan's judgement can be alluded to in the story of Haman and Mordecai, in the book of Ester and in the story of the mighty men of valor who threw Shadrach, Meshach and Abed-Nego into the furnace in the book of Daniel. Though Mordecai, Shadrach, Meshach and Abed-Nego were rescued from their fates, Haman and the mighty men of valor tasted the punishment that had been meant for their victims. The Old Testament is riddled with adages and proverbs of the consequences of someone who devises evil intent. The evil intent designed for an unsuspecting victim ultimately finds its way home to the deviser of that intent.

Promises of the LORD God Almighty are seen in the following.

> O LORD, You are the portion of my inheritance
> and my cup; You maintain my lot. The lines have
> fallen to me in pleasant places; Yes, I have a good
> inheritance. (Psalms 16:5–6)

Although mankind had lost their inheritance, God has promised that He will be our inheritance.

> Therefore my heart is glad, and my glory rejoices;
> My flesh also will rest in hope. For You will not

> leave my soul in Sheol, Nor will You allow Your
> Holy One to see corruption. (Psalms 16:9–10)

> The key of the house of David I will lay on his
> shoulder; So he shall open, and no one shall shut;
> And he shall shut, and no one shall open. I will
> fasten him as a peg in a secure place. And he will
> become a glorious throne to his father's house.
> (Isaiah 22:22–23)

This is the greatest promise that God has ever made. This is the promise that we are able to stake our salvation on. This is the peg that we are able to hang all of our hopes.

On the seventh day of creation before any covenants were enacted God the Father made a promise to His only begotten Son that He would never allow Him to see corruption. He would never allow Him to remain in the grave! This is the everything. This is the promise that makes everything possible.

> And this I say, that the law, which was four hundred
> and thirty years later, cannot annul the covenant
> that was confirmed before by God in Christ, that
> it should make the promise of no effect. For if the
> inheritance is of the law, it is no longer of promise;
> but God gave it to Abraham by promise. (Galatians
> 3:17–18)

Everything in the Old Testament is a copy of the True. That God gave Abraham the promise 430 years before the commandment was given to Moses is a reflection of the promise that God gave to His Son prior to the Commandment that was given in the Garden of Eden. And just as the promise to Abraham superseded the commandment given to Moses, God's promise to His Son superseded the Commandment that was given in the Garden of

Eden. Our eternity hangs on a promise and this promise is in Jesus Christ our Lord.

> Now it shall come to pass in the latter days That the mountain of the LORD's house Shall be established on the top of the mountains, And shall be exalted above the hills; And peoples shall flow to it. Many nations shall come and say, "Come, and let us go up to the mountain of the LORD, To the house of the God of Jacob; He will teach us His ways, And we shall walk in His paths." For out of Zion the law shall go forth, And the word of the LORD from Jerusalem. He shall judge between many peoples, And rebuke strong nations far off; They shall beat their swords into plowshares, And their spears into pruning hooks; Nation shall not lift up sword against nation, Neither shall they learn war anymore. But everyone shall sit under his vine and under his fig tree, And no one shall make them afraid; For the mouth of the LORD of hosts has spoken. For all people walk each in the name of his god, But we will walk in the name of the LORD our God Forever and ever. In that day says the LORD, "I will assemble the lame, I will gather the outcast And those whom I have afflicted; I will make the lame a remnant, And the outcast a strong nation." So the LORD will reign over them in Mount Zion From now on, even forever. (Micah 4:1–7)

> He will again have compassion on us, And will subdue our iniquities. You will cast all our sins Into the depths of the sea. You will give truth to Jacob And mercy to Abraham, Which You have sworn to our fathers From days of old. (Micah 7:19–20)

"I will gather those who sorrow over the appointed assembly, Who are among you, To whom its reproach is a burden. Behold, at that time I will deal with all who afflict you; I will save the lame, And gather those who were driven out; I will appoint them for praise and fame In every land where they were put to shame. At that time I will bring you back, Even at the time I gather you; For I will give you fame and praise Among all the peoples of the earth, When I return your captives before your eyes," says the LORD. (Zephaniah 3:18–20)

For thus says the LORD of hosts: "Once more (it is a little while) I will shake heaven and earth, the sea and dry land; and I will shake all nations, and they shall come to the Desire of All Nations, and I will fill this temple with glory," says the LORD of hosts. "The silver is Mine, and the gold is Mine," says the LORD of hosts. "The glory of the latter temple shall be greater than the former," says the LORD of hosts. "And in this place I will give peace," says the Lord of hosts. (Haggai 2:6–9)

Speak to Zerubbabel, governor of Judah, saying: "I will shake heaven and earth. I will overthrow the throne of kingdoms; I will destroy the strength of the Gentile kingdoms. I will overthrow the chariots And those who ride in them; The horses and the riders shall come down. Everyone by the sword of his brother." (Haggai 2:21–22)

And there was the angel who talked with me, going out; and another angel was coming out to meet him, who said to him, "Run, speak to this young man, saying: 'Jerusalem shall be inhabited as towns without walls, because of the multitude of men and livestock in it. For I,' says the LORD, 'will be a wall of fire all around her, and I will be the glory in her midst.' Up, up! Flee from the land of the north," says the LORD; "for I have spread you abroad like the four winds of heaven," says the LORD. "Up, Zion! Escape, you who dwell with the daughter of Babylon." For thus says the LORD of hosts: "He sent Me after glory, to the nations which plunder you; for he who touches you touches the apple of His eye. For surely I will shake My hand against them, and they shall become spoil for their servants. Then you will know that the LORD of hosts has sent Me. Sing and rejoice, O daughter of Zion! For behold, I am coming and I will dwell in your midst," says the LORD. "Many nations shall be joined to the LORD in that day, and they shall become My people. And I will dwell in your midst. Then you will know that the LORD of hosts has sent Me to you. And the LORD will take possession of Judah as His inheritance in the Holy Land, and will again choose Jerusalem." (Zechariah 2:3–12)

Behold, the day of the LORD is coming. And your spoil will be divided in your midst. For I will gather all the nations to battle against Jerusalem; The city shall be taken, The houses rifled, And the women ravished. Half of the city shall go into captivity, But the remnant of the people shall not be cut off from the city. Then the LORD will go forth And fight against those nations, As He fights in the day of battle. And in that day His feet will stand on the Mount of Olives, Which faces Jerusalem on the east. And the Mount of Olives shall be split in two, From east to west, Making a very large valley; Half of the mountain shall move toward the north And half of it toward the south. Then you shall flee through My mountain valley, For the mountain valley shall reach to Azal. Yes, you shall flee As you fled from the earthquake In the days of Uzziah king of Judah. Thus the LORD my God will come, And all the saints with You. It shall come to pass in that day That there will be no light; The lights will diminish. It shall be one day Which is known to the LORD—Neither day nor night. But at evening time it shall happen That it will be light. And in that day it shall be That living waters shall flow from Jerusalem, Half of them towards the eastern sea And half of them toward the western sea; In both summer and winter it shall occur. And the LORD shall be King over all the earth. In that day it shall be—"The LORD is one," And His name one. (Zechariah 14:1–9)

And this shall be the plague with which the LORD will strike all the people who fought against Jerusalem: Their flesh shall dissolve while they stand on their feet, Their eyes shall dissolve in their sockets, And their tongues shall dissolve in their mouths. (Zechariah 14:12)

For when God made a promise to Abraham, because He could swear by no one greater, He swore by Himself, saying, "Surely blessing I will bless you, and multiplying I will multiply you." And so, after he had patiently endured, he obtained the promise. For men indeed swear by the greater, and an oath for confirmation is for them an end of all dispute. Thus God, determining to show more abundantly to the heirs of promise the immutability of His council, confirmed it by an oath, that by two immutable things, in which it is impossible for God to lie, we might have strong consolation, who have fled for refuge to lay hold of the hope set before us this hope we have as an anchor of the soul, both sure and steadfast, and which enters the Presence behind the veil, where the forerunner has become High Priest forever according to the order of Melchizedek. (Hebrews 6:13–20)

For this Melchizedek, king of Salem, priest of the Most High God, who met Abraham returning from the slaughter of the kings and blessed him to whom also Abraham gave a tenth part of all, first being translated, "king of righteousness," and then also king of Salem, meaning "king of peace," without father, without mother, without genealogy, having neither beginning of days nor end of life, but made like the Son of God, remains a priest continually. Now consider how great this man was, to whom even the patriarch Abraham gave a tenth of the spoils. (Hebrews 7:1–4)

And this is the promise that He has promised us— eternal life. (1 John 2:25)

Chapter 19

PHYSICAL REPRESENTATIONS OF THE OLD TESTAMENT RESOUNDING IN THE NEW

From the promise to Abraham that God would provide him a son, to the testing of Abraham's obedience, to Joseph's incarceration, to Moses's deliverance of Israel, to all of Israel's and Judah's victories in battle and on and on, the written history of the peoples of Israel in the Old Testament were physical representations of the salvation plan that God has provided to humanity. There is no one that is outside of this invitation. Whatever you think you have done or haven't done; God looks upon us all exactly the same. All have sinned and fall short of the glory of God. No one is righteous.

In many cases, as it was in Jesus's time, it was much easier for a thief, a prostitute, or a murderer to accept that they were sinners than for the average "law-abiding" citizen. The Sermon on the Mount exemplifies true "Christian" behavior. "Christian" and "love" denote attitude—not emotion. You can believe anything and everything, and you can feel anything and everything, and none of it changes a thing.

The next chapter will deal with faith and works. This chapter will focus on what God has promised in the Old Testament and how it is diametrically opposed to His nature for Him to renege on those promises.

The promises made in the Old Testament were fulfilled in phases. There was a phase to be realized in an immediate physical component, and there is a phase to be realized in a future spiritual component.

A major part of that spiritual component was fulfilled on the day of Pentecost, about seven weeks after Jesus's death on the cross. On the day of Pentecost, Jesus received the promise and breathed out onto His disciples His Holy Spirit. Once armed with Christ's Holy Spirit, we are able to realize the promises given to us by God, which allow us to conquer our spiritual enemies. We are now fully armed to triumph over every spiritual enemy that exists in the universe.

Through the name of Jesus Christ of Nazareth, the Way to our salvation is realized. There is nothing that can prevent us from triumphing over sin, other than our unbelief.

> And in the wilderness where you saw how the LORD your God carried you, as a man carries his son, in all the way that you went until you came to this place. Yet, for all that, you did not believe the LORD your God. (Deuteronomy 1:31–32)

> And the LORD your God will drive out those nations before you little by little; you will be unable to destroy them at once, lest the beast of the field become too numerous for you. But the LORD your God will deliver them over to you, and will inflict defeat upon them until they are destroyed. And He will deliver their kings into your hand, and you will destroy their name from under heaven; no one shall be able to stand against you until you have destroyed them. (Deuteronomy 7:22–24)

Hear, O Israel: You are to cross over the Jordan today, and go in to dispossess nations greater and mightier than yourself, cities great and fortified up to heaven, a people great and tall, the descendants of the Anakim, whom you know, and of whom you heard it said, "Who can stand before the descendants of Anak?" Therefore understand today that the LORD your God is He who goes over before you as a consuming fire. He will destroy them and bring them down before you; so you shall drive them out and destroy them quickly, as the LORD has said to you. Do not think in your heart, after the LORD your God has cast them out before you, saying, "Because of my righteousness the LORD has brought me in to possess this land," but it is because of the wickedness of these nations that the LORD is driving them out from before you. It is not because of your righteousness or the uprightness of your heart that you go in to possess their land, but because of the wickedness of these nations that the LORD your God drives them out from before you, and that He may fulfill the word which the LORD swore to your fathers, to Abraham, Isaac, and Jacob. Therefore understand that the LORD your God is not giving you this good land to possess because of your righteousness, for you are a stiff-necked people. (Deuteronomy 9:1–6)

No man shall be able to stand against you; the LORD your God will put the dread of you and the fear of you upon all the land where you tread, just as He has said to you. (Deuteronomy 11:25)

You shall not at all do as we are doing here today—
every man doing whatever is right in his own eyes—
for as yet you have not come to the rest and the
inheritance which the LORD your God is giving
you. But when you cross over the Jordan and dwell
in the land which the LORD your God is giving
you to inherit, and He gives you rest from all your
enemies round about, so that you dwell in safety.
(Deuteronomy 12:8–10)

When you go out to battle against your enemies, and
see horses and chariots and people more numerous
than you, do not be afraid of them; for the LORD
your God is with you, who brought you up from
the land of Egypt. So it shall be, when you are on
the verge of battle, that the priest shall approach
and speak to the people. And he shall say to them,
"Hear, O Israel: Today you are on the verge of battle
with your enemies. Do not let your heart faint, do
not be afraid, and do not tremble or be terrified
because of them; for the LORD your God is He
who goes with you, to fight for you against your
enemies, to save you." (Deuteronomy 20:1–4)

Be strong and of good courage, do not fear nor be
afraid of them; for the LORD your God, He is the
One who goes with you. He will not leave you nor
forsake you. (Deuteronomy 31:6)

But you shall hold fast to the LORD your God, as
you have done to this day. For the LORD has driven
out from before you great and strong nations; but as
for you, no one has been able to stand against you
to this day. One man of you shall chase a thousand,

for the LORD your God is He who fights for you, as He promised you. (Joshua 23:8–10)

But David answered Rechab and Baanah his brother, the sons of Rimmon the Beerothite, and said to them, "As the LORD lives, who has redeemed my life from all adversity." (2 Samuel 4:9)

And he said: "The Lord is my rock and my fortress and my deliverer; The God of my strength, in whom I will trust; My shield and the horn of my salvation, My stronghold and my refuge; My Savior, You save me from violence. I will call upon the LORD, who is worthy to be praised; So shall I be saved from my enemies. When the waves of death surrounded me, The floods of ungodliness made me afraid. The sorrows of Sheol surrounded me; The snares of death confronted me. In my distress I called upon the LORD, And I cried out to my God; He heard my voice from His temple, And my cry entered His ears. Then the earth shook and trembled; The foundations of heaven quaked and were shaken, Because He was angry. Smoke went up from His nostrils, And devouring fire from His mouth; Coals were kindled by it. He bowed the heavens also, and came down With darkness under His feet. He rode upon a cherub, and flew; And He was seen upon the wings of the wind. He made darkness canopies around Him, Dark waters and thick clouds of the skies. From the brightness before Him Coals of fire were kindled. The LORD thundered from heaven, And the Most High uttered His voice. He sent out arrows and scattered them; Lightning bolts, and He vanquished them. Then the channels of the sea were seen, The foundations of the world were uncovered, At the rebuke of the LORD, At the blast of the breath of His nostrils. He sent from above, He took me, He drew me out of many waters. He delivered me from my strong enemy, From those who hated me; For they were too strong for me. They confronted me in the day of my calamity, But the Lord was my support. He also brought me out into a broad place; He delivered me because He delighted in me. The Lord rewarded me according to my righteousness; According to the cleanness of my hands He has recompensed me. For I have kept the ways of the Lord, And have not wickedly departed from my God. For all His judgments were before me; And as for His statutes, I did not depart from them. I was also blameless before Him, And I kept myself from my iniquity. Therefore the Lord has recompensed me according to my righteousness, According to the cleanness in His eyes. With the merciful You will show Yourself merciful; With a blameless man You will show Yourself blameless; With the pure You will show Yourself pure; And with the devious You will show Yourself shrewd. You will save the humble people; But Your eyes are on the haughty, that you may bring them down. For You are my lamp, O LORD; The LORD shall enlighten my darkness. For by You I can run against a troop; By my God I can leap over a wall. As for God, His way is perfect; The word of the LORD is proven; He is a shield to all who trust in Him. For who is God, except the LORD? And who is a rock, except our God? God is my strength and power, And He makes my way perfect. He makes my feet like the feet of deer, And sets me on my high places. He teaches my hand to make war, So that my arms can bend a bow of bronze. You have also given me the shield of Your salvation; Your gentleness has made me great. You enlarged my path under me; So my feet did not slip. I have pursued my enemies and destroyed them; Neither did I turn back again till they were destroyed. And I have destroyed them and wounded them, So that they could not rise; They have fallen under my feet. For You have armed me with strength for the battle; You have subdued under me those who rose against me. You have also given me the necks of my enemies, So that I destroyed those who hated me. They looked, but there was none to save; Even to the LORD, but He did not answer them. Then I beat them as fine as the dust of the earth; I trod them like dust in the streets, And I spread them out. You have also delivered me from the strivings of my people; You have kept me as the head of the nations. A people I have not known shall serve me. The foreigners submit to me; As soon as they hear, they obey me. The foreigners fade away, And come frightened from their hideouts. The LORD lives! Blessed be the Rock! Let God be exalted, The Rock of my salvation! It is God who avenges me, And subdues the peoples under me; He delivers me from my enemies. You also lift me up above those who rise against me; You have delivered me from the violent man. Therefore I will give thanks to You, O LORD, among the Gentiles, And sing praises to Your name. He is the tower of salvation to His king, And shows mercy to His anointed, To David and his descendants forevermore." (2 Samuel 22:2–51)

"You will not need to fight in this battle. Position yourselves, stand still and see the salvation of the LORD, who is with you, O Judah and Jerusalem!" Do not fear or be dismayed; tomorrow go out against them, for the LORD is with you. (2 Chronicles 20:17)

Now because of this King Hezekiah and the prophet Isaiah, the son of Amoz, prayed and cried out to heaven. Then the LORD sent an angel who cut down every mighty man of valour, leader, and captain in the camp of the king of Assyria. (2 Chronicles 32:20–21)

The hand of our God is upon all those for good who seek Him, but His power and His wrath are against all those who forsake Him. (Ezra 8:22)

For the Lord will not forsake His people, for His great name's sake, because it has pleased the Lord to make you His people. (1 Samuel 12:22)

For You will light my lamp; The LORD my God will enlighten my darkness. For by You I can run against a troop, By my God I can leap over a wall. As for God, His way is perfect; The word of the LORD is proven; He is a shield to all who trust in Him. For who is God, except the LORD? And who is a rock, except our God? It is God who arms me with strength, And makes my way perfect. He makes my feet like the feet of deer, And sets me on high places. He teaches my hands to make war, So that my arms can bend a bow of bronze. You have also given me the shield of Your salvation; Your right hand has held me up, Your gentleness has made me great. You enlarge my path under me, So my feet did not slip. (Psalm 18:28–36)

But the salvation of the righteous is from the LORD; He is their strength in the time of trouble And the LORD shall help them and deliver them; He shall deliver them from the wicked, And save them, Because they trust in Him. (Psalm 37:39–40)

I will cry out to God Most High, To God who performs all things for me. He shall send from heaven and save me; He reproaches the one who would swallow me up. God shall send forth His mercy and His truth. (Psalm 57:2–3)

Give us help from trouble, For the help of man is useless. Through God we will do valiantly, For it is He who shall tread down our enemies. (Psalm 60:11–12)

Because You have been my help, Therefore in the shadow of Your wings I will rejoice. (Psalm 63:7)

Deliver me, O my God, out of the hand of the wicked, Out of the hand of the unrighteous and cruel man. For You are my hope, O LORD God; You are my trust from my youth. By You I have been upheld from birth; You are He who took me out of my mother's womb. My praise shall be continually of You. (Psalm 71:4–6)

He who dwells in the secret place of the Most High Shall abide under the shadow of the Almighty. I will say to the LORD, "He is my refuge and my fortress; My God, in Him I will trust." Surely He shall deliver you from the snare of the fowler And from the perilous pestilence. He shall cover you with His feathers, And under His wings you shall take refuge; His truth shall be your shield and buckler. You shall not be afraid of the terror by night, Nor of the arrow that flies by day, Nor of the pestilence that walks in darkness, Nor of the destruction that lays waste at noonday. A thousand may fall at your side, And ten thousand at your right hand; But it shall not come near you. Only with your eyes shall you look, And see the reward of the wicked. Because you have made the LORD, who is my refuge, Even the Most High, your dwelling place, No evil shall befall you, Nor shall any plague come near your dwelling; For He shall give His angels charge over you, To keep you in all your ways. In their hands they shall bear you up, Lest you dash your foot against a stone. You shall tread upon the lion and the cobra, The young lion and the serpent you shall trample underfoot. Because he has set his love upon Me, therefore I will deliver him; I will set him high, because he has known My name. He shall call upon Me, and I will answer him; I will be with him in trouble; I will deliver him and honor him. With long life I will satisfy him, And show him My salvation. (Psalm 91:1–16)

Then they cried out to the LORD in their trouble, And He brings them out of their distresses. He calms the storm, So that its waves are still. Then they are glad because they are quiet; So He guides them to their desired haven. (Psalm 107:28–30)

Give us help from trouble, For the help of man is useless. Through God we will do valiantly, For it is He who shall tread down our enemies. (Psalm 108:12–13)

"For the help of man is useless." All of humanity's philosophies and psychology are useless when attempting to permanently modify or control human nature.

I will lift up my eyes to the hills—From whence comes my help? My help comes from the LORD, Who made heaven and earth. He will not allow your foot to be moved; He who keeps you will not slumber. Behold, He who keeps Israel Shall neither slumber or sleep. The LORD is your keeper; The LORD is your shade at your right hand. The sun shall not strike you by day, Nor the moon by night. The LORD shall preserve you from all evil; He shall preserve your soul. The LORD shall preserve your going out and your coming in From this time forth, and even forevermore. (Psalm 121:1–8)

He destroyed the firstborn of Egypt, Both of man and beast. He sent signs and wonders into the midst of you, O Egypt, Upon Pharaoh and all his servants. He defeated many nations And slew mighty kings—Sihon king of the Amorites, Og king of Bashan, And all the kingdoms of Canaan—And gave their land as a heritage, Heritage to Israel His people. (Psalm 135:8–12)

But my eyes are upon You, O God the LORD; In You I take refuge; Do not leave my soul destitute. Keep me from the snares they have laid for me,

And from the traps of the workers of iniquity. Let the wicked fall into their own nets, While I escape safely. (Psalm 141:8–10)

The LORD upholds all who fall, And raises up all who are bowed down. The eyes of all look expectantly to You, And You give them their food in due season. You open Your hand And satisfy the desire of every living thing. The LORD is righteous in all His ways, Gracious in all His works. The LORD is near to all who call upon Him, To all who call upon Him in truth. He will fulfill the desire of those who fear Him, He also will hear their cry and save them. The LORD preserves all who love Him, But all the wicked He will destroy. My mouth shall speak the praise of the LORD, And all flesh shall bless His holy name Forever and ever. (Psalm 145:14–21)

He is a shield to those who walk uprightly; He guards the paths of justice, And preserves the way of His saints. (Proverbs 2:7–8)

For the LORD has redeemed Jacob, And ransomed him from the hand of one stronger than he. (Jeremiah 31:11)

Chapter 20

FAITH VERSUS WORKS
OF THE LAW

The Law of Faith

Without faith, it is impossible to please God. The Israelites failed in the wilderness because they did not believe God. Adam and Eve succumbed to Satan's temptation because they did not believe God. The entire Gospel is based on faith, on believing God. Salvation is then based on faith, and as a result of our faith, we are able to conquer our spiritual enemies. It is not us who conquers these enemies; it is Christ. We have rested from our works, which are evil, and Jesus is working in us works of righteousness. If you believe and trust in God, He will do the work for you through Jesus Christ of Nazareth. The admonition then is not to "harden your hearts as in the rebellion."

> Behold the proud, His soul is not upright in him;
> But the just shall live by his faith. (Habakkuk 2:4)

> So God, who knows the heart, acknowledged them
> by giving them the Holy Spirit, just as He did to
> us, and made no distinction between us and them,

purifying their hearts by faith. Now therefore, why do you test God by putting a yoke on the neck of the disciples which neither our fathers nor we were able to bear? But we believe that through the grace of the Lord Jesus Christ we shall be saved in the same manner as they. (Acts 15:8–11)

So they said, "Believe on the Lord Jesus Christ, and you will be saved, you and your household." Then they spoke the word of the Lord to him and to all who were in his house. (Acts 16:31–32)

Through Him we have received grace and apostleship for obedience to the faith among all nations for His name. (Romans 1:5)

For I am not ashamed of the gospel of Christ, for it is the power of God to salvation for everyone who believes, for the Jew first and also for the Greek. For in it the righteousness of God is revealed from faith to faith; as it is written, "The just shall live by faith." (Romans 1:16–17)

"From faith to faith." The faith of Abraham regarded physical promises that were promised in Old Testament times, and today, the faith of the spiritual promises, which come to us through Jesus Christ.

Do we then make void the law through faith? Certainly not! On the contrary, we establish the law. (Romans 3:31)

But to him who does not work but believes on Him who justifies the ungodly, his faith is accounted for righteousness. (Romans 4:5)

Blessed are those whose lawless deeds are forgiven, And whose sins are covered; Blessed is the man to whom the Lord shall not impute sin. (Romans 4:7–8)

For the promise that he would be the heir of the world was not to Abraham or to his seed through the law, but through the righteousness of faith. (Romans 4:13)

Therefore it is of faith that it might be according to grace, so that the promise might be sure to all the seed, not only to those who are of the law, but also to those who are of the faith of Abraham, who is the father of us all. (Romans 4:16)

Who, contrary to hope, in hope believed, so that he became the father of many nations, according to what was spoken, "So shall your descendants be." And not being weak in faith, he did not consider his own body, already dead (since he was about a hundred years old), and the deadness of Sarah's womb. He did not waver at the promise of God through unbelief, but was strengthened in faith, giving glory to God, and being fully convinced that what He had promised He was also able to perform. And therefore "it was accounted to him for righteousness." Now it was not written for His sake alone that it was imputed to him, but also for us. It shall be imputed to us who believe in Him who

> raised up Jesus our Lord from the dead, who was
> delivered up because of our offences, and was raised
> because of our justification. (Romans 4:18–25)

"Who was delivered up because of our offences." He was crucified
for past sin—for the termination of the First Covenant. He was
"raised for our justification." He was raised to be High Priest forever
in order to keep us from sin and have Christ formed in us so that we
should be presented pure and undefiled when Jesus Christ returns.

Just as Abraham believed in God, we should likewise believe
in the promises that God provided to us through His Son. He is
justifying us and will never forsake us. When we are in need of help,
He will always be there when we call on His name. From faith to
faith, Abraham had faith in regard to the physical promises, and we
have faith in regard to the Spiritual promises.

> Therefore, having been justified by faith, we have
> peace with God through our Lord Jesus Christ.
> (Romans 5:1)

"We have peace with God." This is the peace that Jesus, His
disciples, and the prophets spoke about. Before the works that
Christ performed in the flesh, there was no peace between God
and humanity. The physical world was—and still is—on a collision
course with destruction. Do not be fooled. Jesus is the Way, the
Truth, and the Life. No one comes to the Father except through
Him, and the Father demands nothing less than perfection. If God
could allow sinners into His kingdom, there would have been no
need for Christ to come in the flesh. There would have been no need
for God to expel Adam and Eve from the Garden of Eden. Satan
himself could be renamed "the loyal opposition."

> Through whom also we have access by faith into
> this grace in which we stand, and rejoice in hope

> of the glory of God. And not only that, but we
> also glory in tribulations, knowing that tribulations
> produce perseverance; and perseverance, character;
> and character, hope. (Romans 5:2–4)

"We glory in tribulations." We glory in trials, and we glory in temptations because we have the Helper to get us through unscathed to present us perfect on that fateful day.

> Now hope does not disappoint, because the love
> of God has been poured out into our hearts by the
> Holy Spirit who was given to us. (Romans 5:5)

The love of God is being poured out into our hearts. One is able to experience the love of God once one has repented, become baptized and received the Holy Spirit. One begins experiencing the love of God when one begins to internalize the experience of the forgiveness of sin and the ability to triumph over temptation. One experiences love once one begins experiencing the workings of Jesus Christ in their lives.

> Love suffers long and is kind; love does not envy;
> love does not parade itself, is not puffed up; does
> not behave rudely, does not seek its own, is not
> provoked, thinks no evil; does not rejoice in iniquity,
> but rejoices in the truth; bears all things, believes
> all things, hopes all things, endures all things. Love
> never fails. (1 Corinthians 13:4–8)

The opportunity is now available for us to share in the divine nature with Jesus Christ. Through the sharing of His nature, He is raising up for Himself a people—or, more aptly—a kingdom of priests that will reign with Him for all of eternity. Experiencing the workings of

Jesus Christ is why we experience joy. Love is a state of mind—or, more precisely—a state of spirit.

> For when we were still without strength, in due time
> Christ died for the ungodly. (Romans 5:6)

He died in order to give us strength through His Spirit, which is made available to us through His name.

> Much more then, having now been justified by His
> blood, we shall be saved from wrath through Him.
> For if when we were enemies we were reconciled to
> God through the death of His Son, much more,
> having been reconciled, we shall be saved by His
> life. (Romans 5:9–10)

"We shall be saved by His life." We now have the opportunity to become members of Christ's body. We are promised to be delivered from all temptation through the power of His name. Through His life as High Priest forever, according to the order of Melchizedek, He is intervening in our lives, raising up for Himself a priesthood, holy and undefiled, a chaste virgin, which He is making ready to stand before Himself and our Sovereign LORD and Father, Almighty God.

> For whatever is not from faith is sin. (Romans
> 14:23)

> For obedience to the faith. (Romans 16:26)

> That your faith should not be in the wisdom of men
> but in the power of God. (1 Corinthians 2:5)

And that power is found in the name of Jesus Christ, His Son, the mystery that has been hidden since the beginning of time, God's rest. Now we can take rest from our enemies.

> Not that we have dominion over your faith, but are fellow workers for your joy; for by faith you stand. (2 Corinthians 1:24)

> And since we have the same spirit of faith, according to what is written, "I believed and therefore I spoke," we also believe and therefore speak. (2 Corinthians 4:13)

> For we walk by faith, not by sight. (2 Corinthians 5:7)

> For when I am weak, then I am strong. (2 Corinthians 12:10)

I am strong through the name of Jesus Christ of Nazareth, the only begotten Son of God who strengthens me through my weaknesses.

> Knowing that a man is not justified by the works of the law but by faith in Jesus Christ, even we have believed in Christ Jesus, that we might be justified by faith in Christ and not by the works of the law; for by the works of the law no flesh shall be justified. (Galatians 2:16)

"The works of the law." Fleshly ordinances, sacrifices, and ceremonial washings do nothing to cleanse the conscience of sin.

> But if, while we seek to be justified by Christ, we ourselves also are found sinners, is Christ therefore a minister of sin? Certainly not! For if I build again

those things which I destroyed, I make myself a transgressor. (Galatians 2:17–18)

We are commanded to be perfect.

> For I through the law died to the law that I might live to God. I have been crucified with Christ; it is no longer I who live, but Christ lives in me; and the life which I now live in the flesh I live by faith in the Son of God, who loved me and gave Himself for me. (Galatians 2:19–20)

"Christ lives in me." Christ lives in us through His Holy Spirit.

> I do not set aside the grace of God; for if righteousness comes through the law, then Christ died in vain. (Galatians 2:21)

> Christ has redeemed us from the curse of the law, having become a curse for us (for it is written, "Cursed is everyone who hangs on a tree"), that the blessing of Abraham might come upon the Gentiles in Christ Jesus, that we might receive the Spirit through faith. (Galatians 3:13–14)

Jesus Christ is God's saving grace from the wrath to come, the High Priest forever, according to the Order of Melchizedek. The penalty of sin is death, but the promise of life is through Jesus Christ. He who commits sin is the slave of sin, and the slave does not abide in the house forever.

> For it is written that Abraham had two sons: the one by a bondwoman, the other by a freewoman. But he who was of the bondwoman was born according

to the flesh, and he of the freewoman through promise, which things are symbolic. For these are the two covenants: the one from Mount Sinai which gives birth to bondage, which is Hagar—for this Hagar is Mount Sinai in Arabia, and corresponds to Jerusalem which now is, and is in bondage with her children—but the Jerusalem above is free, which is the mother of us all. For it is written: "Rejoice, O barren, You who do not bear! Break forth and shout, You who are not in labour! For the desolate has many more children Than she who has a husband." Now we, brethren, as Isaac was are children of the promise. But, as he who was born according to the flesh then persecuted him who was born according to the Spirit, even so it is now. Nevertheless what does the Scripture say? "Cast out the bondwoman and her son, for the son of the bondwoman shall not be heir with the son of the freewoman." So then, brethren, we are not children of the bondwoman but of the free. (Galatians 4:22–31)

The two covenants were given as the result of the condemnation that was placed on humanity in the Garden of Eden. The law of ordinances and sacrifice gave humanity an opportunity to discover their own sinfulness and weaknesses against sin. That First Covenant was a copy of what was required.

The Second Covenant was the fulfillment of all those things the First Covenant was incapable of accomplishing. The section of the Bible referred to as the Old Testament chronicles what had taken place and what was promised. What took place in the Garden of Eden was that Adam and Eve decided to reject God and instead, they attempted to manage their own lives without God's help. Later, the divine nature was not available to humanity because of their rebellion.

Metaphorically speaking, the divine nature was represented as the Tree of Life, and access to the Tree of Life was now denied, removing their opportunity to live forever because of sin. As long as they were in a sinful state, the fruit of the Tree of Life would be denied, regardless of what was otherwise opted by Satan.

After an educational period of some four thousand years in which humanity should have realized that they are completely incapable of managing their own lives, God revealed His promise to us in the person of Jesus Christ, His only begotten Son. Jesus Christ is the mystery that had been hidden since the beginning of time. Jesus Christ is the embodiment of the Second Covenant—a covenant in which those chosen would submit to and rely on Jesus Christ to manage their lives.

> Stand fast therefore in the liberty by which Christ has made us free, and do not be entangled again with a yoke of bondage. (Galatians 5:1)

> As you therefore have received Christ Jesus the Lord, so walk in Him, rooted and built up in Him and established in the faith, as you have been taught, abounding in it with thanksgiving. Beware lest anyone cheat you through philosophy and empty deceit, according to the tradition of men, according to the basic principles of the world, and not according to Christ. For in Him dwells all the fullness of the Godhead bodily; and you are complete in Him, who is the head of all principality and power. In Him you were also circumcised with the circumcision made without hands, by putting off the body of the sins of the flesh, by the circumcision of Christ, buried with Him in baptism, in which you also were raised with Him through faith in the working of God, who raised Him from the dead. And you, being

211

dead in your trespasses and the uncircumcision of
your flesh, He has made alive together with Him,
having forgiven you all trespasses, having wiped out
the handwriting of requirements that was against
us. And He has taken it out of the way, having
nailed it to the cross. Having disarmed principalities
and powers. He made a public spectacle of them,
triumphing over them in it. (Colossians 2:6–15)

"Having disarmed principalities and powers." Every spirit in heaven
and earth is subject to the name of Jesus Christ of Nazareth. He has
disarmed them through the New Covenant. What has changed is
that those who are baptized into this New Covenant have entered
into a place of spiritual security. This spiritual security is referred to
as the body of Christ and the church of God. These principalities
and powers have been disarmed by this New Covenant of spiritual
security that is being offered to us. They are rendered helpless, and
we are rendered victorious. This redemption is only provided to
humanity—not to the angels. Today, humanity has the opportunity
to choose between life and death, but the principalities and powers
have no choice; they must submit to the power of the name of Jesus
Christ of Nazareth.

This spiritual security is actually the rest that was created on the
seventh day of creation. This rest was available to Adam and Eve in
the Garden of Eden. This is the rest in which we allow God to share
His divine nature in us through His only begotten Son.

This was the original setting in the Garden of Eden: God had
created everything through His only begotten Son, and God took
an appraisal of all that was created and He saw that it was all good;
not perfect, but good.

Man had been created in God's image. Man was created as a
copy or image of God. It wasn't an exact image, it was a vessel that
could be found overflowing with the full measure of the nature of
God. The divine nature needs to be formed. It needs to be molded

and shaped and sometimes crushed and reshaped. Trust needs to be developed as does hope and love. Time becomes the medium in which the divine nature can be formed.

It is only God who can use our individual life's experiences to develop the nature of God within us. Trial and adversity becomes the anvil on which God's nature is formed. As the spirit of a Christian matures we will invariably arrive at the realization that, "Our worst days are our best days".

As this realization slowly seeps into our inner most beings, we slowly begin to develop a willingness. We begin to develop the willingness to align our wills with the will of our Sovereign LORD and Father Almighty God. Remember the sometimes overlooked phrase in the Lord's Prayer, "thy will be done; on earth as it is in heaven." Everything that happens is according to God's will. Unfortunately, it is sometimes the greatest of tragedies, that brings us closest to God.

> Knowing this: that the law is not made for a righteous person, but for the lawless and insubordinate, for the ungodly and for sinners, for the unholy and profane, for murderers of fathers and murderers of mothers, for man slayers, for fornicators, for sodomites, for kidnappers, for liars, for perjurers, and if there is any other thing that is contrary to sound doctrine. (1 Timothy 1:9–10)

> This charge I commit to you, son Timothy, according to the prophecies previously made concerning you, that by them you may wage the good warfare, having faith and a good conscience, which some having rejected, concerning the faith have suffered shipwreck. (1 Timothy 1:18–19)

"Having suffered shipwreck." They do not believe that, through faith, Christ is able to present us perfect in this current life because they have been seduced by the sinful passions of this world. They don't want to believe. They have been blinded by Satan.

> But you, O man of God, flee these things and pursue righteousness, godliness, faith, love, patience, gentleness. Fight the good fight of faith, lay hold on eternal life, to which you were called and have confessed the good confession in the presence of many witnesses. (1 Timothy 6:11–12)

"Fight the good fight of faith." This refers to overcoming sin through faith in Jesus's name. "The good confession" is the testimony that Jesus Christ is the only begotten Son of God, the Firstborn of Creation, the Mystery that has been hidden since the beginning of time. "Lay hold on eternal life" can only be accomplished by someone who is pure and undefiled.

> O Timothy! Guard what was committed to your trust, avoiding the profane and idle babbling and contradictions of what is falsely called knowledge— by professing it some have strayed concerning the faith. (1 Timothy 6:20–21)

> Hold fast the pattern of sound words which you have heard from me, in faith and love which are in Christ Jesus. That good thing which was committed to you, keep by the Holy Spirit who dwells in us. (2 Timothy 1:13–14)

> Therefore, as the Holy Spirit says: "Today, if you will hear His voice, Do not harden your hearts as in the rebellion, In the day of trial in the wilderness,

Where your fathers tested Me, tried Me, And saw My works forty years. Therefore I was angry with that generation, And said, 'They always go astray in their heart, And they have not known My ways.' So I swore in My wrath, 'They shall not enter My rest.'" (Hebrews 3:7–11)

God is the same yesterday, today, and tomorrow. Do not think that believing that Jesus is the Christ, the Son of God gives you a license to sin. The consequence of sin is death—whether you are reading the Old Testament or the New Testament. Actually, our spiritual journey begins at our baptism. Baptism figuratively translates into us dying together with Christ on the cross and being raised together with Him. This is accomplished so that we might be counted as new creatures with Him and that together with Him we might be found worthy to stand before our Sovereign LORD and Father, Almighty God. There is no place for sin in the presence of God.

Beware, brethren, lest there be in any of you an evil heart of unbelief in departing from the living God; but exhort one another daily, while it is called "Today," lest any of you be hardened through the deceitfulness of sin. (Hebrews 3:12–13)

"While it is called Today." We are expected to reach this level of spiritual perfection while it is still called today—not in some distant future moment when we are changed into spiritual beings at the return of Jesus Christ. Today—while it is still called today—we are to put on the new man, even Jesus Christ, in whom there is no sin.

For we have become partakers of Christ if we hold the beginning of our confidence steadfast to the end, while it is said: "Today, if you will hear His voice, Do not harden your hearts as in the

215

rebellion." For who, having heard, rebelled? Indeed, was it not all who came out of Egypt, led by Moses. Now with whom was He angry forty years? Was it not with those who sinned, whose corpses fell in the wilderness? And to whom did He swear that they would not enter His rest, but to those who did not obey? So we see that they could not enter in because of unbelief. (Hebrews 3:14–19)

"Unbelief" is rebellion, and rebellion is sin.

Therefore, since a promise remains of entering His rest, let us fear lest any of you seem to have come short of it. For indeed the gospel was preached to us as well as to them; but the word which they heard did not profit them, not being mixed with faith in those who heard it. For we who have believed do enter that rest, as He has said: "So I swore in My wrath, 'They shall not enter My rest,'" Although the works were finished from the foundation of the world. For He has spoken in a certain place of the seventh day in this way: "And God rested on the seventh day from all His works"; and again in this place: "They shall not enter My rest." Since therefore it remains that some must enter it, and those to whom it was first preached did not enter because of disobedience, again He designates a certain day, saying in David, "Today," after such a long time, as it has been said: "Today, if you will hear His voice, Do not harden your hearts." For if Joshua had given them rest, then He would not afterward have spoken of another day. There remains therefore a rest for the people of God. For he who has entered

His rest has himself also ceased from his works as God did from His. (Hebrews 4:1–10)

"Ceased from his works." All of humanity's works are evil.

Let us therefore be diligent to enter that rest, lest anyone fall according to the same example of disobedience. For the word of God is living and powerful, and sharper than any two-edged sword, piercing even to the division of soul and spirit, and of joints and marrow, and is a discerner of the thoughts and intents of the heart. And there is no creature hidden from His sight, but all things are naked and open to the eyes of Him to whom we must give account. Seeing then that we have a great High Priest who has passed through the heavens, Jesus the Son of God, let us hold fast our confession. For we do not have a High Priest who cannot sympathize with our weaknesses, but was in all points tempted as we are, yet without sin. Let us therefore come boldly to the throne of grace, that we may obtain mercy and find grace to help in time of need. (Hebrews 4:11–16)

For every high priest taken from among men is appointed for men in things pertaining to God, that he may offer both gifts and sacrifices for sins. He can have compassion on those who are ignorant and going astray, since he himself is also subject to weakness. (Hebrews 5:1–2)

"Subject to weakness." For Christ to become a suitable High Priest, He had to be subjected to the same temptations that every person coming into the world is subjected to. As the result of the life that Jesus lived in physical form, He now knows exactly what it means to be tempted. Through His temptations and harrowing life experiences, Jesus developed the empathy that now affords Him the compassion and sympathy to deal with us as someone would deal with friends. He has now become a suitable High Priest. It is important to point out one overlooked aspect of what Jesus's life in His physical form was to accomplish. Eli the priest had a conversation with his sons in an effort to correct his sons' bad behavior:

> If one man sins against another, God will judge him. But if a man sins against the LORD, who will intercede for him? (Samuel 2:25)

Remembering that God is right and just, God cannot make a judgment in a case in which He is the plaintiff. For all moral and ethical purposes, God would need to recuse Himself from making any judgment between Himself and humanity. In order for God and humanity to move forward through this impasse, it was necessary for God to appoint an Arbitrator between God and man. The qualifications of this Arbitrator needed to be more than impeccable. He had to have a thorough understanding of both parties as well as being completely impartial and completely without sin:

> He who is without sin among you, let him throw a stone at her first. (John 8:7)

Because Jesus is the only begotten Son of God—and actually the only person who shares in the divine nature with God—He is the only person in creation who can fully appreciate who and what God really is. Having become fully man and having shared with man all of the life experiences that go into shaping and developing a man, gives Jesus the full appreciation of what it means to be a man. Now that Jesus has returned to His former position and has been seated at the right hand of God, His abilities to arbitrate between God and man cannot be disputed.

> Because of this he is required as for the people, so also for himself to offer sacrifices for sins. And no man takes this honour to himself, but he who is called by God, just as Aaron was. So also Christ did not glorify Himself to become High Priest, but it was He who said to Him: "You are My Son, Today I have begotten You." As He also says in another place: "You are a priest forever According to the order of Melchizedek"; who, in the days of His flesh, when He had offered up prayers and supplications, with vehement cries and tears to Him who was able to save Him from death, and was heard because of His godly fear, though He was a Son, yet He learned obedience by the things which He suffered. And having been perfected, He became the author of eternal salvation to all who obey Him, called by God as High Priest "according to the order of Melchizedek." (Hebrews 5:3–10)

> For you have need of endurance, so that after you have done the will of God, you may receive the promise: "For yet a little while, And He who is coming will come and will not tarry. Now the just shall live by faith; But if anyone draws back, My soul has no pleasure in him." But we are not of those who draw back to perdition, but of those who believe to the saving of the soul. (Hebrews 10:36–39)

> Now faith is the substance of things hoped for, the evidence of things not seen. For by it the elders

obtained a good testimony. By faith we understand that the worlds were framed by the word of God, so that the things which are seen were not made of things which are visible. By faith Abel offered to God a more excellent sacrifice than Cain, through which he obtained witness that he was righteous, God testifying of His gifts; and through it he being dead still speaks. By faith Enoch was taken away so that he did not see death, "and was not found, because God had taken him"; for before he was taken he had this testimony, that he pleased God. But without faith it is impossible to please Him, for he who comes to God must believe that He is, and that He is a rewarder of those who diligently seek Him. By faith Noah, being divinely warned of things not yet seen, moved with Godly fear, prepared an ark for the saving of his household, by which he condemned the world and became the heir of righteousness which is according to faith. By faith Abraham obeyed when he was called to go out to the place which he would receive as an inheritance. And he went out, not knowing where he was going. By faith he dwelt in the land of promise as in a foreign country, dwelling in tents with Isaac and Jacob, the heirs with him of the same promise; for he waited for the city which has foundations, whose builder and maker is God. By faith Sarah herself also received strength to conceive seed, and she bore a child when she was past the age, because she judged Him faithful who had promised. Therefore from one man, and him as good as dead, were born as many as the stars of the sky in multitude—innumerable as the sand which is by the seashore. These all died in faith, not having received the promises, but having seen them afar off were assured of them, embraced them and confessed that they were strangers and pilgrims on the earth. For those who say such things declare plainly that they seek a homeland. And truly if they had called to mind that country from which they had come out, they would have had opportunity to return. But now they desire a better, that is, a heavenly country. Therefore, God is not ashamed to be called their God, for He has prepared a city for them. By faith Abraham, when he was tested, offered up Isaac, and he who had received the promises offered up his only begotten son, of whom it was said, "In Isaac your seed shall be called." concluding that God was able to raise him up, even from the dead, from which he also received him in a figurative sense. By faith Isaac blessed Jacob and Esau concerning things to come. By faith Jacob, when he was dying, blessed each of the sons of Joseph, and worshipped, leaning on the top of his staff. By faith Joseph, when he was dying, made mention of the departure of the children of Israel, and gave instructions concerning his bones. By faith Moses, when he was born, was hidden three months by his parents, because they saw he was a beautiful child; and they were not afraid of the king's command. By faith Moses, when he became of age, refused to be called the son of Pharaoh's daughter, choosing rather to suffer affliction with the people of God than to enjoy the passing pleasures of sin, esteeming the reproach of Christ greater riches than the treasures in Egypt; for he looked to the reward. By faith he forsook Egypt, not fearing the wrath of the king; for he endured as seeing Him who is invisible. By faith he kept the

Passover and the sprinkling of blood, lest he who destroyed the firstborn should touch them. By faith they passed through the Red Sea as by dry land, whereas the Egyptians, attempting to do so, were drowned. By faith the walls of Jericho fell down after they were encircled for seven days. By faith the harlot Rahab did not perish with those who did not believe, when she had received the spies with peace. And what more shall I say? For the time would fail me to tell of Gideon and Barak and Samson and Jephthah, also of David and Samuel and the prophets: who through faith subdued kingdoms, worked righteousness, obtained promises, stopped the mouths of lions, quenched the violence of fire, escaped the edge of the sword, out of weakness were made strong, became valiant in battle, turned to flight the armies of the aliens. Women received their dead raised to life again. Others were tortured, not accepting deliverance, that they might obtain a better resurrection. Still others had trial of mocking and scourging, yes, and of chains and imprisonment. They were stoned, they were sawn in two, were tempted, were slain with the sword. They wandered about in sheepskins and goatskins, being destitute, afflicted, tormented—of whom the world was not worthy. They wandered in deserts and mountains, in dens and caves of the earth. And all these, having obtained a good testimony through faith, did not receive the promise, God having provided something better for us, that they should not be made perfect apart from us. (Hebrews 11:1–40)

Therefore we also, since we are surrounded by so great a cloud of witnesses, let us lay aside every weight, and the sin which so easily ensnares us, and let us run with endurance the race that is set before us, looking unto Jesus, the author and finisher of our faith, who for the joy that was set before Him endured the cross, despising the shame, and has sat down at the right hand of the throne of God. For consider Him who endured such hostility from sinners against Himself, lest you become weary and discouraged in your souls. You have not yet resisted to bloodshed, striving against sin. (Hebrews 12:1–4)

What does it profit, my brethren, if someone says he has faith but does not have works? Can faith save him? If a brother or sister is naked and destitute of daily food, and one of you says to them, "Depart in peace, be warmed and filled," but you do not give them the things which are needed for the body, what does it profit? Thus also faith by itself, if it does not have works, is dead. But someone will say, "You have faith, and I have works." Show me your faith without your works, and I will show you my faith by my works. You believe that there is one God. You do well. Even the demons believe— and tremble! But do you want to know, O foolish man, that faith without works is dead? Was not Abraham our father justified by works when he offered Isaac his son on the alter? Do you see that faith was working together with his works, and by works faith was made perfect? And the Scripture was fulfilled which says, "Abraham believed God, and it was accounted to him for righteousness." And he was called the friend of God. You see that a man is justified by works, and not by faith only. Likewise, was not Rahab the harlot also justified by works when she received the messengers and sent them out another way? For as the body without the spirit is dead, so faith without works is dead also. (James 2:14–26)

Elect according to the foreknowledge of God the Father, in sanctification of the Spirit, for obedience and sprinkling of the blood of Jesus Christ: Grace to you and peace be multiplied. Blessed be the God and Father of our Lord Jesus Christ, who according to His abundant mercy has begotten us again to a living hope through the resurrection of Jesus Christ from the dead to an inheritance incorruptible and undefiled and that does not fade away, reserved in heaven for you, who are kept by the power of God through faith for salvation ready to be revealed in the last time. In this you greatly rejoice, though now for a little while, if need be, you have been grieved by various trials, that the genuineness of your faith, being much more precious than gold that perishes, though it is tested by fire, may be found to praise, honour, and glory at the revelation of Jesus Christ, whom having not seen you love. Though now you do not see Him, yet believing, you rejoice with joy inexpressible and full of glory, receiving the end of your faith—the salvation of your souls. (1 Peter 1:2–9)

Therefore gird up the loins of your mind, be sober, and rest your hope fully upon the grace that is to be brought to you at the revelation of Jesus Christ; as obedient children, not conforming yourselves to the former lusts, as in your ignorance; but as He who called you is holy, you also be holy in all your conduct, because it is written, "Be holy, for I am holy." And if you call on the Father, who without partiality judges according to each one's work, conduct yourselves throughout the time of your stay here in fear; knowing that you were not redeemed with corruptible things, like silver or gold, from your aimless conduct received by tradition from your fathers, but with the precious blood of Christ, as of a lamb without blemish and without spot. He indeed was foreordained before the foundation of the world, but was manifested in these last times for you who through Him believe in God who raised Him from the dead and gave Him glory, so that your faith and hope are in God. Since you have purified your souls in obeying the truth through the Spirit, in sincere love of the brethren, love one another fervently with a pure heart, having been born again, not of corruptible seed but incorruptible, through the word of God which lives and abides forever. (1 Peter 1:13–23)

Whoever believes that Jesus is the Christ is born of God, and everyone who loves Him who begot also loves him who is begotten of Him. By this we know that we love the children of God, when we love God and keep His commandments. For this is the love of God, that we keep His commandments. And His commandments are not burdensome. For whatever is born of God overcomes the world. And this is the victory that has overcome the world—our faith. Who is he who overcomes the world, but he who believes that Jesus is the Son of God? This is

Michael J. Byrne

He who came by water and blood—Jesus Christ;
not only by water, but by water and blood. And it
is the Spirit who bears witness, because the Spirit is
truth. (1 John 5:1–6)

Chapter 21

GRACE

The entirety of Your word is truth, And every one of Your righteous judgments endures forever. (Psalm 119:160)

Therefore, having been justified by faith, we have peace with God through our Lord Jesus Christ, through whom also we have access by faith into this grace in which we stand, and rejoice in hope of the glory of God. And not only that, but we also glory in tribulations, knowing that tribulation produces perseverance; and perseverance, character; and character, hope. (Romans 5:1–4)

"Into this grace in which we stand." This grace was created before time began, and God rested on the seventh day from all His works. This is the grace afforded to us through the name of Jesus Christ of Nazareth. Christ's Spirit is joining with our spirit. We are betrothed as chaste virgins. The battle is won, and we are members of the New Covenant of the Spirit. We have been freed from sin and death.

What shall we say then? Shall we continue in sin that grace may abound? Certainly not! How shall we who died to sin live any longer in it? Or do you not know that as many of us as were baptized into Christ Jesus were baptized into His death? Therefore we were buried with Him through baptism into death, that just as Christ was raised from the dead by the glory of the Father, even so we also should walk in newness of life. For if we have been united together in the likeness of His death, certainly we also shall be in the likeness of His resurrection, knowing this, that our old man was crucified with Him, that the body of sin might be done away with, that we should no longer be slaves of sin. For he who has died has been freed from sin. Now if we died with Christ, we believe that we shall also live with Him, knowing that Christ, having been raised from the dead, dies no more. Death no longer has dominion over him. For the death that He died, He died to sin once for all; but the life that He lives, He lives to God. Likewise you also, reckon yourself to be dead indeed to sin, but alive to God in Christ Jesus our Lord. Therefore do not let sin reign in your mortal body, that you should obey it in its lusts. And do not present your members as instruments of unrighteousness to sin, but present yourselves to God as being alive from the dead, and your members as instruments of righteousness to God. For sin shall not have dominion over you, for you are not under law but under grace. What then? Shall we sin because we are not under law but under grace? Certainly not! Do you not know that to whom you present yourselves slaves to obey, you are that one's slaves whom you obey, whether of sin leading to death, or of obedience leading to righteousness? But God be thanked that though you were slaves of sin, yet you obeyed from the heart that form of doctrine to which you were delivered. And having been set free from sin, you became slaves of righteousness. I speak in human terms because of the weakness of your flesh. For just as you presented your members as slaves of uncleanness, and of lawlessness leading to more lawlessness, so now present your members as slaves of righteousness for holiness. For when you were slaves of sin, you were free in regard to righteousness. What fruit did you have then in the things of which you are now ashamed? For the end of those things is death. But now having been set free from sin, and having become slaves of God, you have your fruit to holiness, and the end, everlasting life. For the wages of sin is death, but the gift of God is eternal life through Jesus Christ our Lord. (Romans 6:1–23)

For He says to Moses, "I will have mercy on whomever I will have mercy, and I will have compassion on whomever I will have compassion." So then it is not of him who wills, nor of him who runs, but of God who shows mercy. For the Scripture says to the Pharaoh, "For this very purpose I have raised you up, that I may show My power in you, and that My name may be declared in all the earth." Therefore He has mercy on whom He wills, and whom He wills He hardens. You will say to me then, "Why does He still find fault? For who has resisted His will?" But indeed, O man, who are you to reply against God? Will the thing formed say to him who formed it, "Why have you made me like this?" Does not the potter have power over the clay, from the same lump to make one vessel for honour and another for dishonour? What if God, wanting to show His wrath and to make His power known, endured with much long-suffering the vessels of wrath prepared for destruction, and that He might make known the riches of His glory on the vessels of mercy, which He had prepared beforehand for glory, even us whom He called, not of the Jews only, but also of the Gentiles? As He says also in Hosea: "I will call them My people, who were not my people, And her beloved, who was not beloved. And it shall come to pass in the place where it was said to them, 'You are not My people,' There they shall be called sons of the living God." Isaiah also cries out concerning Israel: "Though the number of the children of Israel be as the sand of the sea, The remnant will be saved. For He will finish the work and cut it short in righteousness, Because the Lord will make a short work upon the earth." And as Isaiah said before: "Unless the Lord of Sabbath had left us a seed, We would have become like Sodom, And we would have been made like Gomorrah." What shall we say then? That Gentiles, who did not pursue righteousness, have attained to righteousness, even the righteousness of faith; but Israel, pursuing the law of righteousness, has not attained to the law of righteousness. Why? Because they did not seek it by faith, but as it were, by the works of the law. For they stumbled at that stumbling stone. As it is written: "Behold, I lay in Zion a stumbling stone and rock of offence, And whoever believes on Him will not be put to shame." (Romans 9:15–33)

For Christ is the end of the law for righteousness to everyone who believes. For Moses writes about the righteousness which is of the law, "The man who does those things shall live by them." But the righteousness of faith speaks in this way, "Do not say in your heart, 'Who will ascend into heaven?'" (That is, to bring Christ down from above) or, "'Who will descend into the abyss?'" (That is, to bring Christ up from the dead). But what does it say? "The word is near you, in your mouth and in your heart" (that is, the word of faith which we preach): that if you confess with your mouth the Lord Jesus and believe in your heart that God raised Him from the dead, you will be saved. For with the heart one believes unto righteousness, and with the mouth confession is made unto salvation. For the Scripture says, "Whoever believes on Him will not be put to shame. (Romans 10:4–11)

It is imperative that a person believes that Jesus of Nazareth is the Christ, the only begotten Son of God, the Firstborn of creation, and that He came by water and blood. By water, in that He was born of a woman, and by blood, in that He was crucified on the cross. This confession must be believed in the heart in order to call on the name of Jesus Christ if we are expecting Him to rescue us from temptation and share the divine nature with us. We can be assured of our rescue in that He promises that all who call on the name of our Lord Jesus Christ will be saved.

God has not cast away His people whom He foreknew. Or do you not know what the Scripture says of Elijah, how he pleads with God against Israel, saying, "Lord, they have killed Your prophets and torn down Your altars, and I alone am left, and they seek my life"? But what does the divine response say to him? "I have reserved for Myself seven thousand men who have not bowed the knee to Baal." Even so then, at this present time there is a remnant according to the election of grace. And if by grace, then it is no longer of works; otherwise grace is no longer grace. But if it is of works, it is no longer grace; otherwise work is no longer work. (Romans 11:2–6)

I thank my God always concerning you for the grace of God which was given to you by Christ Jesus. (1 Corinthians 1:4)

But by the grace of God I am what I am, and His grace toward me was not in vain; but I laboured more abundantly than they all, yet not I but the grace of God which was with me. (1 Corinthians 15:10)

And by their prayer for you, who long for you because of the exceeding grace of God in you. Thanks be to God for His indescribable gift! (2 Corinthians 9:14–15)

Not having my own righteousness, which is from the law, but that which is through faith in Christ, the righteousness which is from God by faith. (Philippians 3:9)

You therefore, my son, be strong in the grace that is in Christ Jesus. (2 Timothy 2:1)

For the grace of God that brings salvation has appeared to all men, teaching us that, denying ungodliness and worldly lusts, we should live soberly, righteously, and godly in the present age, looking for the blessed hope and glorious appearing of our great God and Savior Jesus Christ, who gave Himself for us, that He might redeem us from every lawless deed and purify for Himself His own special people, zealous for good works. (Titus 2:11–14)

Chapter 22

THE HOLY SPIRIT

Isaiah admonished Israel not to worry themselves with the things of the flesh but to come to God and to the nourishment that God provides: His Holy Spirit. These, as were the entirety of the Old and New Testament, were written for our understanding so that they should not be made perfect apart from us.

> And all these, having obtained a good testimony through faith, did not receive the promise, God having provided something better for us, that they should not be made perfect apart from us. (Hebrews 11:39–40)

> "Ho! Everyone who thirst, Come to the waters; And you who have no money, Come, buy and eat. Yes, come, buy wine and milk Without money and without price. Why do you spend money for what is not bread, And your wages for what does not satisfy? Listen carefully to Me, and eat what is good, And let your soul delight itself in abundance. Incline your ear, and come to Me. Hear, and your soul shall live; And I will make an everlasting covenant with you—The mercies of David. Indeed I have

given him as a witness to the people, A leader and commander for the people. Surely you shall call a nation you do not know, And nations who do not know you shall run to you, Because of the LORD your God, And the Holy One of Israel; For He has glorified you. Seek the LORD while He may be found, Call upon Him while He is near. Let the wicked forsake his way, And the unrighteous man his thoughts; Let him return to the LORD, And He will have mercy on him; And to our God, For He will abundantly pardon. For My thoughts are not your thoughts, Nor are your ways My ways," says the LORD. "For as the heavens are higher than the earth, So are My ways higher than your ways, And My thoughts than your thoughts. For as the rain comes down, and the snow from heaven, And do not return there, But water the earth, And make it bring forth and bud, That it may give seed to the sower And bread to the eater, So shall My word be that goes forth from My mouth; It shall not return to Me void, But it shall accomplish what I please, And it shall prosper in the thing for which I sent it. For you shall go out with joy, And be led out with peace; The mountains and the hills Shall break forth into singing before you, And all the trees of the field shall clap their hands. Instead of the thorn shall come up the cypress tree, And instead of the brier shall come up the myrtle tree; And it shall be to the LORD for a name, For an everlasting sign that shall not be cut off." (Isaiah 55:1–13)

Who can understand his errors? Cleanse me from secret faults. Keep back Your servant also from presumptuous sins; Let them not have dominion over me. Then I shall be blameless, And I shall be innocent of great transgression. Let the words of my mouth and the meditation of my heart Be acceptable in Your sight, O Lord, my strength and my Redeemer. (Psalm 19:12–14)

Create in me a clean heart, O God, And renew a steadfast spirit within me. (Psalm 51:10)

And it shall come to pass afterward That I will pour out My Spirit on all flesh; Your sons and your daughters shall prophecy, Your old men shall dream dreams, Your young men shall see visions. And also on My menservants and on My maidservants I will pour out My Spirit in those days. (Joel 2:28–29)

Now his father Zacharias was filled with the Holy Spirit, and prophesied, saying: "Blessed is the Lord God of Israel, For He has visited and redeemed His people, And has raised up a horn of salvation for us In the house of His servant David, As He spoke by the mouth of His holy prophets, Who have been since the world began, That we should be saved from our enemies And from the hand of all who hate us, To perform the mercy promised to our fathers And to remember His holy covenant, The oath which He swore to our father Abraham: To grant us that we, Being delivered from the hand of our enemies, Might serve Him without fear, In holiness and righteousness before Him all the days of our life. And you, child, will be called the prophet of the Highest; For you will go before the face of the Lord to prepare His ways, To give knowledge of salvation to His people By the remission of their sins, Through the tender mercy of our God, with which the Dayspring from on high has visited us: To give light to those who sit in darkness and the shadow of death, To guide our feet into the way of peace." (Luke 1:67–79)

You send forth Your Spirit, they are created; And You renew the face of the earth. (Psalm 104:30)

For who is greater, he who sits at the table, or he who serves? Is it not he who sits at the table? Yet I am among you as the One who serves. (Luke 22:27)

Jesus serves by coming to us as the Helper in the form of the Holy Spirit, sharing with us the divine nature, delivering us from this evil age.

On the last day, that great day of the feast, Jesus stood and cried out, saying, "If anyone thirsts, let him come to Me and drink. (John 7:37)

"Let him come to Me and drink." Drink in the Holy Spirit.

"He who believes in Me, as the Scripture has said, out of His heart will flow rivers of living water." But He spoke concerning the Spirit, whom those believing in Him would receive; for the Holy Spirit was not yet given, because Jesus was not yet glorified. (John 7:38–39)

Then Jesus said to those Jews who believed in Him, "If you abide in My word, you are My disciples indeed. And you shall know the truth, and the truth shall make you free." They answered Him, "We are Abraham's descendants, and have never been in bondage to anyone. How can You say, 'You will be made free'? Jesus answered them, "Most assuredly, I say to you, whoever commits sin is a slave of sin. And a slave does not abide in the house forever, but a son abides forever. Therefore if the Son makes you free, you shall be free indeed." (John 8:31–36)

But Jesus answered them, saying, "The hour has come that the Son of Man should be glorified. Most assuredly, I say to you, unless a grain of wheat falls into the ground and dies, it remains alone; but if it dies, it produces much grain." (John 12:23–24)

"It produces much grain." This signifies the sending out of the Holy Spirit. Jesus had to die in order to receive His inheritance, establish the New Covenant and send out His Holy Spirit.

"Let not your heart be troubled; you believe in God, believe also in Me. In My Father's house are many mansions; if it were not so, I would have told you. I go to prepare a place for you. And if I go and prepare a place for you, I will come again and receive you to Myself; that where I am, there you may be also. And where I go you know, and the way you know." Thomas said to Him, "Lord, we do not know where You are going, and how can we know the way?' Jesus said to him, "I am the way, the truth, and the life. No one comes to the Father except through Me. If you had known Me, you would have known My Father also; and from now on you know Him and have seen Him." (John 14:1–7)

Jesus is the image of God, and just as Jesus is the image of God, those who have been baptized into the name of Jesus Christ of Nazareth are being transformed into that same image. God and Jesus share in the divine nature, and this is the same divine nature that Jesus is offering to share with us through His Holy Spirit.

For Jesus to be an acceptable High Priest, He had to be found completely in the form of a man. Jesus has been described in scripture as the second Adam. He had to have been tempted—just as every man suffers temptation—yet be found innocent. He had to be found innocent because the consequence of guilt and sin is death.

Humanity was condemned in the Garden of Eden; therefore, because Jesus was a man, He was also under that same condemnation. Jesus had the same inner man that He had as the Son of God. He had the same self-awareness of who He was.

Christ had to be found in the same circumstances as was the first Adam in the Garden of Eden. He was presented with the same choices that the first Adam had. He had the choice to rebel and receive all that Satan promised or be obedient. Jesus never gave into Satan's temptations and, therefore, never became a slave to Satan. After Jesus's temptation in the wilderness, the angels came to minister to Him—just as they were originally designed.

In the Garden of Eden, the spiritual ideal was there in the person of the Christ for humans to follow; later, the temptation came through Satan's rebellion. Eve did not believe God and succumbed to Satan's lies. Having fallen from their pristine state into sin, and thereby becoming divorced from God, it was impossible for God to share the divine nature with them. Because the divine nature could no longer be shared with them, they were, in essence, denied access to the Tree of Life. The denied access to the Tree of Life left them denied eternal life.

There is a relative relationship, but a distinct difference between the Tree of Life and mortality. Mortality came through the transgression of God's command—the person who sins will die. Exclusion from the Tree of Life also came through the transgression of God's command. "We became alienated and enemies in our mind by wicked works."(Colossians 1:21)

The Tree of Life is representative of the divine nature, the character or Spirit of God. In theory one can have access to, although not be in possession of, the Tree of Life and still be subject to physical death. Humanity was immediately cut off from the Tree of Life after the fall because of sin. As a consequence of being cut off from the Tree of Life, man became alienated from God and lost the entitlement of sharing the divine nature with God. In addition to becoming alienated from God, mankind became mortal. The soul who sins will die.

The resulting removal from God's presence in our physical sense—the divorce between God and man—is the loss of our inheritance that has been passed down to us through Adam. This divorce is permanent: "'Til death do us part." The situation that has been passed down to humanity is irreparable. What's done is done, and there's no turning back. God has devised something new.

As previously discussed, the Son of God needed to give up His Godhead. He had to strip Himself of everything that made Him God and take on the form of a man. Therefore, Jesus in the flesh was 100 percent man, while having the conscious awareness that He was the only begotten Son of God.

Just as Adam had to stand under the temptations exacted upon him by Satan, Jesus also needed to stand and face all of Satan's temptations. Jesus—having been born a man through His mother Mary—inherited the curse that had been imposed upon all of humanity in the Garden of Eden.

Jesus's final condition prior to dying on the cross was that He was still the only begotten Son of God, the Christ, completely undefiled by the world, pure and innocent, sharing in God's nature, but He was under the same condemnation imposed upon all of humanity: cursed because He had been born a man. He shared in God's nature because He was free from sin and therefore still had access to the Tree of Life.

Jesus's self-awareness did not prevent Him from becoming 100 percent man. During His time on earth, Christ had shed Himself of anything and everything that could be considered to be God. We can understand exactly what He was like because we also were created in God's image, holding our consciousnesses in vessels of clay. He was the same as us except for the fact that He had the self-awareness that He was the Son of God and was free from sin. During those last moments of Jesus's time on the cross, God the Father completed the overflowing of Jesus's Spiritual vessel with the full measure of God's Holy Spirit.

He was in the same state as was Adam in the Garden of Eden. Just as Adam was created in a 'natural state of neutrality'—in which it was possible for God to share in the divine nature with him, it was necessary for Christ to shed Himself of everything that did not correspond to the natural state of neutrality that was found in the first Adam. Christ shed everything from Himself other than His Spirit. For Jesus to become 100 percent man, while retaining the Spirit that He was in possession of as a Divine Being testifies to the fact that man and God share the same spirit. The spirit of man and the Spirit of God are mechanically the same. 'Jesus answered them, "Is it not written in your law, 'I said, "You are gods"'? If He called them gods, to whom the word of God came (and the Scripture cannot be broken), do you say of Him whom the Father sanctified and sent into the world, 'You are blaspheming,' because I said, 'I am the Son of God'?"' (John 10:34–36) The spirit can be better viewed as an operating system. Mankind is in the possession of the same operating system as God. The soul, which can be better defined as our emotions can be viewed as a program. The body can be better understood as our senses; taste, touch and seeing, etc. Through mankind's rebellion in the Garden of Eden, the soul of mankind or mankind's program has been corrupted. Mankind's corrupted soul has in turn corrupted mankind's spirit. Because Christ never ate from the Tree of the Knowledge of Good and Evil, He has never been corrupted nor has He ever been deprived access to the Tree of

Life and has never fallen from the Grace that Adam and Eve were originally created in. Once baptized by John, Jesus received the Holy Spirit through God the Father, just as today we receive Christ's Holy Spirit once we are baptized into His name. Remember Christ has the Pre-eminence in all things.

The temptation that Adam and Eve faced were dull in comparison to the fiery darts that Satan used to tempt Jesus. Eve was seduced by the desire to become like God. The temptations that have since entered into the world since Eve's transgression are incalculable. This is one of the reasons why Christ had to wait on the sidelines before making His appearance to Israel. It was necessary for temptation and sin to reach their full zenith before Christ could be introduced into the equation. In order for Christ to be made a suitable High Priest it was necessary that He suffer all of the temptations that could possibly plague humanity.

> (For if by one man's offense death reigned through the one, much more those who receive abundance of grace and of the gift of righteousness will reign in life through the One, Jesus Christ.) Therefore, as through one man's offense judgement came to all men, resulting in condemnation, even so through one Man's righteous act the free gift came to all men, resulting in justification of life. For as by one man's disobedience many were made sinners, so also by one Man's obedience many will be made righteous. Moreover the law entered that the offense might abound. But where sin abounded, grace abounded much more, so that as sin reigned in death, even so grace might reign through righteousness to eternal life through Jesus Christ our Lord. (Romans 5:17–21)

God the Father Almighty used all of Satan's temptations and all of the experiences Jesus experienced in His time on earth to further enhance the divine nature that was within Him. Through that enhancement, God brought about the perfection that was required for Jesus to lay hold of the High Priesthood. And just as God the Father used all that the world could throw at Jesus to perfect the divine nature within Him, Jesus now uses all that the world can muster, in order to develop the divine nature within us.

> I said, "You are gods, And all of you are children of the Most High. But you shall die like men, And fall like one of the princes." (Psalm 82:6)

> Jesus answered them, "Is it not written in your law, 'I said, "You are gods"'? If He called them gods, to whom the word of God came (and the Scripture cannot be broken), do you say of Him whom the Father sanctified and sent into the world, 'You are blaspheming,' because I said, 'I am the Son of God'"? (John 10:34–36)

Now, we can use that same understanding to realize how the Spirit of Jesus Christ can become imprinted upon our consciousness, which allows us to develop the same Spirit that is in Christ Jesus while maintaining the curse that has been placed upon our physical selves, the old man.

Therefore, when we are baptized, we are baptized into the death of Jesus Christ; our physical selves have figuratively died. By taking advantage of the grace that is being offered to us, the tether that joins our physical selves with our conscious selves, or inner man—through emotions and senses—becomes severed. This physical self could better be described as the "flesh" or the "processor" between the conscious mind and the senses. Therefore, when we become baptized into the name of Jesus Christ of Nazareth, the "flesh" or the "processor" is replaced with the Spirit of Christ. Jesus Christ's Holy Spirit becomes the buffer between us and the world.

We are no longer susceptible to sin because that genetic predisposition to sin is fading. We now have an opportunity to enter into a state of grace. Now that Jesus Christ has been allowed to institute a New Covenant, His Spirit is able to join with our spirit, which adds a dimension to our spirit that allows us the ability to reject any and all temptations. We can still be tempted and lured back into sin, but the grace that is afforded to us through the name of Jesus Christ of Nazareth is always there. We need only to call upon the name of Jesus Christ of Nazareth to triumph over temptation. Remember, Satan is still prowling around and looking for those whom he may devour. We are still subject to temptation, but as was told to Cain after he killed his brother, Abel: "You should rule over it."

> Philip said to Him, "Lord, show us the Father, and it is sufficient for us." Jesus said to him, "Have I been with you so long, and yet you have not known Me, Philip? He who has seen Me has seen the Father; so how can you say, 'Show us the Father'? Do you not believe that I am in the Father, and the Father in Me? The words that I speak to you I do not speak on My own authority; but the Father who dwells in Me does the works." (John 14:8–10)

Jesus is the image of the Father, and just as Jesus bears the image of the Father, we have the opportunity to bear the image of Jesus in the Spirit. The works that Jesus did were actually God the Father working through Him. Jesus had never sinned and therefore had never been denied access to the Tree of Life.

> Believe Me that I am in the Father and the Father in Me, or else believe Me for the sake of the works

themselves. Most assuredly, I say to you, he who
believes in Me the works that I do he will do also;
and greater works than these he will do, because I
go to My Father. (John 14:11–12)

"The works that I do he will do also." The works through the Spirit,
removing oneself from sin, overcoming temptation, sharing in the
divine nature and becoming perfect.

"And whatever you ask in My name, that I will
do, that the Father may be glorified in the Son. If
you ask anything in My name, I will do it. If you
love Me, keep My commandments. And I will pray
the Father, and He will give you another Helper,
that He may abide with you forever—the Spirit
of truth, whom the world cannot receive, because
it neither sees Him or knows Him; but you know
Him, for He dwells with you and will be in you."
(John 14:13–17)

"If you ask anything in My name ...And I will pray the Father."
Jesus is telling us to pray to Him and He will pray to the Father.
Jesus Christ is the Mediator between God and man.

Just as the Father was with Jesus. "But you know Him, for He
dwells with you and will be in you." You know Him; they knew
Jesus. He dwells with you; Jesus dwelt with them. Jesus is the Holy
Spirit.

"I will not leave you orphans: I will come to you.
(John 14:18)

"I will come to you." He reiterates again and again that He is the
Holy Spirit.

"A little while longer and the world will see Me no more, but you will see Me. Because I live, you will live also. At that day you will know that I am in My Father, and you in Me, and I in you. He who has My commandments and keeps them, it is he who loves Me. And he who loves Me will be loved by My Father, and I will love him and manifest Myself to him." Judas (not Iscariot) said to Him, "Lord, how is it that You will manifest Yourself to us, and not to the world?" Jesus answered and said to him, "If anyone loves Me, he will keep My word; and My Father will love him, and We will come to him and make Our home with him. (John 14:19–23)

Jesus purifies us so that the Spirit that Jesus shares with the Father can come and dwell with us. Forgiveness and victory over sin and death are only one aspect of the Gospel. The most important and most crucial aspect of the Gospel is the cultivation of love. Once one is baptized and has received Christ's Spirit it is necessary that the love of God be cultivated in each and everyone of us. Jesus using a parable describes the consequences of someone repenting and being baptized but not having God's love cultivated in them;

"When an unclean spirit goes out of a man, he goes through dry places, seeking rest, and finds none. Then he says, 'I will return to my house from which I came.' And when he comes, and finds it empty, swept, and put in order. Then he goes and takes with him seven other spirits more wicked than himself, and they enter and dwell there; and the last state of that man is worse than the first. So shall it also be with this wicked generation." Matthew 12:43–45)

The Father is the Vinedresser who prunes the vine. As we give up our dead works through the name of Jesus Christ of Nazareth, the Father prunes off the dead branches, giving us complete access to the divine nature.

> He who does not love Me does not keep My words; and the word which you hear is not Mine but the Father's who sent Me. These things I have spoken to you while being present with you. But the Helper, the Holy Spirit, whom the Father will send in My name, He will teach you all things, and bring to your remembrance all things that I said to you. Peace I leave with you, My peace I give to you; not as the world gives do I give to you. Let not your heart be troubled, neither let it be afraid. You have heard Me say to you, "I am going away and coming back to you." If you loved Me, you would rejoice because I said, "I am going to the Father," for My Father is greater than I. And now I have told you before it comes, that when it does come to pass, you may believe. (John 14:24–29)

> Abide in Me, and I in you. As the branch cannot bear fruit of itself, unless it abides in the vine, neither can you, unless you abide in Me. I am the vine, you are the branches. He who abides in Me, and I in him, bears much fruit; for without Me you can do nothing. If anyone does not abide in Me, he is cast out as a branch and is withered; and they gather them and throw them into the fire, and they are burned. If you abide in Me, and My words abide in you, you will ask what you desire, and it shall be done for you. By this My Father is glorified, that you bear much fruit, so you will be My disciples. As

the Father loved Me, I also have loved you; abide in My love. (John 15:4–9)

Nevertheless I tell you the truth. It is to your advantage that I go away; for if I do not go away, the Helper will not come to you; but if I depart, I will send Him to you. (John 16:7)

Jesus is the Helper.

However, when He, the Spirit of truth; has come, He will guide you into all truth; for He will not speak on His own authority, but whatever He hears He will speak; and He will tell you things to come. He will glorify Me, for He will take of what is Mine and declare it to you. All things that the Father has are Mine. Therefore I said that He will take of Mine and declare it to you. (John 16:13–15)

"Assuredly, I say to you, all sins will be forgiven the sons of men, and whatever blasphemies they may utter; but he who blasphemes against the Holy Spirit never has forgiveness, but is subject to eternal condemnation"—because they said, "He has an unclean spirit." (Mark 3:28–30)

This Jesus God has raised up, of which we are all witnesses. Therefore being exalted to the right hand of God, and having received from the Father the promise of the Holy Spirit, He poured out this which you now see and hear. (Acts 2:32–33)

Jesus received the promise, which is in addition to His inheritance, specifically: "I will put My laws into their minds, and in their hearts,

write them, and I will be their God and they shall be My people."
This is what is being poured out.

> Now when the apostles who were at Jerusalem heard
> that Samaria had received the word of God, they
> sent Peter and John to them, who, when they had
> come down, prayed for them that they might receive
> the Holy Spirit. For as yet He had fallen upon none
> of them. They had only been baptized in the name
> of the Lord Jesus. Then they laid hands on them,
> and they received the Holy Spirit. (Acts 8:14–17)

> Then I remembered the Word of the Lord, how
> He said, "John indeed baptized with water, but you
> shall be baptized with the Holy Spirit." (Acts 11:16)

> For when we were in the flesh, the sinful passions
> which were aroused by the law were at work in our
> members to bear fruit to death. But now we have
> been delivered from the law, having died to what
> we were held by, so that we should serve in newness
> of the Spirit and not in the oldness of the letter.
> (Romans 7:5–6)

> There is therefore now no condemnation to those
> who are in Christ Jesus, who do not walk according
> to the flesh, but according to the Spirit. For the law
> of the Spirit of life in Christ Jesus has made me free
> from the law of sin and death. For what the law
> could not do in that it was weak through the flesh,
> God did by sending His own Son in the likeness
> of sinful flesh, on account of sin: He condemned
> sin in the flesh, that the righteous requirements of
> the law might be fulfilled in us who do not walk

according to the flesh but according to the Spirit. For those who live according to the flesh set their minds on the things of the flesh, but those who live according to the Spirit, the things of the Spirit. For to be carnally minded is death, but to be spiritually minded is life and peace. Because the carnal mind is enmity against God; for it is not subject to the law of God, nor indeed can be. So then, those who are in the flesh cannot please God. But you are not in the flesh but in the Spirit, if indeed the Spirit of God dwells in you. Now if anyone does not have the Spirit of Christ, he is not His. And if Christ is in you, the body is dead because of sin, but the Spirit is life because of righteousness. But if the Spirit of Him who raised Jesus from the dead dwells in you, He who raised Christ from the dead will also give life to your mortal bodies through His Spirit who dwells in you. Therefore, brethren, we are debtors— not to the flesh, to live according to the flesh. For if you live according to the flesh you will die; but if by the Spirit you put to death the deeds of the body, you will live. For as many as are led by the Spirit of God, these are sons of God. For you did not receive the spirit of bondage again to fear, but you received the Spirit of adoption by whom we cry out, "Abba, Father." The Spirit Himself bears witness with our spirit that we are children of God, (Romans 8:1–16)

He bears witness by keeping us from sin and developing the love of God in us.

and if children, then heirs—heirs of God and joint heirs with Christ, if indeed we suffer with Him, that we may also be glorified together. For I consider that

the sufferings of this present time are not worthy to
be compared with the glory which shall be revealed
in us. (Romans 8:17–18)

Jesus's sufferings were the sufferings against the flesh, against
temptation, and against everything that separates us from God.
Jesus's sufferings armed Him with the inheritance of the name that is
above every other name, which is in heaven and on earth and under
the earth. This is the grace in which we stand. This grace allows us
to be victorious over the sufferings of temptation.

Likewise the Spirit helps in our weaknesses. For we
do not know what we should pray for as we ought,
but the Spirit Himself makes intercession for us
with groaning which cannot be uttered. Now He
who searches the hearts knows what the mind of
the Spirit is, because He makes intercession for the
saints according to the will of God. And we know
that all things work together for good to those who
love God, to those who are the called according
to His purpose. For whom He foreknew, He also
predestined to be conformed to the image of His
Son, that He might be the firstborn among many
brethren. Moreover whom He predestined, these
He also called; whom He called, these He also
justified; and whom He justified, these He also
glorified. What then shall we say to these things?
If God is for us, who can be against us? He who
did not spare His own Son, but delivered Him up
for us all, how shall He not with Him also freely
give us all things? Who shall bring a charge against
God's elect? It is God who justifies. Who is he who
condemns? It is Christ who died, and furthermore is
also risen, who is even at the right hand of God, who

also makes intercession for us. Who shall separate us from the love of Christ? Shall tribulation, or distress, or persecution, or famine, or nakedness, or peril, or sword? As it is written: "For Your sake we are killed all day long; We are accounted as sheep for the slaughter." Yet in all these things we are more than conquers through Him who loved us. For I am persuaded that neither death nor life, nor angels nor principalities nor powers, nor things present nor things to come, nor height nor depth, nor any other created thing, shall be able to separate us from the love of God which is in Christ Jesus our Lord. (Romans 8:26–39)

Therefore do not let your good be spoken of as evil; for the kingdom of God is not eating and drinking, but righteousness and peace and joy in the Holy Spirit. For he who serves Christ in these things is acceptable to God and approved by men. (Romans 14:16–18)

Now may the God of hope fill you with all joy and peace in believing, that you may abound in hope by the power of the Holy Spirit. (Romans 15:13)

That the offering of the Gentiles might be acceptable, sanctified by the Holy Spirit. (Romans 15:16)

But of Him you are in Christ Jesus, who became for us wisdom from God—and righteousness and sanctification and redemption—that, as it is written, "He who glories, let Him glory in the LORD." (1 Corinthians 1:30–31)

Now we have received, not the spirit of the world, but the Spirit who is from God, that we might know the things that have been freely given to us by God. (1 Corinthians 2:12)

For "who has known the mind of the LORD that he may instruct Him?" But we have the mind of Christ. (1 Corinthians 2:16)

Do you not know that you are the temple of God and that the Spirit of God dwells in you? (1 Corinthians 3:16)

And you are Christ's, and Christ is God's. (1 Corinthians 3:23)

For the kingdom of God is not in word but in power. (1 Corinthians 4:20)

Or do you not know that your body is the temple of the Holy Spirit who is in you, whom you have from God, and you are not your own? For you were bought at a price: therefore glorify God in your body and in your spirit, which are God's. (1 Corinthians 6:19–20)

Therefore I make known to you that no one speaking by the Spirit of God calls Jesus accursed, and no one can say that Jesus is Lord except by the Holy Spirit. (1 Corinthians 12:3)

For as the body is one and has many members, but all the members of that one body, being many, are one body, so also is Christ. For by one Spirit we were all baptized into one body—whether Jews or Greeks, whether slaves or free—and have all been made to drink into one Spirit. For in fact the body is not one member but many. (1 Corinthians 12:12–14)

Now He who establishes us with you in Christ and has anointed us is God, who also has sealed us and given us the Spirit in our hearts as a guarantee. (2 Corinthians 1:21–22)

Therefore, since we have such hope, we use great boldness of speech—unlike Moses, who put a veil over his face so that the children of Israel could not look steadily at the end of what was passing away. But their minds were blinded. For until this day the same veil remains unlifted in the reading of the Old Testament, because the veil is taken away in Christ. But even to this day, when Moses is read, a veil lies on their heart. Nevertheless when one turns to the Lord, the veil is taken away. Now the Lord is the Spirit; and where the Spirit of the Lord is, there is liberty. But we all, with unveiled face, beholding as in a mirror the glory of the Lord, are being transformed into the same image from glory to glory, just as by the Spirit of the Lord. (2 Corinthians 3:12–18)

For it is the God who commanded light to shine out of darkness, who has shone in our hearts to give the light of the knowledge of the glory of God in the face of Jesus Christ. But we have this treasure in earthen vessels, that the excellence of the power may be of God and not us. We are hard-pressed on every side, yet not crushed; we are perplexed, but not in despair; persecuted, but not forsaken; struck down, but not destroyed—always carrying about in the body the dying of the Lord Jesus, that the life of Jesus also may be manifested in our body. (2 Corinthians 4:6–10)

Therefore we do not lose heart. Even though our outward man is perishing, yet the inward man is being renewed day by day. (2 Corinthians 4:16)

For we who are in this tent groan, being burdened, not because we want to be unclothed, but further clothed, that mortality may be swallowed up by life. Now He who has prepared us for this very thing is God, who also has given us the Spirit as a guarantee. (2 Corinthians 5:4–5)

Examine yourselves as to whether you are in the faith. Test yourselves. Do you not know yourselves, that Jesus Christ is in you?—unless indeed you are disqualified. (2 Corinthians 13:5)

Jesus Christ is the Holy Spirit. It is through Jesus Christ that all of God's works have been and are being realized.

But when it pleased God, who separated me from my mother's womb and called me through His grace, to reveal His Son in me. (Galatians 1:15–16)

I have been crucified with Christ; it is no longer I who live, but Christ lives in me; and the life which I now live in the flesh I live by faith in the Son of God, who loved me and gave Himself for me. (Galatians 2:20)

For as many as are of the works of the law are under the curse; for it is written, "Cursed is everyone who does not continue in all things which are written in the book of the law, to do them." But that no one is justified by the law in the sight of God is evident, for "the just shall live by faith." Yet the law is not of faith, but "the man who does them shall live by them." (Galatians 3:10–12)

Christ has redeemed us from the curse of the law, having become a curse for us (for it is written, "Cursed is everyone who hangs on a tree"), that the blessing of Abraham might come upon the Gentiles in Christ Jesus, that we might receive the Spirit through faith. (Galatians 3:13–14)

The blessing is the Holy Spirit who is Jesus Christ. "I will put My laws into their mind, and into their hearts write them, and I shall be a God to them, and they shall be My people."

For as many of you as were baptized into Christ have put on Christ. There is neither Jew nor Greek, there is neither slave nor free, there is neither male nor female; for you are all one in Christ Jesus. And if you are Christ's, then you are Abraham's seed, and heirs according to the promise. (Galatians 3:27–29)

Now I say that the heir, as long as he is a child, does not differ at all from a slave, though he is master of all, but is under guardians and stewards until the time appointed by the Father. Even so

we, when we were children, were in bondage under
the elements of the world. But when the fullness of
the time had come, God sent forth His Son, born
of a woman, born under the law, to redeem those
who were under the law, that we might receive the
adoption as sons. And because you are sons, God
has sent forth the Spirit of His Son into your hearts,
crying out, "Abba, Father!" Therefore you are no
longer a slave but a son, and if a son, then an heir of
God through Christ. (Galatians 4:1–7)

We were slaves to the natural elements of the world, which dictated
our behavior. God has now freed us by sending the Spirit of Jesus
Christ into our hearts in order to transform us into sons of God.

My little children, for whom I laboured in birth
again until Christ is formed in you. (Galatians 4:19)

For we through the Spirit eagerly wait for the hope
of righteousness by faith. For in Christ Jesus neither
circumcision nor uncircumcision avails anything,
but faith working through love. (Galatians 5:5–6)

For you, brethren, have been called to liberty; only
do not use liberty as an opportunity for the flesh,
but through love serve one another. For all the law
is fulfilled in one word, even in this: "You shall love
your neighbour as yourself." But if you bite and
devour one another, beware lest you be consumed
by one another! I say then: Walk in the Spirit, and
you shall not fulfill the lusts of the flesh. For the
flesh lusts against the Spirit, and the Spirit against
the flesh; and these are contrary to one another, so
that you do not do the things that you wish. But

if you are led by the Spirit, you are not under the law. Now the works of the flesh are evident, which are adultery, fornication, uncleanness, lewdness, idolatry, sorcery, hatred, contentions, jealousies, outbursts of wrath, selfish ambitions, dissensions, heresies, envy, murders, drunkenness, revelries, and the like; of which I tell you beforehand, just as I also told you in time past, that those who practice such things will not inherit the kingdom of God. But the fruit of the Spirit is love, joy, peace, long-suffering, kindness, goodness, faithfulness, gentleness, self-control. Against such there is no law. And those who are Christ's have crucified the flesh with its passions and desires. If we live in the Spirit, let us also walk in the Spirit. Let us not become conceited, provoking one another, envying one another. (Galatians 5:13–26)

Blessed be the God and Father of our Lord Jesus Christ, who has blessed us with every spiritual blessing in the heavenly places in Christ. (Ephesians 1:3)

In Him you also trusted, after you heard the word of truth, the gospel of your salvation; in whom also, having believed, you were sealed with the Holy Spirit of promise, who is the guarantee of our inheritance until the redemption of the purchased possession, to the praise of His glory. (Ephesians 1:13–14)

But now in Christ Jesus you who were far off have been brought near by the blood of Christ. For He Himself is our peace, who has made both one, and

has broken down the wall of separation, having
abolished in His flesh the enmity, that is, the law
of commandments contained in ordinances, so as
to create in Himself one new man from the two,
thus making peace, and that He might reconcile
them both to God in one body through the cross,
thereby putting to death the enmity. And He came
and preached peace to you who were afar off and
to those who were near. For through Him we both
have access by one Spirit to the Father. (Ephesians
2:13–18)

The Spirit of Christ is the divine nature. There is only One divine
nature, hence only One Spirit as opposed to the one spirit of
humanity, the spirit of lawlessness. The peace that Jesus preached,
the "Gospel of peace," is the "New" Testament that God is providing
humanity through the death and resurrection of His only begotten
Son—the Christ.

There was a covenant made between Christ and humanity in
the Garden of Eden regarding the Tree of the Knowledge of Good
and Evil. After this covenant was broken, a promise was given to
Abraham that God would save humanity through the One who
would be Abraham's Heir.

After the promise, the Law was given to teach us about sin and
our need to be purified from sin. There was only one way that God
could purify us from sin. That way was through the death and
resurrection of His only begotten Son, Jesus Christ. There is only
One Testament. A testament is a will. Christ, in the first week of
creation, made a last Will and Testament. He willed His possessions,
which included titles and authorities and powers. In *Abingdon's
Strong's Exhaustive Concordance of the Bible*, the translation for the
Greek word "new" in reference to the "New" Testament—is *kainos*—
(2537)—meaning—of uncertain affin.; (especially in freshness). The
word "new" does not imply that it is replacing something old. There

is only one death that bears any significance in the Bible. The death and resurrection of Jesus Christ is the fulfillment of the promise given to Abraham and the prophets prior to Jesus's appearance two thousand years ago.

For this Jesus to have any significance in regard to the saving grace that God is offering the world, it is necessary that He is who He claims to be: the only begotten Son of God, the Firstborn of creation, the Christ. Otherwise, His death and resurrection would have no significance whatsoever. If He was just a man or an angel, He would not have an inheritance—and He would not be in possession of the divine nature. We could not figuratively die through Him. We could not figuratively be raised through Him, and He could not share the divine nature with us. We could not become children of God or participate in the kingdom of God.

If you do not believe that Jesus of Nazareth is the Christ, the only begotten Son of God, the Firstborn of creation, who through whom God created the worlds, then your faith is useless. You are dead in your sins. Jesus saves us from the wrath to come—at least those who believe. Jesus is the peace that God has provided. In this world, you will know no peace.

> In whom you also are being built together for a dwelling place of God in the Spirit. (Ephesians 2:22)

> That He would grant you, according to the riches of His glory, to be strengthened with might through His Spirit in the inner man, that Christ may dwell in your hearts through faith; that you, being rooted and grounded in love, may be able to comprehend with all the saints what is the width and length and depth and height—to know the love of Christ which passes knowledge; that you may be filled with all the fullness of God. Now to Him who is able to do exceedingly abundantly above all that we

ask or think, according to the power that works in us, to Him be glory in the church by Christ Jesus to all generations, forever and ever. Amen. (Ephesians 3:16–21)

There is one body and one Spirit, just as you were called in one hope of your calling; one Lord, one faith, one baptism; one God and Father of all, who is above all, and through all, and in you all. (Ephesians 4:4–6)

From whom the whole body, joined and knit together by what every joint supplies, according to the effective working by which every part does its share, causes growth of the body for the edifying of itself in love. (Ephesians 4:16)

That you may approve the things that are excellent, that you may be sincere and without offence till the day of Christ, being filled with the fruits of righteousness which are by Jesus Christ, to the glory and praise of God. (Philippians 1:10–11)

For I know that this will turn out for my deliverance through your prayer and the supply of the Spirit of Jesus Christ, according to my earnest expectation and hope that in nothing I shall be ashamed, but with all boldness, as always, so now also Christ will be magnified in my body, whether by life or by death. For to me, to live is Christ, and to die is gain. (Philippians 1:19–21)

That you stand fast in one spirit, with one mind striving together for the faith of the gospel. (Philippians 1:27)

For it is God who works in you both to will and to do for His good pleasure. (Philippians 2:13)

For we are the circumcision, who worship God in the Spirit, rejoice in Christ Jesus, and have no confidence in the flesh. (Philippians 3:3)

I press toward the goal for the prize of the upward call of God in Christ Jesus. (Philippians 3:14)

And the peace of God, which surpasses all understanding, will guard your hearts and minds through Christ Jesus. (Philippians 4:7)

I can do all things through Christ who strengthens me. (Philippians 4:13)

And my God shall supply all your need according to His riches in glory by Christ Jesus. (Philippians 4:19)

To them God willed to make known what are the riches of the glory of this mystery among the Gentiles: which is Christ in you, the hope of glory. (Colossians 1:27)

Let no one cheat you of your reward, taking delight in false humility and worship of angels, intruding into those things which he has not seen, vainly puffed up by his fleshly mind, and not holding fast to the Head, from whom all the body, nourished and knit together by joints and ligaments, grows with the increase that is from God. (Colossians 2:18–19)

For you died, and your life is hidden with Christ in God. When Christ who is our life appears, then you also will appear with Him in glory. Therefore put to death your members which are on the earth: fornication, uncleanness, passion, evil desire, and covetousness, which is idolatry. Because of these things the wrath of God is coming upon the sons of disobedience, in which you yourselves once walked when you lived in them. But now you yourselves are to put off all these: anger, wrath, malice, blasphemy, filthy language out of your mouth. Do not lie to one another, since you have put off the old man with his deeds, and have put on the new man who is renewed in knowledge according to the image of Him who created him, where there is neither Greek nor Jew, circumcised nor uncircumcised, barbarian, Scythian, slave nor free, but Christ is all and in all. Therefore, as the elect of God, holy and beloved, put on tender mercies, kindness, humility, meekness, long-suffering; bearing with one another, and forgiving one another, if anyone has a complaint against another; even as Christ forgave you, so you also must do. But above all these things put on love, which is the bond of perfection. And let the peace of God rule in your hearts, to which also you were called in one body; and be thankful. Let the word of Christ dwell in you richly in all wisdom, teaching and admonishing one another in psalms and hymns and spiritual songs, singing with grace in your hearts to the Lord. And whatever you do in word or deed, do all in the name of the Lord Jesus, giving thanks to God the Father through Him. (Colossians 3:3–17)

We pray to the Father through Jesus Christ. We pray to Jesus. If you were to buy a house from a builder, you would buy it through the builder's agent or broker. The purchase would be handled by the agent. If you were to meet the builder, you would certainly want to shake his hand, but whatever dealings you had with the builder would be taken care of by the agent. Christ is God's agent; Christ is the Mediator between God and humanity. One should respect His person and position. "You serve the Lord Jesus." At the same time, we cannot ignore our Sovereign Lord and Father, Almighty God.

The analogy is portrayed between Jesus and Jacob's son Joseph. And Joseph was released from prison and brought before Pharaoh in order to decipher a dream. And when Joseph's interpretation of the dream pleased Pharaoh, Pharaoh made a proclamation concerning Joseph.

So that advice was good in the eyes of Pharaoh and in the eyes of all his servants. And Pharaoh said to his servants, "Can we find such a one as this, a man in whom is the Spirit of God?" Then Pharaoh said to Joseph, "Inasmuch as God has shown you all this, there is no one as discerning and wise as you. You shall be over my house, and all my people shall be ruled according to your word; only in regard to the throne will I be greater than you." And Pharaoh said to Joseph, "See, I have set you over all the land of Egypt." Then Pharaoh took his signet ring off his hand and put it on Joseph's hand; and he clothed him in garments of fine linen and put a gold chain around his neck. And he had him ride in the second chariot which he had; and they cried out before him, "Bow the knee!" So he set him over all the land of Egypt. Pharaoh also said to Joseph, "I am Pharaoh, and without your consent no man may lift his hand or foot in all the land of Egypt." (Genesis 41:37–44)

And just as Joseph was raised to be ruler over all of Egypt, Jesus Christ has been raised up to be ruler over all of creation. Nothing can happen in all of creation that isn't authorized by Jesus Christ. There is nothing that does not fall under His authority except for the very throne of our Sovereign LORD and Father Almighty God. Whatever is asked of God must be asked from Jesus Christ. And whatever God wills to be, will be realized through Jesus Christ.

> Knowing that from the Lord you will receive the reward of the inheritance; for you serve the Lord Christ. (Colossians 3:24)

> But the Lord is faithful, who will establish you and guard you from the evil one. (2 Thessalonians 3:3)

> For God has not given us a spirit of fear, but of power and of love and of a sound mind. (1 Timothy 1:7)

> Now may the God of peace who brought up your Lord Jesus from the dead, that great Shepherd of the sheep, through the blood of the everlasting covenant, make you complete in every good work to do His will, working in you, what is well pleasing in His sight, through Jesus Christ, to whom be glory forever and ever. Amen. (Hebrews 13:20–21)

> If any of you lacks wisdom, let him ask of God, who gives to all liberally and without reproach, and it will be given to him. But let Him ask in faith, with no doubting, for he who doubts is like a wave of the sea driven and tossed by the wind. For let not that man suppose that he will receive anything from the Lord. (James 1:5–7)

> Of His own will He brought us forth by the word of truth, that we might be a kind of firstfruits of His creatures. (James 1:18)

James spoke of the first-century church being a kind of firstfruits of God's plan. The end-time harvest prophesied throughout the Old Testament is soon to be upon us.

> Of this salvation the prophets have inquired and searched carefully, who prophesied of the grace that would come to you, searching what, or what manner of time, the Spirit of Christ who was in them was indicating when He testified beforehand the sufferings of Christ and the glories that would follow. To them it was revealed that, not to themselves, but to us they were ministering the things which now have been reported to you through those who have preached the gospel to you by the Holy Spirit sent from heaven—things which angels desire to look into. (1 Peter 1:10–12)

The Spirit of Christ was in them. The Spirit of Christ was in the prophets of the Old Testament. He was the High Priest of God. Although these prophets and holy men of old believed in God's promises and spoke and wrote and did works that confirmed their beliefs—their actions were counted to them as righteousness—they could not be perfected because Jesus had not yet been perfected through His victory over temptation and death. The New Covenant had not yet been established.

> He indeed was foreordained before the foundation of the world, but was manifested in these last times for you who through Him believe in God who raised Him from the dead and gave Him glory, so that your faith and hope are in God. Since you have purified your souls in obeying the truth through the Spirit, in sincere love of the brethren, love one another fervently with a pure heart, having been born again, not of corruptible seed but incorruptible, through the word of God which lives and abides forever. (1 Peter 1:20–23)

> For we did not follow cunningly devised fables when we made known to you the power and coming of our Lord Jesus Christ, but were eye witnesses of His majesty. (2 Peter 1:16)

> My little children, let us not love in word or in tongue, but in deed and in truth. And by this we know that we are of the truth, and shall assure our hearts before Him. For if our heart condemns us, God is greater than our heart, and knows all things. Beloved, if our heart does not condemn us, we have confidence toward God. And whatever we ask we receive from Him, because we keep His commandments and do those things that are pleasing in His sight. And this is His commandment: that we should believe on the name of His Son Jesus Christ and love one another, as He gave us commandment. Now he who keeps His commandment abides in Him, and He in him,

> And by this we know that He abides in us, by the
> Spirit whom He has given us. (1 John 3:18–24)

"We shall assure our hearts before Him." It is our hearts that will judge us. If we are His, there will not be one shred of doubt in our hearts to condemn us. Our consciences will be pure and undefiled. Before we stand before the judgement seat of Christ, our hearts will assure us of our innocence.

> In this the love of God was manifested toward us,
> that God has sent His only begotten Son into the
> world, that we might live through Him. (1 John 4:9)

"That we might live through Him." He lives in us through His Holy Spirit.

> In this is love, not that we loved God, but that He
> loved us and sent His Son to be the propitiation for
> our sins. Beloved, if God so loved us, we also ought
> to love one another. No one has seen God at any
> time. If we love one another, God abides in us, and
> His love has been perfected in us. By this we know
> that we abide in Him, and He in us, because He
> has given us of His Spirit. And we have seen and
> testify that the Father has sent the Son as Savior of
> the world. Whoever confesses that Jesus is the Son
> of God, God abides in him, and he in God. (1 John
> 4:10–15)

> Whoever believes that Jesus is the Christ is born
> of God, and everyone who loves Him who begot
> also loves him who is begotten of Him. By this we
> know that we love the children of God, when we
> love God and keep His commandments. For this is

the love of God, that we keep His commandments. And His commandments are not burdensome. For whatever is born of God overcomes the world. And this is the victory that has overcome the world—our faith. Who is he who overcomes the world, but he who believes that Jesus is the Son of God? This is He who came by water and blood—Jesus Christ; not only by water, but by water and blood. And it is the Spirit who bears witness, because the Spirit is truth. (1 John 5:1–6)

If we receive the witness of men, the witness of God is greater; for this is the witness of God which He has testified of His Son. He who believes in the Son of God has the witness in himself; he who does not believe God has made Him a liar, because he has not believed the testimony that God has given of His Son. And this is the testimony: that God has given us eternal life, and this life is in His Son. He who has the Son has life; he who does not have the Son of God does not have life. These things I have written to you who believe in the name of the Son of God, that you may know that you have eternal life, and that you may continue to believe in the name of the Son of God. Now this is the confidence that we have in Him, that if we ask anything according to His will, He hears us. (1 John 5:9–14)

We know that whoever is born of God does not sin; but he who has been born of God keeps himself, and the wicked one does not touch him. We know that we are of God, and the whole world lies under the sway of the wicked one. And we know that the Son of God has come and has given us an understanding, that we may know Him who is true; and we are in Him who is true, in His Son Jesus Christ. This is the true God and eternal life. (1 John 5:18–20)

Chapter 23

THE NAME OF JESUS CHRIST OF NAZARETH

"Fear not, for I am with you; I will bring your descendants from the east, And gather you from the west; I will say to the north, 'Give them up!' And to the south, 'Do not keep them back!' Bring My sons from afar, And My daughters from the ends of the earth—Everyone who is called by My name, Whom I have created for My glory; I have formed him, yes, I have made him." (Isaiah 43:5–7)

You shall be called by a new name, Which the mouth of the LORD will name. (Isaiah 62:2)

God has witnessed to the name of Jesus Christ of Nazareth:

At that time Jerusalem shall be called The Throne of the LORD, and all the nations shall be gathered to it, to the name of the LORD, to Jerusalem. No more shall they follow the dictates of their evil hearts. (Jeremiah 3:17)

> O LORD, I know the way of man is not in himself;
> It is not in man who walks to direct his own steps.
> O LORD, correct me, but with justice; Not in
> Your anger, lest you bring me to nothing. Pour
> out Your fury on the Gentiles, who do not know
> You, And on the families who do not call on Your
> name; For they have eaten up Jacob, Devoured him
> and consumed him, And made his dwelling place
> desolate. (Jeremiah 10:23–25)

Jesus spent His entire ministry proclaiming the Gospel: that He was the fulfillment of the Scriptures; that He was the Way, the Truth, and the Life; and that no one could come to the Father except through Him. This is the name that Jesus proclaimed. The name of Jesus Christ of Nazareth is above every other name in heaven and on earth. In the Old Testament, calling on the name of the LORD brought about physical benefits. Moses was introduced to a new name for God:

> And God spoke to Moses and said to him: "I am
> the LORD. I appeared to Abraham, to Isaac, and to
> Jacob, as God Almighty, but by My name LORD I
> was not known to them." (Exodus 6:2–3)

Moses introduced a covenant that had promises based on obedience to a law of sacrificial offerings made through a physical priesthood. The New Testament put away the Old Covenant and ushered in the New Covenant, which is based on new promises and new laws. In the commissioning of this New Covenant, the LORD sanctified a new name: the name of Jesus Christ of Nazareth, High Priest forever, according to the order of Melchizedek.

> Then Moses said to God, "Indeed, when I come to
> the children of Israel and say to them, 'The God

of your fathers has sent me to you,' and they say to me, 'What is His name?' What shall I say to them?" And God said to Moses, "I Am Who I Am." And He said, "Thus you shall say to the children of Israel, 'I Am has sent me to you.'" Moreover God said to Moses, "Thus you shall say to the children of Israel: 'The LORD God of your fathers, the God of Abraham, the God of Isaac, and the God of Jacob, has sent me to you. This is My name forever, and this is My memorial to all generations.' "Go and gather the elders of Israel together, and say to them, 'The LORD God of your fathers, the God of Abraham, of Isaac, and of Jacob, appeared to me, saying, "I have surely visited you and seen what is done to you in Egypt."' (Exodus 3:13–16)

God chose to reveal Himself to Israel in stages. Each stage builds on the previous one. The person of God and His character traits never change. He is immutable. We are gradually introduced into the power of His name and His plan of salvation.

Then Moses and the children of Israel sang this song to the LORD, and spoke, saying: "I will sing to the LORD, For He has triumphed gloriously! The horse and its rider He has thrown into the sea! The LORD is my strength and song, And He has become my salvation; He is my God, and I will praise Him; My father's God, and I will exalt Him. The LORD is a man of war; The LORD is His name. Pharaoh's chariots and his army He has cast into the sea; His chosen captains also are drowned in the Red Sea. The depths have covered them; They sank to the bottom like a stone. Your right hand, O LORD, has become glorious in power; Your right hand, O LORD, has dashed the enemy in pieces. And in the greatness of Your excellence You have overthrown those who rose against You; You sent forth Your wrath; It consumed them like stubble. And with the blast of Your nostrils The waters were gathered together; The floods stood upright like a heap; The depths congealed in the heart of the sea. The enemy said, 'I will pursue, I will overtake, I will divide the spoil; My desire shall be satisfied on them. I will draw my sword, My hand shall destroy them.' You blew with Your wind, The sea covered them; They sank like lead in the mighty waters. Who is like You, O LORD, among the gods? Who is like You, glorious in holiness, Fearful in praises, doing wonders? You stretched out Your right hand; The earth swallowed them. You in Your mercy have led forth The people whom You have redeemed; You have guided them in Your strength To Your holy habitation. The people will hear and be afraid; Sorrow will take hold of the inhabitants of Philistia. Then the chiefs of Edom will be dismayed; The mighty men of Moab, Trembling will take hold of them; All the inhabitants of Canaan will melt away. Fear and dread will fall on them; By the greatness of Your arm They will be as still as a stone, Till Your people pass over, O LORD, Till the people pass over Whom You have purchased. You will bring them in and plant them In the mountain of Your inheritance, In the place, O LORD, which You have made For Your own dwelling, The sanctuary, O LORD, which Your hands have established. The LORD shall reign forever and ever." (Exodus 15:1–18)

Moses's psalm denotes how Israel was saved from Pharaoh's attacking armies. It is actually prophetic of the saving grace that we find in the name of Jesus Christ of Nazareth. His name saves us from all of the fiery darts of the devil and his legions. The LORD whom this psalm is dedicated to is the LORD God of Israel.

Throughout the Old Testament, the attributes of the LORD are given. In God's world, in order to ensure credibility and have a sense of modesty and humility, a person waits on someone else to expound their virtues. This can be seen with the Pharisees' response to Jesus's assertion of who He was: "You testify of Yourself, Your testimony is not true."

In that instance, Jesus was merely backing up what God the Father had already witnessed of Jesus through utterances and miracles. The LORD—as was witnessed to in the Old Testament by His True Witness, the Christ—was and is the Almighty God, and there can be no other god before Him. His True Witness, the Christ, pointed out that God the Father was omnipotent and that there was absolutely no one who could challenge His authority or power.

No forces or powers—alone or combined—are able to thwart God's will, authority, or power. It is important to understand this because at no time was Satan or any other entity contradicting the plan of salvation that God had designed through Jesus Christ. His life and death on the cross were all according to design.

The main point from this understanding of God's absolute authority and power is that God, acting as Executor of Christ's Testament, holds a position of power and authority that can never be challenged by spirit or angel in heaven or on earth. He upholds Christ's authority by the power of His might.

Because of Jesus's complete and utter obedience in following God's salvation plan for humanity, He has been raised from the dead and has inherited a name above every other name. He is second only to God the Father Almighty. This claim of Jesus having inherited a name above every other name discourages any argument that the name of Jesus Christ of Nazareth can be defeated or overcome by any temptation, negative emotion, or spirit.

The crux of the problem in calling upon the name of Jesus Christ of Nazareth is that a person needs to believe who Jesus is. They must have faith. This is the admonition made by Jesus: "He who blasphemes the Holy Spirit will not be forgiven in this life or the next."

And just as Christ has given up His Godhead in order to become like man, mankind now has the means to give up their humanity and become like Christ.

Through the name of Jesus Christ of Nazareth we are afforded the Spirit of Christ which now has the ability to bond with our spirit. The bonding of our spirit with Christ's Spirit allows Christ to share the divine nature with us through His Spirit. This sharing of Christ's Spirit through our spirit allows Christ's Spirit to permeate out from our spirit into our soul and body, thereby making our total being blameless until the coming day of our Lord and Savior Jesus Christ. Rather than having sin enter into ourselves through our senses and emotions and corrupting our spirits, today we have the Spirit of Christ entering into ourselves through our spirit and thereby cleansing our spirits and as a result of that inward cleansing, purifying our senses and emotions.

> Now may the God of peace Himself sanctify you
> completely; and may your whole spirit, soul, and
> body be preserved blameless at the coming of our
> Lord Jesus Christ. He who calls you is faithful, who
> also will do it. (1 Thessalonians 5:23–24)

If a person does not believe that Jesus is the person that both He and His Father have testified to, there is absolutely no avenue for that person to take in order for that person to overcome temptation, have the divine nature formed in them or consequentially reap eternal life.

The consequences of sin is death, which has reigned since Adam.

Through sin and death, humanity has figuratively been divorced from God's original plan regarding this physical universe. This plan did not originally include death. This divorce has excluded humanity from eternal life. Through joining in Satan's rebellion, humanity inherited death. Satan introduced sin and death into the world. Remember who the god of this world is. Today, we have the opportunity to enter into a New Covenant that wasn't available to those prior to Jesus's resurrection.

> But Joshua said to the people, "You cannot serve the LORD, for He is a holy God. He is a jealous God; He will not forgive your transgressions nor your sins." (Joshua 24:19)

> And behold, I propose to build a house for the name of the LORD My God, as the LORD spoke to my father David, saying, "Your son, whom I will set on your throne in your place, he shall build the house for My name." (1 Kings 5:5)

> He also built altars in the house of the LORD, of which the LORD had said, "In Jerusalem I will put My name." (2 Kings 21:4)

> In the house of which the LORD had said to David and to Solomon his son, "In this house and in Jerusalem, which I have chosen out of all the tribes of Israel, I will put My name forever." (2 Kings 21:7)

> On that day David first delivered this psalm into the hand of Asaph and his brethren, to thank the LORD: Oh, give thanks to the LORD! Call upon His name; Make known His deeds among the peoples! Sing to Him, sing psalms to Him; Talk of

all His wondrous works! Glory in His holy name;
Let the hearts of those rejoice who seek the LORD!
Seek the LORD and His strength; Seek His face
evermore! Remember His marvellous works which
He has done, His wonders, and the judgments
of His mouth, O seed of Israel His servant, You
children of Jacob, His chosen ones! (1 Chronicles
16:7–13)

Sing to the LORD, all the earth; Proclaim the good
news of His salvation from day to day. Declare His
glory among the nations, His wonders among all
peoples. (1 Chronicles 16:23–24)

So let it be established, that Your name may be
magnified forever, saying, "The LORD of hosts,
the God of Israel, is Israel's God." And let the house
of Your servant David be established before You. (1
Chronicles 17:24)

And God sent an angel to Jerusalem to destroy
it. As he was destroying, the LORD looked and
relented of the disaster, and said to the angel who
was destroying, "It is enough; now restrain your
hand." And the angel of the LORD stood by the
threshing floor of Ornan the Jebusite. (1 Chronicles
21:15)

Therefore, the angel of the LORD commanded
Gad to say to David that David should go and erect
an altar to the LORD on the threshing floor of
Ornan the Jebusite. (1 Chronicles 21:18)

Then David said, "This is the house of the LORD God, and this is the altar of burnt offering for Israel." (1 Chronicles 22:1)

"Since the day that I brought My people out of the land of Egypt, I have chosen no city from any tribe of Israel in which to build a house, that My name might be there, nor did I choose any man to be a ruler over My people Israel. Yet I have chosen Jerusalem, that My name may be there, and I have chosen David to be over My people Israel. "Now it was in the heart of my father David to build a temple for the name of the LORD God of Israel. But the LORD said to my father David, 'Whereas it was in your heart to build a temple for My name, you did well in that it was in your heart. Nevertheless you shall not build the temple, but your son who will come from your body, he shall build the temple for My name.'" (2 Chronicles 6:5–9)

"Behold, the former things are come to pass, And new things do I declare; Before they spring forth I tell you of them." (Isaiah 42:9) God had His prophets reveal where His salvation plan would take place. The story of Abraham sacrificing his son Isaac on the Mount of Moriah. The story of how God had compassion on Israel and stopped the destroying angel from going any further on his path of destruction at the threshing floor of Ornan the Jebusite. The story of how David was directed to build an altar on Ornan's threshing floor. All witnesses to God's testimony that He had appointed the city of Jerusalem, on the Mount of Moriah, at Ornan's threshing floor, to be where He would reveal the name that is above every other name that is in heaven and on earth. The name that we have discovered to be the name of Jesus Christ of Nazareth. The name and only name in which lies the only hope for humanity.

This physical temple that David's son Solomon built is again a copy of the True. The True Temple would be raised up by David's Heir, Jesus Christ. This True Temple is the one that shall never be shaken or ever be destroyed. This True Temple has its reflection in the church of God, the body of Christ and shines in the hearts of those being saved. The True Temple shall be glorified once Christ has made His final appearance.

> When the heavens are shut up and there is no rain because they have sinned against You, when they pray toward this place and confess Your name, and turn from their sin because You afflict them, then hear in heaven, and forgive the sin of Your servants, Your people Israel, that You may teach them the good way in which they should walk. (2 Chronicles 6:26–27)

> And Asa cried out to the LORD his God, and said, "Lord, it is nothing for You to help, whether with many or with those who have no power; help us, O LORD our God, for we rest on You, and in Your name we go against this multitude. O LORD, You are our God; do not let man prevail against You!" (2 Chronicles 14:11)

> In this house and in Jerusalem, which I have chosen out of all the tribes of Israel, I will put My name forever. (2 Chronicles 33:7)

> Yes, in the way of Your judgments, O Lord, we have waited for You; The desire of our soul is for Your name And for the remembrance of You. (Isaiah 26:8)

And those who know Your name will put their trust in You; For You, LORD, have not forsaken those who seek You. (Psalm 9:10)

Some trust in chariots, and some in horses; But we will remember the name of the LORD our God. (Psalm 20:7)

Through You we will push down our enemies; Through Your name we will trample those who rise up against us. (Psalm 44:5)

Save me, O God, by Your name, And vindicate me by Your strength. (Psalm 54:1)

So I will sing praise to Your name forever, That I may daily perform my vows. (Psalm 61:8)

Pour out Your wrath on the nations that do not know You, And on the kingdoms that do not call on Your name. (Psalm 79:6)

Fill their faces with shame, That they may seek Your name, O LORD. Let them be confounded and dismayed forever; Yes, let them be put to shame and perish. That they may know that You, whose name alone is the LORD, Are the Most High over all the earth. (Psalm 83:16–18)

All nations surrounded me, But in the name of the LORD I will destroy them. They surrounded me, Yes, they surrounded me; But in the name of the LORD I will destroy them. They surrounded me like bees; They were quenched like a fire of thorns;

For in the name of the LORD I will destroy them. You pushed me violently, that I might fall, But the LORD helped me. The LORD is my strength and song, And He has become my salvation. (Psalm 118:10–14)

Our help is in the name of the LORD, Who made heaven and earth. (Psalm 124:8)

The name of the LORD is a strong tower; The righteous run to it and are safe. (Proverbs 18:10)

"Then you shall know that I am the LORD, when I have dealt with you for My name's sake, not according to your wicked ways nor according to your corrupt doings, O house of Israel," says the LORD God. (Ezekiel 20:44)

And it shall come to pass That whoever calls on the name of the LORD Shall be saved. For in Mount Zion and in Jerusalem there shall be deliverance, As the remnant whom the LORD calls. (Joel 2:32)

I will leave in your midst A meek and humble people, And they shall trust in the name of the LORD. The remnant of Israel shall do no unrighteousness And speak no lies, Nor shall a deceitful tongue be found in their mouth; For they shall feed their flocks and lie down, And no one shall make them afraid. (Zephaniah 3:12–13)

Christ was not the God of the Old Testament. The God of the Old Testament and the New Testament is and always will be our Sovereign Lord and Father Almighty God. Whoever has attempted to masquerade as God and receive the worship that is reserved for God throughout both the Old and New Testaments is the one who has been identified as the "god of this world." Angels cannot be trusted.

Whatever God has shown humanity in regard to His salvation plan, Satan has twisted and manipulated it in order to keep humanity firmly planted in the mire of their existence. Humanity is firmly planted in the physical here and now. Jesus Christ bears the image of God, His Father, and the offspring of the god of this world bear the same image as their god and father.

Now that Jesus has inherited a name above every other name, He deserves to be worshipped just as the Father is worshipped. Because Jesus inherited this name above every other name, it means that the Testator who bequeathed this inheritance to Him was originally in possession of this name, which is above every other name. Therefore, the only begotten Son of God, the Firstborn of creation, was in possession of the name that is above every other name. He, through His Testament, bequeathed that name to His Heir. Therefore, because Jesus has inherited a name that entitles Him to be worshipped, the One who bequeathed this name to Him was deserving to be worshipped as well.

This seems to be a contradiction in terms but it actually further defines the character of Christ and the relationship between the Father and the Son. To explain it in human terms we can imagine a man owning a department store. The man appoints his son to manage the affairs of the store. The son has the authority to buy, sell and carry out all of the normal business practices on a daily basis. Title to the store is still held by the Father. A buyer or seller would have their business dealings with the son but the entire enterprise is still owned by the father.

> Let this mind be in you which was also in Christ Jesus, who, being in the form of God, did not consider it robbery to be equal to God, but made

> Himself of no reputation, taking the form of a bondservant, and coming in the likeness of men. And being found in the appearance as a man, He humbled Himself and became obedient to the point of death, even the death of the cross. Therefore God also has highly exalted Him and given Him the name that is above every name, that at the name of Jesus every knee should bow, of those in heaven, and of those on earth, and that every tongue should confess that Jesus Christ is Lord, to the glory of God the Father. (Philippians 2:5–11)

This is extremely revealing about the character of Christ. Notice "who, being in the form of God, did not consider it robbery to be equal to God, but made Himself of no reputation." In the Old Testament as well as in the time that Christ spent in the flesh, Christ made Himself of no reputation. The manner in which He conducted Himself in the flesh is the manner in which He conducted Himself while in the person of the High Priest forever, according to the order of Melchizedek. He passed all honor and glory over to His Father, our Sovereign LORD and Father, Almighty God.

Christ, in every aspect of His person, is humble, harmless, and meek. In the Old Testament—as well as during His sojourn on this earth—Christ was inconspicuous. He deflected all honor and glory to His Father in heaven. As did Joseph when he took the form of a servant, went out from his father, Jacob, and ministered to his brothers. Christ has also gone out from our Sovereign LORD and Father and ministered to Israel. In some respects, Christ could be considered to be the God of the Old Testament, but His whole persona would not allow Him to be viewed as such. Certainly one of the reasons why God our Father loves Him so much.

> Take My yoke upon you and learn from Me, for I
> am gentle and lowly in heart, and you will find rest
> for your souls. (Matthew 11:29)

Those in the Spirit are having this Spirit formed in them.

Christ, at that time, was the betrothed to humanity. As stated in the law, a father and a son cannot go into the same woman; therefore, humanity could never have been betrothed to God the Father. In the Old Testament, because Christ was the Son of God and the betrothed, He was deserving of honor. In the same way, we are reminded in 1 Peter 3:6 that Sarah obeyed her husband, Abraham, calling him lord. In Joshua 5:13–15, when Christ presented Himself in the person of the Commander of the army of the LORD, Joshua fell down and worshipped Him.

In the Bible, whenever someone is in the presence of an angel from God and that someone attempts to worship them, they are immediately admonished—except for Satan who craves to be worshipped. In the Old Testament, Christ was the True Witness of God. He testified to the prophets of God, concerning God's salvation plan, through His Spirit.

The Pharisees admonished Jesus for testifying of Himself. The testimony of yourself is not considered accurate because it could possibly be impaired by ego. Therefore, when all of the benevolent characteristics attributed to God are recited, someone other than God is doing the reciting. Jesus stated that no one had ever seen or heard God at any time.

> Then the seventy returned with joy, saying, "Lord,
> even the demons are subject to us in Your name."
> And He said to them, "I saw Satan fall like lighting
> from heaven. Behold, I give you the authority to
> trample on the power of the enemy, and nothing
> shall by any means hurt you." (Luke 10:17–19)

> All things have been delivered to Me by My Father,
> and no one knows who the Son is except the Father,
> and who the Father is except the Son, and the one
> to whom the Son wills to reveal Him. (Luke 10:22)

All things were delivered to Jesus by the Father through the inheritance of the name that is above every other name—even the name, Jesus Christ of Nazareth. Before Jesus's death on the cross He was in possession of all of the authority that He had been in possession of in the Old Testament. All demons, evil spirits and even Satan, when in Jesus's presence had to submit to Jesus's command; as all of Jesus's commands were being upheld by the Power of God. God the Father is the Executor of His Son's Estate or Testament. Salvation can only happen according to the way that God has laid it out. After Jesus's death and resurrection, on the day of Pentecost, Jesus received His inheritance and God granted Him the authority to establish a New Covenant. That New Covenant realizes the promise that was promised to Abraham. And Jesus breathed out His Spirit onto His disciples.

> For as the Father raises the dead and gives life to
> them, even so the Son gives life to whom He will.
> "For the Father judges no one, but has committed
> all judgment to the Son, "that all should honour the
> Son just as they honour the Father. He who does
> not honour the Son does not honour the Father who
> sent Him. (John 5:21–23)

> You did not choose Me, but I chose you and
> appointed you that you should go and bear fruit,
> and that your fruit should remain, that whatever
> you ask the Father in My name He may give you.
> (John 15:16)

And in that day you will ask Me nothing. Most assuredly, I say to you, whatever you ask the Father in My name He will give you. Until Now you have asked nothing in My name. Ask, and you will receive, that your joy may be full. (John 16:23–24)

In that day you will ask in My name, and I do not say to you that I shall pray the Father for you. (John 16:26)

Jesus is commanding that we pray directly to Jesus. He is the Mediator between God and man. God knows what you need before you ask Jesus.

For the Father Himself loves you, because you have loved Me, and have believed that I came forth from God. (John 16:27)

I have manifested Your name to the men whom You have given Me out of the world. (John 17:6)

Now I am no longer in the world, but these are in the world, and I come to You. Holy Father, keep through Your name those whom You have given Me, that they may be one as We are. While I was with them in the world, I kept them in Your name. (John 17:11–12)

The name the Father has sanctified above every other name is Jesus Christ of Nazareth. The apostles claimed they had power over all of the unclean spirits through Jesus's name.

And I have declared to them Your name, and will declare it, that the love with which You loved Me may be in them. (John 17:26)

And truly Jesus did many other signs in the presence of His disciples, which are not written in this book; but these are written that you may believe that Jesus is the Christ, the Son of God, and that believing you may have life in His name. (John 20:30–31)

And it shall come to pass That whoever calls on the name of the LORD Shall be saved. (Acts 2:21)

All prophecies in the Old Testament pointed to Christ. The references to the "name of the Lord" were actually pointing to Christ. Christ's name is the name that God has ordained to offer salvation to the world.

For David did not ascend into the heavens, but he says himself: "The LORD said to my Lord, 'Sit at My right hand, Till I make Your enemies Your footstool.' Therefore let all the house of Israel know assuredly that God has made this Jesus, whom you crucified, both Lord and Christ." (Acts 2:34–36)

Now when they heard this, they were cut to the heart, and said to Peter and the rest of the apostles, "Men and brethren, what shall we do?" Then Peter said to them, "Repent, and let every one of you be baptized in the name of Jesus Christ for the remission of sins; and you shall receive the gift of the Holy Spirit. "For the promise is to you and to your children, and to all who are afar off, as many as the Lord our God will call." (Acts 2:37–39)

> And a certain man lame from his mother's womb was carried, whom they laid daily at the gate of the temple which is called Beautiful, to ask alms from those who entered the temple; who, seeing Peter and John about to go into the temple, asked for alms. And fixing his eyes on him, with John, Peter said, "Look at us." So Peter said, "Silver and gold I do not have, but what I do have I give you: In the name of Jesus Christ of Nazareth, rise up and walk." (Acts 3:2–5)

The apostles did physical miracles in the name of Jesus Christ of Nazareth in order to prove the authenticity of Jesus's name. These miracles were physical manifestations of the spiritual miracles that Jesus is doing in the Christian community today. Today, we look to Jesus—the Author and Finisher of our faith—to purify for Himself a people that He is making holy and acceptable, in order that we may be able to stand before our Sovereign LORD and Father Almighty God at Christ's return.

> And His name, through faith in His name, has made this man strong, whom you see and know. Yes, the faith which comes through Him has given him this perfect soundness in the presence of you all. (Acts 3:16)

> Then Peter, filled with the Holy Spirit, said to them, "Rulers of the people and elders of Israel: If we this day are judged for a good deed done to a helpless man, by what means he has been made well, let it be known to you all, and to all the people of Israel, that by the name of Jesus Christ of Nazareth, whom you crucified, whom God raised from the dead, by Him this man stands here before you whole. This

is the 'stone which was rejected by you builders, which has become the chief cornerstone.' Nor is there salvation in any other, for there is no other name under heaven given among men by which we must be saved." (Acts 4:8–12)

So one came and told them, saying, "Look, the men whom you put in prison are standing in the temple and teaching the people!" Then the captain went with the officers and brought them without violence, for they feared the people, lest they should be stoned. And when they had brought them, they set them before the council. And the high priest asked them, saying, "Did we not strictly command you not to teach in this name? And look, you have filled Jerusalem with your doctrine, and intend to bring this Man's blood on us!" (Acts 5:25–28)

Him God has exalted to His right hand to be Prince and Saviour, to give repentance to Israel and forgiveness of sins. And we are His witnesses to these things, and so also is the Holy Spirit whom God has given to those who obey Him. (Acts 5:31–32)

They commanded that they should not speak in the name of Jesus, and let them go. So they departed from the presence of the council, rejoicing that they were counted worthy to suffer shame for His name. (Acts 5:40–41)

And they stoned Stephen as he was calling on God and saying, "Lord Jesus, receive my spirit." (Acts 7:59)

Stephen, the first documented Christian martyr, prayed directly to Jesus—as we are commanded.

> But when they believed Philip as he preached the things concerning the kingdom of God and the name of Jesus Christ, Both men and women were baptized. (Acts 8:12)

> To Him all the prophets witness that, through His name, whoever believes in Him will receive remission of sins. (Acts 10:43)

> And he commanded them to be baptized in the name of the Lord. (Acts 10:48)

> With our beloved Barnabas and Paul, men who have risked their lives for the name of our Lord Jesus Christ. (Acts 15:25–26)

> Now it happened, as we went to prayer, that a certain slave girl possessed with a spirit of divination met us, who brought her masters much profit by fortune-telling. This girl followed Paul and us, and cried out, saying, "These men are the servants of the Most High God, who proclaim to us the way of salvation." And this she did for many days. But Paul, greatly annoyed, turned and said to the spirit, "I command you in the name of Jesus Christ to come out of her." And he came out that very hour. (Acts 15:16–18)

> Then Paul answered, "What do you mean by weeping and breaking my heart? For I am ready

not only to be bound, but also to die at Jerusalem for the name of the Lord Jesus." (Acts 21:13)

"And now why are you waiting? Arise and be baptized, and wash away your sins, calling on the name of the Lord." (Acts 22:16)

We should call on the name of the Lord Jesus Christ.

For "whoever calls on the name of the Lord shall be saved." (Romans 10:13)

With all who in every place call on the name of Jesus Christ our Lord. (1 Corinthians 1:2)

No temptation has overtaken you except such is common to man; but God is faithful, who will not allow you to be tempted beyond what you are able, but with the temptation will also make the way of escape, that you may be able to bear it. (1 Corinthians 10:13)

Jesus said to His disciples, "I will not leave you orphans." Jesus promised to send the Helper. God has provided us a Way to bear every temptation. The Way is the name of Jesus Christ of Nazareth! All who call upon the name of Jesus Christ will be saved from any and all temptation. Those who believe in the name of the only begotten Son of God, the Firstborn of creation, the High Priest forever, according to the order of Melchizedek, the Christ, will be saved.

And what is the exceeding greatness of His power toward us who believe, according to the working of His mighty power which He worked in Christ when

> He raised Him from the dead and seated Him at
> His right hand in the heavenly places, far above all
> principality and power and might and dominion,
> and every name that is named, not only in this age
> but also in that which is to come. And He put all
> things under His feet, and gave Him to be head
> over all things to the church. which is His body,
> the fullness of Him who fills all in all. (Ephesians
> 1:19–23)

Every spirit and angel in heaven and earth and under the earth must
submit to the name of Jesus Christ of Nazareth. We are counted as
children of God, and through the name of Jesus, we have been freed
from the rulers of this age—even Satan and His legions—through
faith in His name. You must believe that He is the only begotten
Son of God, Firstborn of all creation, through whom all things were
created.

We do not ask Jesus to deliver us from temptation, but we thank
Him for having delivered us. All of the works have been completed.
One must have faith. Without faith, it is impossible to please God.
Once baptized into the name of Jesus Christ of Nazareth and having
received His Spirit, we have entered into His rest. This rest was
created in the beginning of creation and is the True Sabbath. We
will still suffer temptation, but the instant we call on the name of
Jesus, giving thanks to Him and our Sovereign LORD and Father,
Almighty God, for this freedom, we shall be freed. He has promised
not to leave us orphans.

> Rejoice always, pray without ceasing, in everything
> give thanks; for this is the will of God in Christ
> Jesus for you. (1 Thessalonians 5:16–18)

"Pray without ceasing." As Christ exemplified in His life, prayer
is a weapon where faith is the ammunition. We will be tempted.

Remember Jesus's temptation in the Garden of Gethsemane. "His sweat became like great drops of blood falling down to the ground." It is doubtful that many have suffered the anxiety and stress that Jesus did before His arrest. He did not just recite a passage from the bible and give up. He cried, He begged and He pleaded. Sin is still sin and temptation is still temptation, but God has provided us a way out and He has promised that we will not be tempted beyond what we're able to withstand. The battles that were fought in the Old Testament times were analogous to the battles we fight on the spiritual front today. These are real battles against a foe that we are completely unmatched against on our own. We are encouraged to wage the good warfare. It is only through the name of Jesus Christ of Nazareth that affords us any hope in this battle. Remember this battle is to the death.

Another dimension of prayer is fasting. Jesus was quick to point out:

> "However, this kind does not go out except by prayer and fasting." (Matthew 17:21)

What should be assumed to be a common practice in first century Judaism was the practice of fasting two days a week. Jesus spoke a parable in Luke 18:11–12, of a Pharisee boasting to fasting twice a week. Although this particular Pharisee's attitude toward fasting prevented him from receiving a favourable accounting for his efforts, fasting is considered to be a mainstay in a Christian's arsenal of prayer tactics. Jesus actually spent the time to instruct His disciples on how one should comport oneself while one is fasting. Paul in 1&2 Corinthians exhorted his followers to fast often. It can be concluded that fasting is an important facet to enrich a Christian's prayer life. Remember, that Jesus admonished His disciples that their righteousness should exceed the righteousness of the Pharisees.

And you He made alive, who were dead in trespasses and sins, in which you once walked according to the course of this world, according to the prince of the power of the air, the spirit who now works in the sons of disobedience, among whom also we all once conducted ourselves in the lusts of our flesh, fulfilling the desires of the flesh and of the mind, and were by nature children of wrath, just as the others. But God, who is rich in mercy, because of His great love with which He loved us, even when we were dead in trespasses, made us alive together with Christ (by grace you have been saved), and raised us up together, and made us sit together in the heavenly places in Christ Jesus, that in the ages to come He might show the exceeding riches of His grace in His kindness toward us in Christ Jesus. For by grace you have been saved through faith, and that not of yourselves; it is the gift of God, not of works, lest anyone should boast. For we are His workmanship, created in Christ Jesus for good works, which God prepared beforehand that we should walk in them. (Ephesians 2:1–10)

Therefore God also has highly exalted Him and given Him the name which is above every name, that at the name of Jesus every knee should bow, of those in heaven, and of those on earth, and of those under the earth, and that every tongue should confess that Jesus Christ is Lord, to the glory of God the Father. Therefore, my beloved, as you have always obeyed, not as in my presence only, but now much more in my absence, work out your own salvation with fear and trembling; for it is God who works in you both to will and to do for His good pleasure. (Philippians 2:9–13)

Therefore we also pray always for you that our God would count you worthy of this calling, and fulfill all the good pleasure of His goodness and the work of faith with power, that the name of our Lord Jesus Christ may be glorified in you, and you in Him, according to the grace of our God and the Lord Jesus Christ. (2 Thessalonians 1:11–12)

But we are bound to give thanks to God always for you, brethren beloved by the Lord, because God from the beginning chose you for salvation through sanctification by the Spirit and belief in the truth. (2 Thessalonians 1:13)

But we command you, brethren, in the name of our Lord Jesus Christ. (2 Thessalonians 3:6)

Flee also youthful lusts; but pursue righteousness, faith, love, peace with those who call on the Lord out of a pure heart. (2 Timothy 2:22)

For God is not unjust to forget your work and labor of love which you have shown toward His name, in that you have ministered to the saints, and do minister. (Hebrews 6:10)

We have an alter from which those who serve the tabernacle have no right to eat. For the bodies of those animals, whose blood is brought into the sanctuary by the high priest for sin, are burned outside the camp. Therefore Jesus also, that He might sanctify the people with His own blood, suffered outside the gate. Therefore let us go forth to Him, outside the camp, bearing His reproach. For here we have no continuing city, but we seek the one to come. Therefore by Him let us continually offer the sacrifice of praise to God, that is, the fruit of our lips, giving thanks to His name. (Hebrews 13:10–15)

We give thanks to His name because all of this design was completed from the foundation of the world. We enter into the rest that was created on the seventh day. The battle has already been won. Jesus won the battle when God the Father raised Him from the dead and seated Him at His right hand.

When a person is tempted, they don't pray to be delivered from temptation; instead, they give thanks and praise to Jesus Christ of Nazareth and our Sovereign LORD and Father Almighty God that they have been counted worthy to enter into God's rest. They are miraculously freed from temptation. This Sabbath rest was created on the seventh day of creation. This Sabbath rest, God's salvation plan, is the mystery that has been hidden since the foundation of the world. We find this rest in the name of Jesus Christ of Nazareth. Jesus is the Sabbath rest.

He indeed was foreordained before the foundation of the world, but was manifested in these last times for you who through Him believe in God who raised Him from the dead and gave Him glory, so that your faith and hope are in God. Since you have purified your souls in obeying the truth through the Spirit, in sincere love of the brethren, love one another fervently with a pure heart, having been born again, not of corruptible seed but incorruptible, through the word of God which lives and abides forever. (1 Peter 1:20–23)

There is also an antitype which now saves us—baptism (not the removal of the filth of the flesh, but the answer of a good conscience toward God), through the resurrection of Jesus Christ, who has gone into heaven and is at the right hand of God, angels and authorities and powers having been made subject to Him. (1 Peter 3:21–22)

If anyone speaks, let him speak as the oracles of God. If anyone ministers, let him do it as with the ability which God supplies, that in all things God may be glorified through Jesus Christ, to whom belong the glory and the dominion forever and ever. Amen. (1 Peter 4:11)

My little children, let us not love in word or in tongue, but in deed and in truth. And by this we know that we are of the truth, and shall assure our hearts before Him. For if our heart condemns us, God is greater than our heart, and knows all things. Beloved, if our heart does not condemn us, we have confidence toward God. And whatever we ask we receive from Him, because we keep His commandments and do those things that are pleasing in His sight. And this is His commandment: that we should believe on the name of His Son Jesus Christ and love one another, as He gave us commandment. Now he who keeps His commandment abides in Him, and He in him, And by this we know that He abides in us, by the Spirit whom He has given us. (1 John 3:18–24)

The Spirit keeps us from sin—even the Spirit of our Lord Jesus Christ.

> In this the love of God was manifested toward us, that God has sent His only begotten Son into the world, that we might live through Him. In this is love, not that we loved God, but that He loved us and sent His Son to be the propitiation for our sins. Beloved, if God so loved us, we also ought to love one another. No one has seen God at any time. If we love one another, God abides in us, and His love has been perfected in us. By this we know that we abide in Him, and He in us, because He has given us of His Spirit. And we have seen and testify that the Father has sent the Son as Savior of the world. Whoever confesses that Jesus is the Son of God, God abides in him, and he in God. (1 John 4:9–15)

> If we receive the witness of men, the witness of God is greater; for this is the witness of God which He has testified of His Son. He who believes in the Son of God has the witness in himself; he who does not believe God has made Him a liar, because he has not believed the testimony that God has given of His Son. And this is the testimony: that God has given us eternal life, and this life is in His Son. He who has the Son has life; he who does not have the Son of God does not have life. These things I have written to you who believe in the name of the Son of God, that you may know that you have eternal life, and that you may continue to believe in the name of the Son of God. Now this is the confidence that we have in Him, that if we ask anything according to His will, He hears us. (1 John 5:9–14)

"Ask anything according to His will"—not according to our fleshly lusts. Ask anything according to sin and redemption. Once baptized, we can have confidence that we have received forgiveness from past sins because Jesus—through His Holy Spirit—keeps us from committing sins today. We no longer have a conscience of sin because we are no longer living in it.

Chapter 24

GIVING OF THANKS

Call upon Me in the day of trouble; I will deliver you, and you shall glorify Me. (Psalm 50:15)

Oh, that men would give thanks to the LORD for His goodness, And for His wonderful works to the children of men! Let them sacrifice the sacrifice of thanksgiving, And declare His works with rejoicing. (Psalm 107:21–22)

Oh, give thanks to the LORD, for He is good! For His mercy endures forever. Oh, give thanks to the God of gods! For His mercy endures forever. Oh, give thanks to the LORD of lords! For His mercy endures forever: To Him who alone does great wonders, For His mercy endures forever; To Him who by wisdom made the heavens, For His mercy endures forever; To Him who laid out the earth above the waters, For His mercy endures forever; To Him who made great lights, For His mercy endures forever—The sun to rule by day, For His mercy endures forever; The moon and stars to rule by night, For His mercy endures forever. To Him who struck Egypt in their firstborn, For His mercy endures forever; And brought out Israel from among them, For His mercy endures forever; With a strong hand, and with an outstretched arm, For His mercy endures forever; To Him who divided the Red Sea in two, For His mercy endures forever; And made Israel pass through the midst of it, For His mercy endures forever; But overthrew Pharaoh and His army in the Red Sea, For His mercy endures forever; To Him who led His people through the wilderness, For His mercy endures forever; To Him who struck down great kings, For His mercy endures forever; And slew famous kings, For His mercy endures forever—Sihon king of the Amorites, For His mercy endures forever; And Og King of Bashan, For His mercy endures forever—And gave their land as a heritage, For His mercy endures forever; A heritage to Israel His servant, For His mercy endures forever. Who remembered us in our lowly state, For His mercy endures forever; And rescued us from our enemies, For His mercy endures forever; Who gives food to all flesh, For His mercy endures forever. Oh, give thanks to the God of heaven! For His mercy endures forever. (Psalm 136:1–26)

The firstborn of Egypt represents the first Adam. Israel represents the LORD's firstborn, the Christ. The parting of the Red Sea represents baptism and the rejection of the flesh (Egypt).

Giving thanks always for all things to God the Father in the name of our Lord Jesus Christ. (Ephesians 5:20)

"The giving of thanks" occurs because all of the works have been completed. We pray directly to Jesus, the Mediator between God and man. When we are tempted, we don't just give thanks to God for providing us the means by which we are saved from temptation. Instead, we give thanks to both Jesus Christ of Nazareth and our Sovereign LORD and Father Almighty God for providing us the deliverance. All things are done by the will of God and Jesus is the personification of God's will. Draw close to Jesus, and the devil will flee from you. The just shall live by faith. There is no ego with God. God is glorified in His Son, Jesus Christ of Nazareth. God's glory is in seeing all of creation worshipping His Son.

Chapter 25

SUFFERING

The sacrifices of God are a broken spirit, A broken and a contrite heart—These, O God, You will not despise. (Psalm 51:17)

For to you it has been granted on behalf of Christ, not only to believe in Him, but also to suffer for His sake, having the same conflict which you saw in me and now hear is in me. (Philippians 1:29–30)

And you have forgotten the exhortation which speaks to you as to sons: "My son, do not despise the chastening of the LORD, Nor be discouraged when you are rebuked by Him; For whom the LORD loves He chastens, And scourges every son whom He receives." If you endure chastening, God deals with you as with sons; for what son is there whom a father does not chasten? But if you are without chastening, of which all have become partakers, then you are illegitimate and not sons. Furthermore, we have had human fathers who corrected us, and we paid them respect. Shall we not much more readily be in subjection to the Father of spirits and live? For they indeed for a few days chastened us as seemed best to them, but He for our profit, that we may be partakers of His holiness. Now no chastening seems to be joyful for the present, but painful; nevertheless, afterward it yields the peaceable fruit of righteousness to those who have been trained by it. Therefore strengthen the hands which hang down, and the feeble knees, and make straight paths for your feet, so that what is lame may not be dislocated, but rather be healed. Pursue peace with all people, and holiness, without which no one will see the Lord. (Hebrews 12:5–14)

Therefore, since Christ suffered in the flesh, arm yourselves also with the same mind, for he who has suffered in the flesh has ceased from sin. (1 Peter 4:1)

He "suffered in the flesh." He suffered and overcame temptation in order to help us in our times of temptation. He who gives in to temptation has not suffered.

That he no longer should live the rest of his time in the flesh for the lusts of men, but for the will of God. For we have spent enough of our past lifetime in doing the will of the Gentiles—when we walked in lewdness, lusts, drunkenness, revelries, drinking parties, and abominable idolatries. In regard to these, they think it strange that you do not run with them in the same flood of dissipation, speaking evil of you. They will give an account to Him who is ready to judge the living and the dead. (1 Peter 4:2–5)

They will accuse you of all manner of evil.

> Yet if anyone suffers as a Christian, let him not be
> ashamed, but let him glorify God in this matter. (1
> Peter 4:16)

What you suffer has nothing to do with the person or events that are
causing your suffering. Remember everything that is done is done
by the will of God. Everything that a convert or Christian suffers,
suffers by the will of God. It is through suffering that we come to
repentance and through suffering that the Spirit of God is formed
in our lowly bodies. When Joseph's brothers were reunited with
Him after He had become ruler over all of Egypt, He did not take
vengeance on them for selling him into slavery and making his life a
living hell. He realized the years he spent in slavery and incarceration
were God's will and had absolutely nothing to do with his brothers
at all. They may have very well acted out of the jealousy that they
felt toward their brother Joseph, but at the end of the day it was
God's will that allowed Satan to fester the emotions that incited his
brothers to behave as they did. All things work for the glory of God
and those who love Him.

Remember Paul when He stood guard over the clothes of those
who were stoning Stephen. Remember all of the early Christians
who Paul threw his lot against, and had incarcerated and murdered.
God was even able to use the evil intent that Paul held for these
early Christians to convert Paul and make him possibly one of the
greatest of Apostles.

Oh, how wonderful is our God and His ways past finding out.

> Who, in the days of His flesh, when He had offered
> up prayers and supplications, with vehement cries
> and tears to Him who was able to save Him from
> death, and was heard because of His godly fear,

though He was a Son, yet He learned obedience by the things which He suffered. And having been perfected, He became the author of eternal salvation to all who obey Him. (Hebrews 5:7–9)

Chapter 26

FORGIVENESS

Thus says the LORD God: "When I have gathered the house of Israel from the peoples among whom they are scattered, and am hallowed in them in the sight of the Gentiles, then they will dwell in their own land which I gave to My servant Jacob. And they will dwell safely there, build houses, and plant vineyards; yes, they will dwell securely, when I execute judgments on all those around them who despise them. Then they shall know that I am the LORD their God." (Ezekiel 28:25–26)

But go and learn what this means: "I desire mercy and not sacrifice." For I did not come to call the righteous, but sinners, to repentance. (Matthew 9:13)

Then Peter came to Him and said, "Lord, how often shall my brother sin against me, and I forgive him? Up to seven times?" Jesus said to him, "I do not say to you, up to seven times, but up to seventy times seven. "Therefore the kingdom of heaven is like a certain king who wanted to settle accounts with his servants. And when he had begun to settle accounts, one was brought to him who owed him ten thousand talents. But as he was not able to pay, his master commanded that he be sold, with his wife and children and all that he had, and that payment be made. The servant therefore fell down before him, saying, 'Master, have patience with me, and I will pay you all.' Then the master of that servant was moved with compassion, released him, and forgave him the debt. But that servant went out and found one of his fellow servants who owed him a hundred denarii; and he laid hands on him and took him by the throat, saying, 'Pay me what you owe!' So his fellow servant fell down at his feet and begged him, saying, 'Have patience with me, and I will pay you all.' And he would not, but went and threw him into prison till he should pay the debt. So when his fellow servants saw what had been done, they were very grieved, and came and told their master all that had been done. Then his master, after he had called him, said to him, 'You wicked servant! I forgave you all that debt because you begged me. Should you not also have had compassion on your fellow servant, just as I had pity on you?' And his master was angry, and delivered him to the torturers until he should pay all that was due to him. So My heavenly Father also will do to you if each of you, from his heart, does not forgive his brother his trespasses." (Matthew 18:21–35)

And forgive us our debts, As we forgive our debtors. (Matthew 6:12)

As we forgive affects our ability to be delivered from temptation and our sinful behavior.

> And do not lead us into temptation, But deliver us from the evil one, For Yours is the kingdom and the power and the glory forever. Amen. For if you forgive men their trespasses, your heavenly Father will also forgive you. But if you do not forgive men their trespasses, neither will your Father forgive your trespasses. (Matthew 6:13–15)

> And whenever you stand praying, if you have anything against anyone, forgive him, that your Father in heaven may also forgive you your trespasses. But if you do not forgive, neither will your Father in heaven forgive your trespasses. (Mark 11:25–26)

It is Christ in us who gives us the strength to forgive. Our responsibility is to forgive. We are not responsible for people forgiving us, though we are commanded not to cause offence. The more Christ is formed in us, the more we will see how all things have always worked for, and how all things always will work for good to those who love God.

> Now when they bring you to the synagogues and magistrates and authorities, do not worry about how or what you should answer, or what you should say. For the Holy Spirit will teach you in that very hour what you ought to say. (Luke 12:11–12)

> But love your enemies, do good, and lend, hoping for nothing in return; and your reward will be great, and you will be sons of the Most High. For He is kind to the unthankful and evil. Therefore be

merciful, just as your Father also is merciful. Judge not, and you shall not be judged, Condemn not, and you shall not be condemned. Forgive, and you will be forgiven. (Luke 6:35–37)

And Jesus answered and said to him, "Simon, I have something to say to you." So he said, "Teacher, say it." "There was a certain creditor who had two debtors. One owed five hundred denarii, and the other fifty. And when they had nothing with which to repay, he freely forgave them both. Tell Me, therefore, which of them will love him more?" Simon answered and said, "I suppose the one whom he forgave more." And He said to him, "You have rightly judged." Then He turned to the woman and said to Simon, "Do you see this woman? I entered your house; you gave Me no water for My feet, but she has washed My feet with her tears and wiped them with the hair of her head. You gave Me no kiss, but this woman has not ceased to kiss My feet since the time I came in. You did not anoint My head with oil, but this woman has anointed My feet with fragrant oil. Therefore I say to you, her sins, which are many, are forgiven, for she loved much. But to whom little is forgiven, the same loves little." (Luke 7:40–47)

Chapter 27

PERFECTION

So Samuel said: "Has the LORD as great delight in burnt offerings and sacrifices, As in obeying the voice of the LORD? Behold, to obey is better than sacrifice, And to heed than the fat of rams. For rebellion is as the sin of witchcraft, And stubbornness is as iniquity and idolatry, Because you have rejected the word of the LORD, He also has rejected you from being king." (1 Samuel 15:22–23)

My eyes shall be on the faithful of the land, That they may dwell with me; He who walks in a perfect way, He shall serve me. He who works deceit shall not dwell within my house; He who tells lies shall not continue in my presence. Early I will destroy all the wicked of the land, That I may cut off all the evildoers from the city of the LORD. (Psalm 101:6–8)

Having disarmed principalities and powers. He made a public spectacle of them, triumphing over them in it. (Colossians 2:15)

No one puts a piece of un-shrunk cloth on an old garment; for the patch pulls away from the garment, and the tear is made worse. Nor do they put new wine into old wineskins, or else the wineskins break, the wine is spilled, and the wineskins are ruined. But they put new wine into new wineskins, and both are preserved. (Matthew 9:16–17)

One must first repent and then be baptized in order to receive the Holy Spirit. "Then the LORD God said, 'Behold, the man has become like one of Us, to know good and evil. And now, lest he put out his hand and take also of the tree of life, and eat, and live forever"—.' (Genesis 3:22) Unless one believes the Gospel and repents, the Tree of Life, the Holy Spirit of God and the offer to live forever is denied.

Therefore consider the goodness and severity of God: on those who fell severity; but toward you, goodness, if you continue in His goodness. Otherwise you also will be cut off. And they also, if they do not continue in unbelief, will be grafted in, for God is able to graft them in again. For if you were cut out of the olive tree which is wild by nature, and were grafted contrary to nature into a cultivated olive tree, how much more will these, who are natural branches, be grafted into their own olive tree? For I do not desire, brethren, that you should be ignorant of this mystery, lest you should be wise in your own opinion, that blindness in part has happened to Israel until the fullness of the Gentiles has come in. And so all Israel will be saved, as it is written: "The Deliverer will come out of Zion, And He will turn away ungodliness from Jacob; For this is My covenant with them, When I take

away their sins." Concerning the gospel they are
enemies for your sake, but concerning the election
they are beloved for the sake of the fathers. For the
gifts and the calling of God are irrevocable. For as
you were once disobedient to God, yet have now
obtained mercy through their disobedience, even so
these also have been disobedient, that through the
mercy shown you they also may obtain mercy. For
God has committed them all to disobedience, that
He might have mercy on all. (Romans 11:22–32)

Originally the Jews were disobedient to the Gospel message. As a
result of their disobedience, salvation was offered to the Gentiles.
Now the Gentiles have fallen into disobedience and salvation is
returning full circle back to the Jews.

Oh, the depth of the riches both of the wisdom
and knowledge of God! How unsearchable are His
judgments and His ways past finding out! "For who
has known the mind of the Lord? Or who has been
His councillor? Or who has first given to Him And
it shall be repaid to him?" For of Him and through
Him and to Him are all things, to whom be glory
forever. Amen. (Romans 11:33–36)

I beseech you therefore, brethren, by the mercies of
God, that you present your bodies a living sacrifice,
holy, acceptable to God, which is your reasonable
service. And do not be conformed to this world, but
be transformed by the renewing of your mind, that
you may prove what is that good and acceptable and
perfect will of God. (Romans 12:1–2)

Let love be without hypocrisy. Abhor what is evil. Cling to what is good. Be kindly affectionate to one another with brotherly love, in honour giving preference to one another; not lagging in diligence, fervent in spirit, serving the Lord; rejoicing in hope, patient in tribulation, continuing steadfastly in prayer; distributing to the needs of the saints, given to hospitality. Bless those who persecute you; bless and do not curse. Rejoice with those who rejoice, and weep with those who weep. Be of the same mind toward one another. Do not set your mind on high things, but associate with the humble. Do not be wise in your own opinion. Repay no one evil for evil. Have regard for good things in the sight of all men. If it is possible, as much as depends on you, live peaceably with all men. Beloved, do not avenge yourselves, but rather give place to wrath; for it is written, "Vengeance is Mine, I will repay," says the Lord. Therefore "If your enemy is hungry, feed him; If he is thirsty, give him a drink; For in so doing you will heap coals of fire on his head." Do not be overcome by evil, but overcome evil with good. (Romans 12:9–21)

Let every soul be subject to the governing authorities. For there is no authority except from God, and the authorities that exist are appointed by God. Therefore whoever resists the authority resists the ordinance of God, and those who resist will bring judgment on themselves. For rulers are not a terror to good works, but to evil. Do you want to be unafraid of the authority? Do what is good, and you will have praise from the same. For he is God's minister to you for good. But if you do evil, be afraid; for he does not bear the sword in vain; for he is God's minister, an avenger to execute wrath on him who practices evil. Therefore you must be subject, not only because of wrath but also for conscience' sake. For because of this you also pay taxes, for they are God's ministers attending continually to this very thing. Render therefore to all their due: taxes to whom taxes are due, customs to whom customs, fear to whom fear, honour to whom honour. Owe no one anything except to love one another, for he who loves another has fulfilled the law. For the commandments, "You shall not commit adultery," "You shall not murder," "You shall not steal." "You shall not bear false witness," "You shall not covet," and if there is any other commandment, are all summed up in this saying, namely, "You shall love your neighbour as yourself." Love does no harm to a neighbour; therefore love is the fulfillment of the law. And do this, knowing the time, that now it is high time to awake out of sleep; for now our salvation is nearer than when we first believed. The night is far spent, the day is at hand. Therefore let us cast off the works of darkness, and let us put on the armour of light. Let us walk properly, as in the day, not in revelry and drunkenness, not in lewdness and lust, not in strife and envy. But put on the Lord Jesus Christ, and make no provisions for the flesh, to fulfill its lusts. (Romans 13:1–14)

I thank my God always concerning you for the grace of God which was given to you by Christ Jesus, that you were enriched in every thing by Him in all utterance and all knowledge, even as the testimony of Christ was confirmed in you, so that you come short in no gift, eagerly waiting for the revelation of our Lord Jesus Christ, who will also confirm you to the end, that you may be blameless in the day of our Lord Jesus Christ. (1 Corinthians 1:4–8)

Therefore, whether you eat or drink, or whatever you do, do all to the glory of God. Give no offence, either to the Jews or to the Greeks or to the church of God, just as I also please all men in all things, not seeking my own profit, but the profit of many, that they may be saved. (1 Corinthians 10:31–33)

Imitate me, just as I also imitate Christ. (1 Corinthians 11:1)

But earnestly desire the best gifts. And yet I show you a more excellent way. (1 Corinthians 12:31)

Though I speak with the tongues of men and of angels, but have not love, I have become sounding brass or a clanging cymbal. And though I have the gift of prophecy, and understand all mysteries and all knowledge, and though I have all faith, so that I could remove mountains, but have not love, I am nothing. And though I bestow all my goods to feed the poor, and though I give my body to be burned, but have not love, it profits me nothing. Love suffers long and is kind; love does not envy; love does not parade itself, is not puffed up; does not behave rudely, does not seek its own, is not provoked, thinks no evil; does not rejoice in iniquity, but rejoices in the truth; bears all things, believes all things, hopes all things, endures all things. Love never fails. But whether there are prophecies, they will fail; whether there are tongues, they will cease; whether there is knowledge, it will vanish away. For we know in part and we prophesy in part. But when that which is perfect has come, then that which is in part will be done away. When I was a child, I spoke as a child, I understood as a child, I thought as a child; but when I became a man, I put away childish things. For now we see in a mirror, dimly, but then face to face. Now I know in part, but then I shall know just as I also am known. And now abide faith, hope, love, these three; but the greatest of these is love. (1 Corinthians 13:1–13)

Now thanks be to God who always leads us in triumph in Christ. (2 Corinthians 2:14)

Our sufficiency is from God. (2 Corinthians 3:5)

For He says: "In an acceptable time I have heard you. And in the day of salvation I have helped you." Behold, now is the accepted time; behold, now is the day of salvation. (2 Corinthians 6:2)

For though we walk in the flesh, we do not war according to the flesh. For the weapons of our warfare are not carnal but mighty in God for pulling down strongholds, casting down arguments and every high thing that exults itself against the knowledge of God, bringing every thought into captivity to the obedience of Christ. (2 Corinthians 10:3–5)

But "he who glories, let him glory in the LORD." For not he who commends himself is approved, but whom the Lord commends. (2 Corinthians 10:17–18)

And this also we pray, that you may be made complete. (2 Corinthians 13:9)

My little children, for whom I laboured in birth again until Christ is formed in you. (Galatians 4:19)

Stand fast therefore in the liberty by which Christ has made us free, and do not be entangled again with a yoke of bondage. (Galatians 5:1)

Walk worthy of the calling with which you were called, with all lowliness and gentleness, with long-suffering, bearing with one another in love, endeavouring to keep the unity of the Spirit in the bond of peace. (Ephesians 4:1–3)

Till we all come to the unity of the faith and of the knowledge of the Son of God, to a perfect man, to the measure of the stature of the fullness of Christ; that we should no longer be children, tossed to and fro and carried about with every wind of doctrine, by the trickery of men, in the cunning craftiness of deceitful plotting, but, speaking the truth in love, may grow up in all things into Him who is the head—Christ—from whom the whole body, joined and knit together by what every joint supplies, according to the effective working by which every part does its share, causes growth of the body for the edifying of itself in love. This I say, therefore, and testify in the Lord, that you should no longer walk as the rest of the Gentiles walk, in the futility of their mind. (Ephesians 4:13–17)

That you put off, concerning your former conduct, the old man which grows corrupt according to the deceitful lusts, and be renewed in the spirit of your mind, and that you put on the new man which was created according to God, in true righteousness and holiness. (Ephesians 4:22–24)

"According to God." According to the God kind.

Therefore, putting away lying, "Let each one of you speak truth with his neighbour," for we are members of one another. "Be angry, and do not sin": do not let the sun go down on your wrath, nor give place to the devil. Let him who stole steal no longer, but rather let him labor, working with his hands what is good, that he may have something to give him who has need. Let no corrupt word proceed out of your mouth, but what is good for necessary edification, that it may impart grace to the hearers. And do not grieve the Holy Spirit of God, by whom you were sealed for the day of redemption. Let all bitterness, wrath, anger, clamor, and evil speaking be put away from you, with all malice. And be kind to one another, tenderhearted, forgiving one another, even as God in Christ forgave you. (Ephesians 4:25–32)

Therefore be imitators of God as dear children. (Ephesians 5:1)

Husbands, love your wives, just as Christ also loved the church and gave Himself for her, that He might sanctify and cleanse her with the washing of water by the word, that He might present her to Himself a glorious church, not having spot or wrinkle or any such thing, but that she should be holy and without blemish. (Ephesians 5:25–27)

Put on the whole armour of God, that you may be able to stand against the wiles of the devil. For we do not wrestle against flesh and blood, but against principalities, against powers, against the rulers of the darkness of this age, against spiritual hosts of wickedness in the heavenly places. Therefore take up the whole armour of God, that you may be able to withstand in the evil day, and having done all, to stand. Stand therefore, having girded your waist with truth, having put on the breastplate of righteousness, and having shod your feet with the preparation of the gospel of peace; above all, taking the shield of faith with which you will be able to quench all the fiery darts of the wicked one. And take the helmet of salvation, and the sword of the Spirit, which is the word of God; praying always with all prayer and supplication in the Spirit, being watchful to this end with all perseverance and supplication for all the saints. (Ephesians 6:11–18)

That you may become blameless and harmless, children of God without fault in the midst of a crooked and perverse generation, among whom you shine as lights in the world. (Philippians 2:15)

Him we preach, warning every man and teaching every man in all wisdom, that we may present every man perfect in Christ Jesus. (Colossians 1:28)

Always labouring fervently for you in prayers, that you may stand perfect, and complete in all the will of God. (Colossians 4:12)

And may the Lord make you increase and abound in love to one another and to all, just as we do to you, so that He may establish your hearts blameless in holiness before our God and Father at the coming of our Lord Jesus Christ with all His saints. (1 Thessalonians 3:12–13)

Test all things; hold fast what is good. Abstain from every form of evil. Now may the God of peace Himself sanctify you completely; and may your whole spirit, soul, and body be preserved blameless at the coming of our Lord Jesus Christ. He who calls you is faithful, who also will do it. (1 Thessalonians 5:21–24)

Now may our Lord Jesus Christ Himself, and our God and Father, who has loved us and given us everlasting consolation and good hope by grace, comfort your hearts and establish you in every good word and work. (2 Thessalonians 2:16–17)

But shun profane and idle bablings, for they will increase to more ungodliness. And their message will spread like cancer. Hymenaeus and Philetus are of this sort, who have strayed concerning the truth, saying that the resurrection is already past; and they overthrew the faith of some. (2 Timothy 2:16–18)

The dead are still in the ground. The dead in Christ shall rise first at Christ's return.

I thank my God, making mention of you always in my prayers, hearing of your love and faith, which you have toward the Lord Jesus and toward all the saints, that the sharing of your faith may become effective by the acknowledgement of every good thing which is in you in Christ Jesus. (Philemon 1:4–6)

But you have come to Mount Zion and to the city of the living God, the heavenly Jerusalem, to an innumerable company of angels, to the general assembly and church of the firstborn who are registered in heaven, to God the Judge of all, to the spirits of just men made perfect, to Jesus the Mediator of the new covenant, and to the blood of sprinkling that speaks better things than that of Abel. See that you do not refuse Him who speaks. For if they did not escape who refused Him who spoke on earth, much more shall we not escape if we turn away from Him who speaks from heaven, whose voice then shook the earth; but now He has promised, saying, "Yet once more I shake not only the earth, but also heaven." Now this, "Yet once more," indicates the removal of those things that are being shaken, as of things that are made, that the things which cannot be shaken may remain. Therefore, since we are receiving a kingdom which cannot be shaken, let us have grace, by which we may serve God acceptably with reverence and godly fear. For our God is a consuming fire. (Hebrews 12:22–29)

My brethren, count it all joy when you fall into various trials, knowing that the testing of your faith produces patience, But let patience have its perfect work. That you may be perfect and complete, lacking nothing. (James 1:2–4)

Blessed is the man who endures temptation; for when he has been approved, he will receive the crown of life which the Lord has promised to those who love Him. Let no one say when he is tempted, "I am tempted by God"; for God cannot be tempted by evil, nor does He Himself tempt anyone. But each one is tempted when he is drawn away by his own desires and enticed. Then, when desire has conceived, it gives birth to sin; and sin, when it is full grown, brings forth death. (James 1:12–15)

Therefore lay aside all filthiness and overflow of wickedness, and receive with meekness the implanted word, which is able to save your souls. But be doers of the word, and not hearers only, deceiving yourselves. For if anyone is a hearer of the word and not a doer, he is like a man observing his natural face in a mirror, for he observes himself, goes away, and immediately forgets what kind of man he was, But he who looks into the perfect law of liberty and continues in it, and is not a forgetful hearer but a doer of the work, this one will be blessed in what he does. If anyone among you thinks he is religious, and does not bridle his tongue but deceives his own heart, this one's religion is useless. Pure and undefiled religion before God and the Father is this: to visit orphans and widows in their trouble, and to keep oneself unspotted from the world. (James 1:21–27)

Who is wise and understanding among you? Let him show by good conduct that his works are done in the meekness of wisdom. But if you have bitter envy and self-seeking in your hearts, do not boast and lie against the truth. This wisdom does not descend from above, but is earthly, sensual, demonic. For where envy and self-seeking exist, confusion and every evil thing are there. But the wisdom that is from above is first pure, then peaceable, gentle, willing to yield, full of mercy and good fruits, without partiality and hypocrisy. Now the fruit of righteousness is sown in peace by those who make peace. (James 3:13–18)

He indeed was foreordained before the foundation of the world, but was manifested in these last times for you who through Him believe in God who raised Him from the dead and gave Him glory, so that your faith and hope are in God. Since you have purified your souls in obeying the truth through the Spirit, in sincere love of the brethren, love one another fervently with a pure heart, having been born again, not of corruptible seed but incorruptible, through the word of God which lives and abides forever. (1 Peter 1:20–23)

Therefore submit yourselves to every ordinance of man for the Lord's sake, whether to the king as supreme, or to governors, as to those who are sent by him for the punishment of evildoers and for the praise of those who do good. For this is the will of God, that by doing good you put to silence the ignorance of foolish men—as free, yet not using liberty as a cloak for vice, but as bondservants of God. Honour all people, Love the brotherhood. Fear God, Honour the king. Servants, be submissive to your masters with all fear, not only to the good and gentle, but also to the harsh. For this is commendable, if because of conscience toward God one endures grief, suffering wrongfully. For what credit is it if, when you are beaten for your faults, you take it patiently? But when you do good and suffer, if you take it patiently, this is commendable before God. For to this you were called, because Christ also suffered for us, leaving us an example, that you should follow His steps: "Who committed no sin, Nor was deceit found in His mouth"; who, when He was reviled, did not revile in return; when He suffered, He did not threaten, but committed Himself to Him who judges righteously; who, Himself bore our sins in His own body on the tree, that we, having died to sins, might live for righteousness—by whose stripes you were healed. For you were like sheep going astray, but have now returned to the Shepard and Overseer of your souls. (1 Peter 2:13–25)

Finally, all of you be of one mind, having compassion for one another; love as brothers, be tenderhearted, be courteous; not returning evil for evil or reviling for reviling, but on the contrary blessing, knowing that you were called to this, that you may inherit a blessing. (1 Peter 3:8–9)

We have the opportunity to share in the inheritance with Jesus Christ, not just receive the promise but to share in the inheritance with Jesus.

For "He who would love life And see good days, Let him refrain his tongue from evil, And his lips from speaking deceit. Let him turn away from evil and do good: Let him seek peace and pursue it. For the eyes of the LORD are on the righteous, And His ears are open to their prayers; But the face of the LORD is against those who do evil." And who is he who will harm you if you become followers of what is good? But even if you suffer for righteousness' sake, you are blessed. "And do not be afraid of their threats, nor troubled." But sanctify the Lord God in your hearts, and always be ready to give a defence to everyone who asks you a reason for the hope that is in you, with meekness and fear: having a good conscience, that when they defame you as evildoers, those who revile your good conduct in Christ may be ashamed. For it is better, if it is the will of God, to suffer for doing good than for doing evil. For Christ also suffered once for sins, the just for the unjust, that He might bring us to God, being put to death in the flesh but made alive by the Spirit. (1 Peter 3:10–18)

Now "if the righteous one is scarcely saved, Where will the ungodly and the sinner appear?" (1 Peter 4:18)

Likewise you younger people, submit yourselves to your elders. Yes, all of you be submissive to one another, and be clothed with humility, for "God resists the proud, But gives grace to the humble." Therefore humble yourselves under the mighty hand of God, that He may exalt you in due time, casting all your care upon Him, for He cares for you. Be sober, be vigilant; because your adversary the devil walks about like a roaring lion, seeking whom he may devour. Resist him, steadfast in the faith, knowing that the same sufferings are experienced by your brotherhood in the world. But may the God of all grace who called us to His eternal glory by Christ Jesus, after you have suffered awhile, perfect, establish, strengthen, and settle you. (1 Peter 5:5–10)

But also for this very reason, giving all diligence, add to your faith virtue, to virtue knowledge, to knowledge self control, to self control perseverance, to perseverance godliness, to godliness brotherly kindness, and to brotherly kindness love. For if these are yours and abound, you will be neither barren nor unfruitful in the knowledge of our Lord Jesus Christ. For he who lacks these things is shortsighted, even to blindness, and has forgotten that he was cleansed from his old sins. Therefore, brethren, be even more diligent to make your call and election sure, for if you do these things you will never stumble; for so an entrance will be supplied to you abundantly into the everlasting kingdom of our Lord and Savior Jesus Christ. (2 Peter 1:5–11)

Again, a new commandment I write to you, which thing is true in Him and in you, because the darkness is passing away, and the true light is already shining. He who says he is in the light, and hates his brother, is in darkness until now. He who loves his brother abides in the light, and there is no cause for stumbling in him. But he who hates his brother is in darkness and walks in darkness, and does not know where he is going, because the darkness has blinded his eyes. (1 John 2:8–11)

But the anointing which you have received from Him abides in you, and you do not need that anyone teach you; but as the same anointing teaches you concerning all things, and is true, and is not a lie, and just as it has taught you, you will abide in Him. And now, little children, abide in Him, that when He appears, we may have confidence and not be ashamed before Him at His coming. If you know that He is righteous, you know that everyone who practices righteousness is born of Him. (1 John 2:27–29)

Behold what manner of love the Father has bestowed on us, that we should be called children of God! Therefore the world does not know us, because it did not know Him. Beloved, now we are children of God; and it has not yet been revealed what we shall be, but we know that when He is revealed, we shall be like Him, for we shall see Him as He is. And everyone who has this hope in him purifies himself, just as He is pure. Whoever commits sin also commits lawlessness, and sin is lawlessness. And you know that He was manifested to take away our sins, and in Him there is no sin. Whoever abides in Him does not sin. Whoever sins has neither seen Him nor known Him. Little children, let no one deceive you. He who practices righteousness is righteous, just as He is righteous. He who sins is of the devil, for the devil has sinned from the beginning. For this purpose the Son of God was manifested, that He might destroy the works of the devil. Whoever has been born of God does not sin, for His seed remains in him; and he cannot sin, because he has been born of God. In this the children of God and the children of the devil are manifested: Whoever does not practice righteousness is not of God, nor is he who does not love his brother. (1 John 3:1–10)

We know that whoever is born of God does not sin; but he who has been born of God keeps himself, and the wicked one does not touch him. We know that we are of God, and the whole world lies under the sway of the wicked one. And we know that the Son of God has come and has given us an understanding, that we may know Him who is true; and we are in Him who is true, in His Son Jesus Christ. This is the true God and eternal life. (1 John 5:18–20)

For many deceivers have gone out into the world who do not confess Jesus Christ as coming in the flesh. This is a deceiver and an antichrist. (2 John 7)

The spirit that proclaims the doctrine of the Trinity, which tries to convince us that God has multiple personalities, that the resurrection has already happened, and that the dead go to heaven or hell is the spirit of the antichrist. These lies contradict the person of Jesus Christ, the person of God the Father, and God's salvation plan. All are deceiving and being deceived. The promise of God is eternal life with Him through His only begotten Son. The rejection of His promise is eternal death. Now is the time. Now God is willing to overlook transgressions that were committed in ignorance. Now is the time to repent, to believe the Gospel, and be baptized into the name of our Lord and Saviour, Jesus Christ of Nazareth and receive Christ's Holy Spirit.

> Look to yourselves, that we do not lose those things we worked for, but that we may receive a full reward. Whoever transgresses and does not abide in the doctrine of Christ does not have God. He who abides in the doctrine of Christ has both the Father and the Son. If anyone comes to you and does not bring this doctrine, do not receive him into your house nor greet him; for he who greets him shares in his evil deeds. (2 John 8–11)

> Beloved, do not imitate what is evil, but what is good. He who does good is of God, but he who does evil has not seen God. (3 John 11)

Chapter 28

REJECTION OF THE GOSPEL

Go to this people and say: "Hearing you will hear, and shall not understand; And seeing you will see, and not perceive; For the hearts of this people have grown dull. Their ears are hard of hearing, And their eyes they have closed, Lest they should see with their eyes and hear with their ears, Lest they should understand with their hearts and turn, So that I should heal them." (Acts 28:26–27)

For I know this, that after my departure savage wolves will come in among you, not sparing the flock. Also from among yourselves men will rise up, speaking perverse things, to draw away the disciples after themselves. (Acts 20:29–30)

Whose minds the god of this age has blinded, who do not believe, lest the light of the gospel of the glory of Christ, who is the image of God, should shine on them. (2 Corinthians 4:4)

For Satan himself transforms himself into an angel of light. (2 Corinthians 11:14)

> Indeed I will make those of the synagogue of Satan, who say they are Jews and are not, but lie—I will make them come and bow down at your feet, and make them know that I have loved you. (Revelation 3:9)

> Now the Spirit expressly says that in latter times some will depart from the faith, giving heed to deceiving spirits and doctrines of demons, speaking lies in hypocrisy, having their own conscience seared with a hot iron. (1 Timothy 4:1–2)

> But know this, that in the last days perilous times will come: For men will be lovers of themselves, lovers of money, boasters, proud, blasphemers, disobedient to parents, unthankful, unholy, unloving, unforgiving, slanderers, without self-control, brutal, despisers of good, traitors, headstrong, haughty, lovers of pleasure rather than lovers of God, having a form of godliness but denying its power. And from such people turn away. (2 Timothy 3:1–5)

"Denying its power." They are denying the power of the Holy Spirit, the Spirit of Jesus Christ, to transform us into blameless children of God.

> For of this sort are those who creep into households and make captives of gullible women loaded down with sins, led away by various lusts, always learning and never able to come to the knowledge of the truth. Now as Jannes and Jambres resisted Moses, so do these also resist the truth: men of corrupt minds, disapproved concerning the faith; but they will

progress no further, for their folly will be manifest to all, as theirs also was. (2 Timothy 3:6–9)

But evil men and imposters will grow worse and worse, deceiving and being deceived. (2 Timothy 3:13)

False teachers and false religious leaders.

For the time will come when they will not endure sound doctrine, but according to their own desires, because they have itching ears, they will heap up for themselves teachers; and they will turn their ears away from the truth, and be turned aside to fables. (2 Timothy 4:3–4)

For there are many insubordinate, both idle talkers and deceivers, especially those of the circumcision, whose mouths must be stopped, who subvert whole households, teaching things which they ought not, for the sake of dishonest gain. (Titus 1:10–11)

They profess to know God, but in works they deny Him, being abominable, disobedient, and disqualified for every good work. (Titus 1:16)

For it is impossible for those who were once enlightened, and have tasted the heavenly gift, and have become partakers of the Holy Spirit, and have tasted the good word of God and the powers of the age to come, if they fall away, to renew them again to repentance, since they crucify again for themselves the Son of God, and put Him to an open shame. For the earth which drinks in the rain that often comes upon it, and bears herbs useful for those by whom it is cultivated, receives blessing from God; but if it bears thorns and briers, it is rejected and near to being cursed, whose end is to be burned. (Hebrews 6:4–8)

For if we sin willfully after we have received the knowledge of the truth, there no longer remains a sacrifice of sins, but a certain fearful expectation of judgment, and fiery indignation which will devour the adversaries. Anyone who has rejected Moses' law dies without mercy on the testimony of two or three witnesses. Of how much worse punishment, do you suppose, will he be thought worthy who has trampled the Son of God underfoot, counted the blood of the covenant by which he was sanctified a common thing, and insulted the Spirit of grace? For we know Him who said, "Vengeance is Mine, I will repay," says the Lord. And again, "The LORD will judge His people." It is a fearful thing to fall into the hands of the living God. (Hebrews 10:26–31)

Who is a liar but he who denies that Jesus is the Christ? He is antichrist who denies the Father and the Son. Whoever denies the Son does not have the Father either; he who acknowledges the Son has the Father also. (1 John 2:22–23)

But there were also false prophets among the people, even as there will be false teachers among you, who will secretly bring in destructive heresies, even denying the Lord who bought them, and bringing on themselves swift destruction. And many will follow their destructive ways, because of whom the way of truth will be blasphemed. By covetousness they will exploit you with deceptive words; for a long time their judgment has not been idle, and their destruction does not slumber. For if God did not spare the angels who sinned, but cast them down to hell and delivered them into chains of darkness, to be reserved for judgment; and not spare the ancient world, but saved Noah, one of eight people, a preacher of righteousness, bringing in the flood on the world of the ungodly; and turning the cities of Sodom and Gomorrah into ashes, condemned them to destruction, making them an example to those who afterward would live ungodly; and delivered righteous Lot, who was oppressed by the filthy conduct of the wicked (for that righteous man, dwelling among them, tormented his righteous soul from day to day by seeing and hearing their lawless deeds)—then the Lord knows how to deliver the godly out of temptations and to reserve the unjust under punishment for the day of judgment, and especially those who walk according to the flesh in the lust of uncleanness and despise authority. They are presumptuous, self-willed. They are not afraid to speak evil of dignitaries, whereas angels, who are greater in power and might, do not bring a reviling accusation against them before the Lord. But these, like natural brute beasts made to be caught and destroyed, speak evil of the things they do not understand, and will utterly perish in their own corruption, and will receive the wages of unrighteousness, as those who count it pleasure to carouse in the daytime. They are spots and blemishes, carousing in their own deceptions while they feast with you, having eyes full of adultery and that cannot cease from sin, enticing unstable souls. They have a heart trained in covetous practices, and are accursed children. They have forsaken the right way and gone astray, following the way of Balaam the son of Beor, who loved the wages of unrighteousness; but he was rebuked for his iniquity: a dumb donkey speaking with a man's voice restrained the madness of the prophet. These are wells without water, clouds carried by a tempest, for whom is reserved the blackness of darkness forever. For when they speak great swelling words of emptiness, they allure through the lusts of the flesh, through lewdness, the ones who have actually escaped from those who live in error. While they promise them liberty, they themselves are slaves of corruption; for by whom a person is overcome, by him also he is brought into bondage. For if, after they have escaped the pollutions of the world through the knowledge of the Lord and Savior Jesus Christ, they are again entangled in them and overcome, the latter end is worse for them than the beginning. For it would have been better for them not to have known the way of righteousness, than having known it, to turn from the holy commandment delivered to them. But it has happened to them according to the true proverb: "A dog returns to his own vomit," and, "a sow, having washed, to her wallowing in the mire." (2 Peter 2:1–22)

The ungodly are not so, But are like the chaff which the wind drives away. Therefore the ungodly shall not stand in the judgment, Nor sinners in the congregation of the righteous. (Psalm 1:4–5)

The fool says in his heart, "There is no God." They are corrupt, and have done abominable iniquity; There is none who does good. (Psalm 53:1)

But God will wound the head of His enemies, The hairy scalp of the one who still goes on in his trespasses. (Psalm 68:21)

If the righteous will be recompensed on the earth, How much more the ungodly and the sinner. (Proverbs 11:31)

The LORD has made all Himself, Yes, even the wicked for the day of doom. (Proverbs 16:4)

There is a way that seems right to a man, But its end is the way of death. (Proverbs 16:25)

For thus says the LORD God of Israel to me: "Take this wine cup of fury from My hand, and cause all the nations, to whom I send you, to drink it." (Jeremiah 25:15)

All the kings of the north, far and near, one with another; and all the kingdoms of the world which are on the face of the earth. Also the king of Sheshach shall drink after them. "Therefore you shall say to them, 'Thus says the LORD of hosts, the God of Israel: "Drink, be drunk, and vomit! Fall and rise no more, because of the sword which I will send among you."'" (Jeremiah 25:26–27)

Therefore prophesy against them all these words, and say to them: "The LORD will roar from on high, And utter His voice from His holy habitation; He will roar mightily against His fold. He will give a shout, as those who tread the grapes, Against all the inhabitants of the earth. A noise will come to the ends of the earth—For the LORD has a controversy with the nations; He will plead His case with all flesh. He will give those who are wicked to the sword," says the LORD. Thus says the LORD of hosts: "Behold, disaster shall go forth From nation to nation, And a great whirlwind shall be raised up From the farthest parts of the earth. And at that day the slain of the LORD shall be from one end of the earth even to the other end of the earth. They shall not be lamented, or gathered, or buried; they shall become refuse on the ground. Wail, shepherds, and cry! Roll about in the ashes, You leaders of the flock! For the days of your slaughter and your dispersions are fulfilled; You shall fall like a precious vessel. And the shepherds will have no way to flee, Nor the leaders of the flock to escape. A voice of the cry of the shepherds, And a wailing of the leaders to the flock will be heard. For the LORD has plundered their pasture, And the peaceful dwellings are cut down Because of the fierce anger of the LORD. He has left His lair like the lion; For their land is desolate Because of the fierceness of the Oppressor, And because of His fierce anger." (Jeremiah 25:30–38)

"For I am with you," says the LORD, "to save you; Though I make a full end of all nations where I have scattered you, Yet I will not make a complete end of you. But I will correct you in justice, And will not let you go altogether unpunished." (Jeremiah 30:11)

The fierce anger of the LORD will not return until He has done it, And until He has performed the intents of His heart. In the latter days you will consider it. (Jeremiah 30:24)

For the day of the LORD upon all the nations is near; As you have done, it shall be done to you; Your reprisal shall return upon your own head; For as you drank on My holy mountain, So shall all the nations drink continually; Yes, they shall drink, and swallow, And they shall be as though they had never been. (Obadiah 1:15-16)

The LORD is slow to anger and great in power, And will not at all acquit the wicked. (Nahum 1:3)

"Therefore wait for Me," says the LORD, "Until the day I rise up for nations; My determination is to gather the nations To My assembly of kingdoms, To pour on them My indignation, All My fierce anger; All the earth shall be devoured With the fire of My jealousy." (Zephaniah 3:8)

The field is the world, the good seeds are the sons of the kingdom, but the tares are the sons of the wicked one. The enemy who sowed them is the devil, the harvest is the end of the age, and the reapers are the angels. Therefore as the tares are gathered and burned in the fire, so it will be at the end of this age. The Son of Man will send out His angels, and they will gather out of His kingdom all things that offend, and those who practice lawlessness. and will cast them into the furnace of fire. There will be wailing and gnashing of teeth. (Matthew 13:38–42)

So it will be at the end of the age, The angels will come forth, separate the wicked from among the just, and cast them into the furnace of fire. There will be wailing and gnashing of teeth. (Matthew 13:49–50)

Hear another parable: There was a certain landowner who planted a vineyard and set a hedge around it, dug a winepress in it and built a tower. And he leased it to vinedressers and went into a far country. Now when the vintage-time drew near, he sent his servants to the vinedressers, that they might receive its fruit. And the vinedressers took his servants, beat one, killed one, and stoned another. Again he sent other servants, more than the first, and they did likewise to them. Then last of all he sent his son to them, saying, "They will respect my son." But when the vinedressers saw the son, they said among themselves, "This is the heir. Come let us kill him and seize his inheritance." So they took him and cast him out of the vineyard and killed him. Therefore, when the owner of the vineyard comes, what will he do to those vinedressers? They said to Him, "He will destroy those wicked men miserably, and lease his vineyard to other vinedressers who will render to him the fruits in their seasons." Jesus said to them, "Have you never read in the Scriptures: 'The stone which the builders rejected Has become the chief cornerstone. This was the Lord's doing, And it is marvellous in our eyes'? Therefore I say to you, the kingdom of God will be taken from you and given to a nation bearing the fruits of it. And whoever falls on this stone will be broken; but on whomever it falls, it will grind him to powder." (Matthew 21:33–44)

Then he said to his servants, "The wedding is ready, but those who were invited were not worthy. Therefore go into the highways, and as many as you find, invite to the wedding. So those servants went out into the highways and gathered together all whom they found, both bad and good. And the wedding hall was filled with guests. But when the king came in to see the guests, he saw a man there who did not have on a wedding garment. So he said to him, 'Friend, how did you come in here without a wedding garment?' And he was speechless. Then the king said to the servants, 'Bind him hand and foot, take him away, and cast him into outer darkness; there will be weeping and gnashing of teeth.' For many are called, but few are chosen." (Matthew 22:8–14)

Behold, you despisers, Marvel and perish! For I work a work in your days, A work which you will by no means believe, Though one were to declare it to you. (Acts 13:41)

For the wrath of God is revealed from heaven against all ungodliness and unrighteousness, because what may be known of God is manifest in them, for God has shown it to them. For since the creation of the world His invisible attributes are clearly seen, being understood by the things that are made, even His eternal power and Godhead, so that they are without excuse, because, although they knew God, they did not glorify Him as God, nor were thankful, but became futile in their thoughts, and their foolish hearts were darkened. (Romans 1:18–21)

But even if we, or an angel from heaven, preach any other gospel to you than what we have preached to you, let him be accursed. As we have said before, so now I say again, if anyone preaches any other gospel to you than what you have received, let him be accursed. (Galatians 1:8–9)

Brethren, join in following my example, and note those who so walk, as you have us for a pattern. For many walk, of whom I have told you often, and now tell you even weeping, that they are the enemies of Christ: whose end is destruction, whose god is their belly and whose glory is in their shame—who set their mind on earthly things. For our citizenship is in heaven, from which we also eagerly wait for the Saviour, the Lord Jesus Christ, who will transform our lowly body that it may be conformed to His glorious body, according to the working by which He is able even to subdue all things to Himself. (Philippians 3:17–21)

But I do not want you to be ignorant, brethren, concerning those who have fallen asleep, lest you sorrow as others who have no hope. (1 Thessalonians 4:13)

Since it is a righteous thing with God to repay with tribulation those who trouble you, and to give you

Michael J. Byrne

who are troubled rest with us when the Lord Jesus
is revealed from heaven with His mighty angels,
in flaming fire taking vengeance on those who do
not know God, and on those who do not obey
the gospel of our Lord Jesus Christ. These shall
be punished with everlasting destruction from the
presence of the Lord and from the glory of His
power. (2 Thessalonians 1:6–9)

Chapter 29

CLOSING EXHORTATION

Beloved, while I was very diligent to write to you concerning our common salvation, I found it necessary to write to you exhorting you to contend earnestly for the faith which was once for all delivered to the saints. For certain men have crept in unnoticed, who long ago were marked out for this condemnation, ungodly men, who turn the grace of our God into lewdness and deny the only Lord God and our Lord Jesus Christ. But I want to remind you, though you once knew this, that the Lord, having saved the people out of the land of Egypt, afterward destroyed those who did not believe. And the angels who did not keep their proper domain, but left their own abode, He has reserved in everlasting chains under darkness for the judgment of the great day; as Sodom and Gomorrah, and the cities around them in a similar manner to these, having given themselves over to sexual immorality and gone after strange flesh, are set forth as an example, suffering the vengeance of eternal fire. Likewise also these dreamers defile the flesh, reject authority, and speak evil of dignitaries. Yet Michael the archangel, in

contending with the devil, when he disputed about
the body of Moses, dared not bring against him
a reviling accusation, but said, "The Lord rebuke
you!" But these speak evil of whatever they do not
know; and whatever they know naturally, like brute
beasts, in these things they corrupt themselves. Woe
to them! For they have gone in the way of Cain,
have run greedily in the error of Balaam for profit,
and perished in the rebellion of Korah. These are
spots in your love feasts, while they feast with you
without fear, serving only themselves. They are
clouds without water, carried about by the winds;
late autumn trees without fruit, twice dead, pulled
up by the roots; raging waves of the sea, foaming up
their shame; wandering stars for whom is reserved
the blackness of darkness forever. Now Enoch, the
seventh from Adam, prophesied about these men
also, saying, "Behold, the Lord comes with ten
thousands of His saints, "to execute judgment on
all, to convict all who are ungodly among them of
all their ungodly deeds which they have committed
in a ungodly way, and of all the harsh things which
ungodly sinners have spoken against Him." These
are grumblers, complainers, walking according
to their own lusts; and they mouth great swelling
words, flattering people to gain advantage. But you,
beloved, remember the words which were spoken
before by the apostles of our Lord Jesus Christ: how
they told you that there would be mockers in the
last time who would walk according to their own
ungodly lusts. These are sensual persons, who cause
divisions, not having the Spirit. But you, beloved,
building yourselves up on your most holy faith,
praying in the Holy Spirit, keep yourselves in the

love of God, looking for the mercy of our Lord Jesus Christ unto eternal life. And on some have compassion, making a distinction; but others save with fear, pulling them out of the fire, hating even the garment defiled by the flesh. Now to Him who is able to keep you from stumbling, And to present you faultless Before the presence of His glory with exceeding joy, To God our Saviour, Who alone is wise Be glory and majesty, Dominion and power, Both now and forever. Amen. (Jude 3–24)

For the Lord Himself will descend from heaven with a shout, with the voice of an archangel, and with the trumpet of God. And the dead in Christ will rise first, Then we who are alive and remain shall be caught up together with them in the clouds to meet the Lord in the air. And thus we shall always be with the Lord. (1 Thessalonians 4:16–17)

But you, brethren, are not in darkness, so that this Day should overtake you as a thief. (1 Thessalonians 5:4)

Now, brethren, concerning the coming of our Lord Jesus Christ and our gathering together to Him, we ask you, not to be soon shaken in mind or troubled, either by spirit or by word or by letter, as if from us, as though the day of Christ had come. Let no one deceive you by any means; for that Day will not come unless the falling away comes first, and the man of sin is revealed, the son of perdition, who opposes and exalts himself above all that is called God or that is worshipped, so that he sits as God in the temple of God, showing himself that he is

God. Do you not remember that when I was still with you I told you these things? And now you know what is restraining, that he may be revealed in his own time. For the mystery of lawlessness is already at work; only He who now restrains will do so until He is taken away. And then the lawless one will be revealed, whom the Lord will consume with the breath of His mouth and destroy with the brightness of His coming. The coming of the lawless one is according to the working of Satan, with all power, signs, and lying wonders, and with all unrighteous deception among those who perish, because they did not receive the love of the truth, that they might be saved, And for this reason God will send them strong delusion, that they should believe the lie, that they all may be condemned who did not believe the truth but had pleasure in unrighteousness. (2 Thessalonians 2:1–12)

Remind them to be subject to rulers and authorities, to obey, to be ready for every good work, to speak evil of no one, to be peaceable, gentle, showing all humility to all men. For we ourselves were also once foolish, disobedient, deceived, serving various lusts and pleasures, living in malice and envy, hateful and hating one another. But when the kindness and the love of God our Savior toward man appeared, not by works of righteousness which we have done, but according to His mercy He saved us, through the washing of regeneration and renewing of the Holy Spirit, whom He poured out on us abundantly through Jesus Christ our Savior. That having been justified by His grace we should become heirs according to the hope of eternal life. (Titus 3:1–7)

Therefore I testify to you this day that I am innocent of the blood of all men. For I have not shunned to declare to you the whole council of God. (Acts 20:26–27)

Chapter 30

THE PURPOSE OF LIFE

The purpose of life is one of the Spirit. Our ultimate destiny—should we be found worthy—is to share eternity with God the Father and His Only begotten Son, Jesus Christ. We are destined to become adopted brothers and sisters of Christ and sons and daughters of God. We will share in the divine nature with both the Father and the Son and inherit the same body as that of Jesus Christ.

Now we are able to receive full insight into the symbolism of the Tree of Life. The Tree of Life represents the marriage between Christ and His church. The Tree of Life represents God's original plan since the beginning of time. All of God's intents and purposes have been to bring about this great marriage feast. We have all been invited, we have all been called and we shall all see.

We will be sons and daughters of our Sovereign Lord and Father, Almighty God. In order to take on this role, we must be prepared. We must be justified, and we must be proven and sanctified. We, like Christ, must be obedient to death. Don't be fooled; corruption cannot inherit incorruption. The offering of this inheritance is through the Spirit. God is not going to transform our lowly bodies into spiritual bodies if we have no interest in living holy lives. Where would that leave God?

None who cause offense will be raised to life. We are being created—through the Spirit—to live for all of eternity in peace and harmony with those who are likewise chosen. The remainder of our time on this earth is to be spent cultivating and nurturing the Spirit of Jesus Christ that has been offered to us.

Throughout God's salvation plan, He has used the institution of marriage as the physical representation of that which is to come. Marriage is considered the most joyous of celebrations. For a marriage to be successful, both parties must cultivate and nurture specific attitudes. Unfortunately, experience teaches us of the futility of human relationships and their institutions. All have sinned and fall short of the glory of God. Humanity is completely incapable of governing itself. God is offering us something new. Let's be reminded of the attributes of the Spirit that must be found in each and every one of us if we are to be found worthy to be judged innocent on the day we stand before our Lord and Savior, Jesus Christ.

> Let love be without hypocrisy. Abhor what is evil. Cling to what is good. Be kindly affectionate to one another with brotherly love, in honour giving preference to one another; not lagging in diligence, fervent in spirit, serving the Lord; rejoicing in hope, patient in tribulation, continuing steadfastly in prayer; distributing to the needs of the saints, given to hospitality. Bless those who persecute you; bless and do not curse. Rejoice with those who rejoice, and weep with those who weep. Be of the same mind toward one another. Do not set your mind on high things, but associate with the humble. Do not be wise in your own opinion. Repay no one evil for evil. Have regard for good things in the sight of all men. If it is possible, as much as depends on you, live peaceably with all men. Beloved, do not avenge yourselves, but rather give place to wrath; for it is written, "Vengeance is Mine, I will repay," says the Lord. Therefore "If your enemy is hungry, feed him;

If he is thirsty, give him a drink; For in so doing you will heap coals of fire on his head." Do not be overcome by evil, but overcome evil with good. (Romans 12:9–21)

These attributes must be found in each and every one of us; without them, no one will see God. It is Jesus who will answer our fervent prayers and create this character in us. Our hope is in Christ who assures us that He will complete this work. Do not be downcast or disheartened about the terror that is about to come upon the world; instead, rejoice that you have been called into this indescribable gift we share in Christ.

As for me, I will see Your face in righteousness; I shall be satisfied when I awake in Your likeness. (Psalm 17:15)

Printed in the United States
by Baker & Taylor Publisher Services